THE ESSENTIAL

MIR

Praise for *The Essential Mir*

'*The Essential Mir*, a discerning selection of Mir Taqi Mir's Urdu verses, paired with lucid translation and insightful commentary, offers readers a gentle and illuminating passage into his world. It brings Mir's voice into English with care and also restores the emotional fragrance and cultural cadence that breathe between his lines. A richly rewarding way to read and appreciate Mir's emotional depth and lyrical grace.'

—Khalid Jawed
Former Professor of Urdu and author of the JCB award-winning The Paradise of Food

'Professor Anisur Rahman, the translator of Ghalib, presents here the God of Poetry and unpacks his deceptively simple verses to lay bare the complex mélange of meaning, love, suffering, and the deep empathy that Mir displayed for the human condition and for his turbulent times, but withal in as *sahal* a manner as Mir would have approved of.'

—Mahmood Farooqui
Author, performer and reviver of modern Dastangoi

'Mir is widely acknowledged to be the sincerest, simplest and most "artless" of all the major poets in the three hundred years of Urdu poetry—unlike, for example, Ghalib, who was cerebral, philosophical and more Persianate. In his renderings of Mir into English, Anisur Rahman, in his turn, is natural, sincere and simple; in a felicitous match between the poet and his translator. "Who would not be bowled over by such innocence," as Mir himself asked!'

—Harish Trivedi
Literary critic and translator,
Formerly Professor of English, University of Delhi

'Rahman's informed discourse provides remarkable insights into Mir's oeuvre, his engagement with the mystical and the divine, the intertwining of timeless legends across class and faith and the references to the passage of time, life and living. The whole is enriched further by Rahman's comments on specific verses which have influenced subsequent literary legends, particularly Ghalib, but also many others, ranging from Momin and Dagh to Ahmed Faraz.'

—**Muneeza Shamsie**
Literary historian, bibliographer and memoirist

'This lovely monograph offers precisely what its title promises: it allows any reader to enter the essence of Mir Taqi Mir. In exploring the subtle complexities of Mir's story, his encounters with grief, and openings into joy and possibility, Anisur Rahman lays out pathways through which one finds the poet through a life woven into lyric.'

—**Geeta Patel**
Professor, Department of Middle Eastern and South Asian Languages and Literatures, University of Virginia

'Anisur Rahman has done a commendable job in rendering Mir's poetry into English, while also preserving its original sound in Nastaliq, Devanagari and Roman scripts. His work not only makes Mir accessible to a wider readership but also underscores the pluralistic ethos of Mir's works and the Urdu language. I hope that scholars and students of Urdu will pay more attention to Mir's vocabulary, which not only makes beautiful poetry but also offers valuable insight into the linguistic and cultural milieu of his time.'

—**Timsal Masud**
Lecturer of Hindi-Urdu, translator, editor and textbook author, Middle Eastern, South Asian, and African Studies (MESAAS), Columbia University

ALSO BY THE SAME AUTHOR

The Essential Ghalib
Hazaar Rang Shaairi
Hazaaron Khwahishein Aisi

THE ESSENTIAL MIR

ANISUR RAHMAN

HarperCollins *Publishers* India

First published in India by HarperCollins *Publishers* 2026
HarperCollins *Publishers* India, Cyber City,
Building 10-A, Gurugram, Haryana – 122002, India
www.harpercollins.co.in

2 4 6 8 10 9 7 5 3 1

P-ISBN: 978-93-7307-110-7
E-ISBN: 978-93-7307-547-1

Typeset in 9.5/13.5 HC Arc
by HarperCollins *Publishers* India Pvt. Ltd

Printed and bound at
Manipal Technologies Limited, Manipal

MIX
Paper | Supporting responsible forestry
FSC™ C043100

This book is produced from independently certified FSC® paper to ensure responsible forest management.

HarperCollins *Publishers*, Macken House, 39/40 Mayor Street Upper,
Dublin 1, D01 C9W8, Ireland

for

Tabassum

chalo tuk Mir ko sun'ne ke motii sii pirotaa hai

jaane kaa nahii.n shor suKHan kaa mire hargiz
taa hashr jahaa.n mei.n miraa diivaan rahegaa

The roar of my verses will never fade out, never
My *diivaan* will stay till the doomsday to savour

❖

lutf mujh mei.n bhii hai.n hazaaro.n Mir
diidanii huu.n jo soch kar dekho

There are a thousand delights, Mir, in me
I'm worth a look, if you may think and see

❖

muft yuu.n haath se na kho ham ko
kahii.n paidaa bhii hote hai.n ham se

Don't ever lose me for no gain
Ones like me are not born again

❖

she'r mere hai.n sab KHavaas pasand
go mujhe guftuguu 'avaam se hai

The elites love all my verses, my verses all
But I converse freely with the common folks all

Mir Taqi Mir
(Translated into English by the author)

CONTENTS

FOREWORD BY GEETA PATEL	XI
PREFACE	XIV
SAHL HAI MIR KAA SAMAJHNAA KYAA: AN INTRODUCTION	XVII
MIR TAQI MIR: A BRIEF TIMELINE	XXX
VERSES AND COMMENTARIES	1
TRANSLITERATION KEY	403
ACKNOWLEDGEMENTS	407

The Transliteration Key pertaining to this book is available on the HarperCollins *Publishers* India website. Scan this QR code to access the same.

FOREWORD

This lovely monograph offers precisely what its title promises: it allows any reader to enter the essence of Mir Taqi Mir. In exploring the subtle complexities of Mir's story, his encounters with grief, and openings into joy and possibility, Anisur Rahman lays out pathways through which one finds the poet through a life woven into lyric. A universe of aesthetic feeling is brought into being through the characters peopling Mir's life and poetry. Through the language, the grammar, the metre, the similes, the metaphors, all the nuances that Mir played with and plied in each verse.

The Essential Mir opens its foray into Mir with a series of what I call prolegomenas, one might even think of them as *safarnamas*, invitations into the intricacies of the being of the poet. Sections which comprise the introduction and bring us apposite nuggets from *Zikr-e Mir*—through narratives of times when the worlds around Mir were fissured by war, massacres, the upending of courts and kingdoms, Mir's survival through losses, of patrons, of family members, of his sense of himself, of the ability to cobble a life. But Anisur Rahman also gifts us something else—the ways in which, through all the sorrow, the grind, incessant losses, Mir's life and lyric flourished. Mir found faithful patrons, was inculcated into love as the lodestone and path of life and poetry, '[l]ove, his father taught him, finally lay beyond worship, and it moved the heavens,' was introduced to a *darvesh*, and other spiritual guides who brought him more fully into *Sufiana*. The closing sections unveil Mir the philosopher poet—an incanted typology of Mir's characters, people, objects, scenes, places so suffused with texture that by the time we meet them in the two hundred verses and commentaries, they have already become our familiars. And Mir's linguistic palette, playing between 'the ordinary and extraordinary', the rhythms of everyday speech floating into mystical and philosophical grammars, the complex historical and personal somatics of Rekhta, as the lingua franca, 'the idiom and diction' of Mir's tongue, 'a mouth, a way of speaking, a voice'. Though the introduction is chock-a-block with detail, the heart-blood of this introduction is a gentle refusal of a literal mining for history in Mir's lyric. Rather, Anisur Rahman's entre remains with us as we read, as we come to the next section, offering both a caution and a provocation: 'History, as witnessed, and life, as lived, do not inherently provide the material for poetry. As an imaginative reconstruction of reality, poetry does not adhere to linearity or materiality; instead, it draws upon the anima mundi of images connected to life and time.'

The *intikhaab* of verses, following this beautifully crafted introduction, is an absolute delight. Choosing two hundred verses from an oeuvre of over sixteen hundred is a formidable task. A task that Professor Rahman performs with such care and sensitivity, such love, that even those familiar with Mir finds themselves thoroughly absorbed. The glossaries and commentaries are as nuanced as the lyric, in that they simultaneously serve as an exceptional invitation to a naïve reader while Professor Rahman's intricately exquisite parsing of the philosophical, linguistic, multivocal polysemy of each verse, allows more experienced readers to truly savour what the verses carry, offer, suggest. I could go on at length here, but I will restrain myself. Because once you begin savouring each verse and how they can be thought, you come to quickly understand that the introduction was merely a taste of what fills out with such richness. And that anything I offer would fall far short of what you might glean by falling into the text yourself.

Translating a poet such as Mir, precisely because his phrasing can be so spare, so on the tongue, yet so rich, is as daunting as picking the representative verses. And the translations are wonderful—superbly delicate and sonorous, impish when called upon, subdued when necessary, suffused with sorrow or joy at times, and always gently thoughtful.

I found myself reading the entire book and then, as a gift to myself, mulling over a verse or two with the translations and commentary each day, so that *us hii kaa zarra zuhuur thaa*, from the opening verse of the first ghazal of the first *Diivaan*, through which Professor Rahman brings us to Mir's poetry.

thaa must'aar husn se us ke jo nuur thaa
KHurshiid mei.n bhii us hii kaa zarra zuhuur thaa

The radiance that showed up was borrowed
but only from His beauty
Even the sun showed a speck of the same light,
borrowed from His beauty

Mir Taqi Mir
Translation: Anisur Rahman

Geeta Patel
Professor, Department of Middle Eastern and South Asian Languages and Literatures, University of Virginia

PREFACE

The Essential Mir is my way of fulfilling my promises to Mir Taqi Mir (1723–1810) and his readers. These promises are manifold, and they make multiple demands on their author. To this end, the book addresses, first, the overwhelming desire of Mir's diverse readers, spread across the world, to revisit him three centuries after his birth and discover his relevance to understanding the life, literature, and art of his times and their own, within a broader historical and literary context. Second, it attempts to dispel the erroneous notion, reiterated over the ages, that Mir is predominantly a poet of pain and suffering, even though he transformed the idea of pain into a philosophical realization that enriched life better than pleasure. Third, it aspires to integrate him within the current literary and sociocultural contexts, which look back to the times of Mir in multiple ways and underscore the patterns of the ubiquitous human condition. Fourth, it allows the larger English language readership to appreciate his exclusivity and classic modernity, in addition to his contributions to the development of Urdu as a language and canonization of the Urdu ghazal. Fifth, it opens up new avenues for translating and developing comprehensive critical commentaries on Mir's most representative verses, which would help reveal him as a poet of inclusive human consciousness and unparalleled craftsmanship. Finally, it seeks to enrich the vast corpus of Indian literature in English translation, which can be best appreciated through comparative reading. By addressing these promises, Mir may be suitably positioned at the centre of eighteenth-century India's literary and sociopolitical paradigms that impact us to this day.

I met Mir as if on the way, as one meets a *darvesh* quite rewardingly. This supremely enlightened *darvesh* has kept me mesmerized ever since, and I always find his gentle aura around me. He has helped me walk my way with him in solace and silence. He is pristine, pure and powerful; unassuming, yet undulating, and disarmingly so. Finding him was, in a way, a way of finding myself. My selection of two hundred verses for this book is entirely personal, yet strictly based on the aforementioned promises and parameters. To my understanding, this is the first book of its kind, featuring translations of two hundred select verses along with comprehensive commentaries on them. It is designed to help readers appreciate Mir cumulatively as a poet who could transform the ordinary into the extraordinary, develop a poetic language rooted in secular imagination and evolve a style typically affluent and marked by ease.

It is also important to note that Mir compiled six *diivaans* of his Urdu ghazals over fifty-seven years from 1751 to 1808. As per the history of the published *diivaans*, there are six hundred sixty-three ghazals in *diivaan* 1; three hundred ninety-one ghazals in *diivaan* 2; two hundred fifty-seven ghazals in *diivaan* 3; two hundred twenty-two ghazals in *diivaan* 4; two hundred fifty ghazals in *diivaan* 5; and one hundred thirty-three ghazals in *diivaan* 6. All these add up to a total of 1,916 ghazals. Technically, a ghazal must comprise at least five verses. From this point of view, careful counting tells us that there are one hundred thirty-four ghazals in *diivaan* 1 with less than five verses. Similarly, there are nine ghazals in *diivaan* 2, twelve ghazals in *diivaan* 3, forty-four ghazals in *diivaan* 4, thirty-eight ghazals in *diivaan* 5, and five ghazals in *diivaan* 6 that contain less than five verses. This leads us to the conclusion that out of 1,916 ghazals included and published in his six *diivaans*, there are two hundred thirty-eight ghazals with fewer than five verses, and hence these may not be considered complete ghazals. One may surmise that the compositions with fewer than five verses have also been included as ghazals, as they formed part of the *qaafia* and *radiif* scheme and carried some of Mir's finest verses, which could neither be published separately nor left out entirely. Thus, in technical terms, the total number of ghazals in the six *diivaans* is 1,678 rather than the initially projected 1,916.

Mir did not see the publication of his *diivaans* during his lifetime. The College of Fort William in Calcutta published them in 1811, a year after his passing. Later, Nawal Kishore Press of Lucknow published Mir's *diivaans* in 1868, 1916 and 1941. Several other scholars published their editions later, including the respectable editions by Abdul Bari Aasi (1941), Zille Abbas Abbasi (1968), Ram Narain Lal Beni Madho (1972) and Akbar Haidari (1973). Mir lives on through his six *diivaans* in various print avatars, numerous volumes of his selected ghazals and a vast amount of criticism in Urdu.

The Essential Mir is a modest attempt to represent Mir in yet another manner to readers in English who have known Mir all along but need to know him better still. And also to those who are yet to be initiated into Mir's house of mirrors that reflect the onlooker back and forth as they move ahead, turn backwards or look sideways.

Anisur Rahman

Sahl Hai Mir Kaa Samajhnaa Kyaa: AN INTRODUCTION

sahl hai Mir kaa samajhnaa kyaa
har suKHan us kaa ik maqaam se hai
Is it easy to comprehend Mir; is it easy?
Each verse hails from a high station; it isn't easy

Prologue

History, as witnessed, and life, as lived, do not inherently provide the material for poetry. As an imaginative reconstruction of reality, poetry does not adhere to linearity or materiality; instead, it draws upon the anima mundi of images connected to life and time. In stages, images evolve into similes, similes into metaphors, metaphors into symbols, and ultimately symbols into myths. This suggests that the poet's imaginative vitality enhances the quality of the poem. By reflecting mirrors toward one another, the poet and the poem transform the real into the surreal and the physical into the metaphysical. In this dynamic, the reader remains perpetually and rewardingly engaged in defining his role as a literary quester. This framework of poetics manifests itself most clearly when we appreciate Mir's poetry in its entirety.

As the pursuit of discovering the poet and the poem swung through phases of multiple assumptions, Mohammad Taqi, better known as Mir Taqi Mir, became more of a myth than a man and more of a man than a myth. During the three centuries since his birth, Mir the individual has quizzed the reader just as much as Mir the poet has, and the poet as much as his poetry. In this process, Mir emerged as an image bearer of time and time beyond time, as well as of history and history beyond history. He thus appeared as a curious representative of personal and sociopolitical histories, reflecting on human susceptibilities within a broader frame of time and place.

Ambiguities of Inheritance

To appreciate Mir's status as a participant figure in history and as a lasting icon in poetry, his life can be divided into two periods: personal and historical. Let us begin with his personal time. Mir's ancestors had arrived from Hijaz in the Arabian Peninsula and settled in Ahmedabad and Akbarabad, now known as Agra. Mir was born to his father's second wife in Akbarabad and was endearingly brought up by a dear disciple of his father, Amanullah, who can be considered his first benefactor. Amanullah wished for Mir to grow into the spiritualist tradition, and as he matured over the years, he developed into one, but with a difference. Mir was still a young boy of eleven when his father, Mir Mohammad Ali, died, leaving him with no means to sustain himself. Hoping to find his fortune elsewhere, he travelled from Agra to Delhi—the theatre supreme of all times. With the help of a benefactor, Khvaja Mohammad Basit, a friend of his father, he met one of the three highest-ranking nobles, Khvaja Mohammad Asim, appropriately titled Samsam-ud Daula (1672–1739); meaning 'sword of the state'. He proved to be his first patron. Mir was given a stipend of one rupee per month, which ceased about three years later when Samsam-ud Daula lost his life fighting against the army of the Iranian invader Nadir Shah (r. 1736–1747). Mir was about sixteen years old at the time. Left helpless again and unable to find another way to sustain himself, he returned to Agra in utter despair. When he could not obtain any relief there as well, he returned to Delhi and stayed with his stepmother's brother, Sirajuddin Ali Khan 'Arzu' (1687–1756), popularly known as Khan-e Arzu, who became his next patron. He provided a roof over Mir's head, and Mir quietly cultivated his reading skills with a few like-minded young scholars in the battered city of Delhi. During these days, he remained largely unemployed and disappointed, preferring to live in isolation with the doors of his room mostly closed. Much too obsessed with himself, the brooding Mir eventually transformed into a lunatic. On moonlit nights, he began to see the face of an imagined beloved on the moon and became wild every time it happened. His lunacy persisted for four months, but it intensified during the spring season. Ultimately, a kind female benefactor, Begum Fakhruddin Khan, a devotee of his father, arranged for him to be treated, and he regained normalcy when spring departed and winter arrived. By now, Mir had reached his eighteenth year. That was when he met another kind benefactor, Mir Jafar, who hailed from Azimabad, now known as Patna, and who introduced Mir to the pursuit of knowledge in a more disciplined manner. Yet another kind benefactor from Amroha, Syed Saadat Ali, guided him in the art of poetry and drew his attention to Rekhta, a language he ultimately practised and developed as the finest literary tool for himself, his generation and all subsequent ages. However, Mir still needed help, and this time, he found another patron in Riyaet Ali Khan, an emir, around 1747, who offered him employment. Mir was around twenty-four by then and had found other patrons, including Mahanarayan Diwan in 1751, Amir Khan Anjam in 1754, Raja Jugal Kishore in 1755, Raja Nagar Mal in 1757 and Nawab Imad-ul Mulk later still, as well as some others from time to time. They all acknowledged his genius and rescued him from financial hardship, allowing him to pursue his vocation as a poet. Finally, his most devoted patron, Nawab Asaf-ud Daula (r. 1775–1797), invited him to his court in Lucknow in 1782 and offered him a monthly stipend of two hundred rupees. Mir was around sixty years old by then and stayed there for the rest of his life. It was in Lucknow that he suffered the three most tragic events towards the end of his life—the death of Begum, his daughter, in 1807; then Faiz Ali, his first son, in 1808; and finally, his second wife, in 1809. Mir had turned eighty-six years old by then and was too broken to live with any emotional and physical strength, but he was destined to live another year in that state of decline. As can be estimated, Mir's personal time period offers a window to his life, but he lived yet another life related to his historical time period.

Mir was a sore witness to the decline of the Mughal empire. His historical period spans nearly eight decades, from 1731 to 1809, encompassing the terrible events that occurred during this time. Although a young Mir of around eight years may not have realized the magnitude at the time, he must have understood later how history had started taking on a new course with the Maratha kingdom under Bajirao I (r. 1720–1740) defeating the Mughals in 1731. When he grew up and reached the age of fourteen, he saw the Marathas overcoming the Mughals in the Battle of Delhi in 1737. A far more consequential turn of history was still in the making, which transpired when Nadir Shah pillaged Delhi and looted the Mughal treasury in 1739 during the reign of the debauched Mughal emperor, Mohammad Shah (r. 1719–1748). Mir was sixteen then, an impressionable young poet who could not avoid being shaken to his core by the brutality of the event.

Yet another capture of the seemingly indefatigable Delhi was only fourteen years away. In 1753, Mir witnessed the Jats, under Raja Suraj Mal (r. 1755–1763) of the Bharatpur kingdom, defeating the Mughals and winning control of Delhi. Mir was thirty then, a fully grown observer of history's hostile turns. For decades thereafter, the macabre drama of politicking and pillaging persisted as the plotting for power over the capital amongst rivalling clans thickened. In 1754, Bharatpur defeated the Marathas in the Battle of Kumher, which involved the Jats, Marathas and Mughals. Mir was thirty-one then. Three years later, in 1757, when Mir was thirty-four, the Maratha confederacy defeated the Rohilla Afghans in another Battle of Delhi and captured the city. Only that year, Jats under King Suraj Mal also crushed the Durranis in the Battle of Bharatpur. The biggest battle of all followed four years later in 1761, when Marathas were routed in the third Battle of Panipat by the Afghan army of Ahmad Shah Abdali (r. 1747–1772), also known as Ahmad Shah Durrani. This most horrendous battle of the eighteenth century shook the thirty-eight-year-old Mir completely. In the same year, King Suraj Mal defeated the Mughals and the Rohilla Afghans, capturing the Agra Fort, which dealt yet another blow to the fast-deteriorating authority of the Mughals. A year later, in 1762, Abdali's army massacred thirty thousand Sikhs, which took the legend of his cruelty to a whole new zenith. Two years later, in 1764, when Mir was forty-one, Maharaja Jawahar Singh (r. 1763–1768) of Bharatpur, defeated the Mughals in the Battle of Delhi (1764). Skirmishes and battles continued ceaselessly, and in the year 1771, the Marathas, under the command of Mahadaji Shinde (r. 1768–1794), defeated the Rohilla Afghans and reclaimed control of the dilapidated Delhi; in effect also establishing a stronger hold over the northern part of India. Mir, forty-eight, bore witness to all such machinations for power and profit, but with much sadness and sorrow. Mir's miseries were not yet over; another, and arguably most heinous chapter was still to be added. He was in his mid-sixties when Ghulam Qadir Khan Rohilla (r. 1787–1788), an Afghan Rohilla front runner, occupied Delhi in 1788, plundered the fortress, blinded Mughal emperor Shah Alam II (r. 1759–1806), flogged the princes, brutalized the princesses and left the royal family to suffer without food and water for days. He looted the city for two months. A new phase of history began in 1809 when the East India Company signed the first Treaty of Amritsar with Maharaja Ranjit Singh (r. 1801–1839). Mir was eighty-six then and the messenger of death was looming at the door to take him away a year later in 1810. In the treacherous corridors of history from 1751 to 1808, Mir compiled his six *diivaans*, a testament to his extraordinary ability to document his life and times, even amidst adversity. In verse five of ghazal number 1706 in his fifth *diivaan*, he told himself that he was a poet and it was too difficult for a poet to keep silent. He thus urged himself to speak up, read verses, and tell even the tragic tales. Mir followed this poetic conscience truthfully.

In his book of memories, *Zikr-e Mir*, Mir interspersed his sense of personal time with his experiences of historical events. This book is like a roving eye that captures people and places, blurring the lines between the historical as personal and the personal as historical. It is a pathetic account of the cunning passages of history and politics and a sympathetic chronicle of culture and human conditions. We encounter both the kind and the cruel ones writing both happy and unhappy predicaments. There are references to human empathy and ingratitude, intrigues and politicking, skirmishes and wars, killings and blindings, throning and dethroning. In this tug of war are the Mughals, Afghans and Persians; the Jats, Sikhs and Marathas; and later the British jostling alongside.

Mir chose to locate himself—and develop his worldview with a sense of philosophical detachment—within the intersection of the personal and the historical. His upbringing and association with his father, Mir

Mohammad Ali; his mentor, Amanullah; and Sufis like Ehsanullah, Bayazeed and Asadullah profoundly impacted his life. Living through his uniquely personal and collective histories, Mir ultimately emerged as a *Sufi Manush*.

A Sufi Manush

There are many ways to acknowledge Mir as a Sufi, but it is proper to draw upon two episodes from *Zikr-e Mir*, that are central to our understanding of Mir from this perspective. The first episode relates to his father, Mohammad Ali, known as Ali Muttaqi. Mir recalled that his father was an ardent devotee, praying to God day and night. Whenever he raised his head from prayer, he advised Mir to practice love, for love swayed all as the creator and the consumer, the mover and the moved. He counselled him that love was the measure of perfection, fire and water its ardour and agitation, the earth its repose, death its loftiness, life its temperance, day its consciousness and night its slumber. He taught him that the believers and non-believers were its soothing loveliness and overwhelming splendour, respectively. To each there was a paradise to yearn for (*shauq*) and an ecstasy (*zauq*) to enjoy. Love, his father taught him, finally lay beyond worship and it moved the heavens. This proved much too consequential in the making of Mir the poet in the decades to come.

The second episode relates to his consequential meeting with a *darvesh* called Ehsanullah, to whom his uncle Mir Amanullah had taken Mir when he was still a young boy. The *darvesh* looked at him intently and prophesied that he would cross the heavens in a single leap if he were brought up properly. The *darvesh* advised Mir's uncle that the young boy should keep company with *darveshes* for their blessings. Mir recounted that Ehsanullah picked up a piece of dry bread, moistened it with water, and put it in the young Mir's mouth. He added that he had never tasted anything as delicious; he never forgot its taste and his palate longed for it ever after. It should be pertinent to note that Mir's meeting with Ehsanullah led him to seek the company of other spiritual masters later in his life. Mir found them amongst the hallowed beings, such as Bayazeed, Asadullah, Ahmad Beg Wilaayati and Mir Jafar Azimabadi.

In this context, we may examine what Mir added as his concluding observations at the end of his long and eventful life, as recounted in his reminiscences. He surmised that this world was a place of bizarre incidents and coincidences, where bubbling youngsters lost their lives, gardens turned desolate, animated congregations became stories of the past and beautiful blossoms withered. He added that while the caravans (of time) paced, the dear ones faced humiliation, and the worst grew empowered. He mourned everything that the eyes witnessed and the ears heard. He added pathetically that every skull told the story of a crown and every deserted home was a reminder of some gorgeous doors and walls now turned to ashes. He concluded that this world was a tale, and he had told only a part of it, leaving it to someone else to narrate the rest. Mir was only sixty when he wrote this; he was too unwell already, his vision had deteriorated and he had lost his vitality. But he still had twenty-seven years of suffering to undergo before his passing and bear his hardships with unending patience until then.

A Life in Poetry

Poetry may be a passion for poets, but it has been a vocation for them as well. Especially in the ages past, it was a full-time engagement, a way of sustaining themselves—individually, socially and culturally. In what is considered by many critics and scholars as the golden period of Urdu poetry, Mir found himself amongst some of the most celebrated eighteenth- and nineteenth-century poets: Mirza Mazhar Jane Janaan (1699–1781), born twenty-four years before him, Mohammad Rafi Sauda (1713–1781) born ten years before him, Siraj Aurangabadi (1715–1763) born eight years before him, and Khwaja Mir Dard (1721–1785) born two years before him. Those who followed and created yet another tradition of excellence included Ghulam Hamadani Mushafi (1750–1824) born twenty-seven years after him, Insha Allah Khan Insha (1757–1817) born thirty-four after him, Imam Bakhsh Nasikh (1772–1838) born forty-nine years after him, Bahadur Shah Zafar II (1775–1862) born fifty-two years after him, Haider Ali Atish (1778–1847) born fifty-five years after him, Mirza Asadullah Khan Ghalib (1797-1869) born seventy-four years after him, and Momin Khan Momin (1800–1852) born seventy-seven years after him. His contemporaries and successors, including Ghalib, the poet of exacting standards, praised him for his extraordinariness in terms of his worldview and literary merit. The youngest poets—Ghalib and Momin—were only thirteen and ten years old, respectively, when Mir passed away, leaving a majestic tradition for them to draw from.

Mir has left behind a vast literary treasure of six Urdu *diivaans* upon which his reputation rests predominantly and firmly. He also has a Farsi *diivaan*, one hundred *rubaa'iis* (quatrains), thirty-eight *mathnaviis* (long narrative poems), thirty-four *marsiyaas* (elegies), sixteen *manqabats* (religious eulogies), eight *qasiidas* (panegyrics), seven *salaams* (religious obeisance), four *vaashokhts* (hatred-envy verses), and three *hajvs* (lampoons). Apart from these, he wrote his poems in various metrical constructions, including *musallas* (three-line stanzas), *mukhammas* (five-line stanzas), *musaddas* (six-line stanzas), *haft-band* (seven-line stanzas), *tarj'ii-band* (one-line recurrence compositions) and *tarkiib-band* (end-rhyme symmetric compositions). Three remarkable works in Farsi prose include his subtle notes on Urdu poets, titled *Nukaat-us shu'araa*; his reminiscences, *Zikr-e Mir*; and his journal, *Faiz-e Mir*, which contains stories of Sufis for the moral and mental education of his son, Mir Faiz Ali. Younger poets must have dreamt of having a literary master of this calibre as their mentor. By an average estimate, Mir had over fifty disciples who learned the art and craft of poetry writing from him. The following generations only established him on firmer grounds as *ustad-ul asaataza*, the master of masters for all time.

❖

Mir creates a poetic universe entirely and peculiarly of his own. It is both terrestrial and extraterrestrial; it is a macrocosm composed of and constituted by many microcosms of the earth and the skies, encompassing mysticism and eroticism, emperors and plebeians, bubbling romancers seeking sensual and carnal pleasures and failed romantics craving solace and resolution. His world is populated by personages who turn into institutions and institutions that transform into icons. He brings them in now as Farhaad, now as *Majnuu.n*; now as Laila, now as Qais; now as bulbul, now as bird hunter; now as blossom, now as a garden; now as a temple, now as a mosque; now as the castigated Sheikh, now as a reprimanded Brahmin; now as a believer, and now as a heretic. There is a *Khizr* around to show the path, a messenger nearby to disappoint a lover, a stonecutter somewhere to carve a milk channel, a beloved in sight to induce and seduce, an eternally present *Ghair* (the other) as a helpless onlooker, and central to all these figures, the poet's persona surveying them. In his relationship with the mythic other, the lover becomes a myth in his own right. He is erotic and illicit in his relationship; he even mentions same-sex love but only to suggest that these manifestations, too, are honest and undeniable parts of human desires. The perennial passion that unites them all in a vast cosmos is love—with its multifaceted manifestations. Pain is understood as a composite function of human destiny. Mir deciphers the complexities of the internal and external worlds, distinguishing between right and wrong, reality and illusion, love and rationality and idea and action. He nurses no pretensions about himself and reposes faith in his ideals and individuality. He has hope and faith; humanity is his first principle, love his first credo, man his first concern. Mir is an organic entity—an earthly being, a *darvesh*, a lover, a mystic, a philosopher, a product of history and a victim of personal and historical times.

Mir's six *diivaans* have stood as sacrosanct entities, but most of his readers have often turned to the volumes of his selected ghazals, which are as diverse in their focus as are the choices of the editors who have compiled these collections across various eras. This has made way for many a Mir to enter the readers' imaginations, each different from the other. To say that he is a poet only of suffering is a distortion, as he transcended suffering to achieve mystic realization. To insist that he suffered in pain throughout his life without any relief is to reiterate an untruth, as his pain was never without a panacea. Similarly, to assert that he sought pleasure in wishful romance, verging on the immoral, is spreading a fiction that defies reality. And likewise, arguing that he is too simple to be authentic is to put the very notions of simplicity and complexity in the wrong categories, thereby drawing incorrect conclusions. Mir's stature can be evaluated by examining his merits both individually and comparatively within the context of the grand poetic tradition of the eighteenth century, of which he is undoubtedly the presiding deity, popularly and stereotypically known as *KHuda-i SuKHan*, or the God of poetry. Mir is uniquely conscious of his poetics, which is reflected in a number of his verses. In this sense, he is a propounder and practitioner of his poetics. He did not discard the prevalent eighteenth-century preferences for the Persian language and its poetics; instead, he developed his own linguistic and stylistic models. He created a conversational idiom and mode of expression in his poetry, which represented human dignity and tragic aura. Even the mystical and philosophical subjects found their credibility in the subtle simplicity of his poetic speech. His verses thus turned the insignificant objects into significant and the ordinary into extraordinary. The existential angst of Mir's poetry is made sustainable through the quality of his intimate orality, which remains one of his poetry's distinguishing marks.

Language and Diction

As has been mentioned already, Persian was considered the authentic literary language when Mir appeared on the literary scene in the eighteenth century. He also inherited a nearly ubiquitous language called Rekhta, which was gaining ground rapidly and inflaming the common imagination even faster. He drew his diction from there, and it helped him acquire and hone his identity far more substantially than his contemporaries. Curiously, the word Rekhta, which meant 'scattered' and 'mixed', stood for a creative blending of various dialects into a single language. It cannot be ascertained whether Mir was aware that Rekhta was also a term used in music, which Alauddin Barnavi, in his 1655 treatise on musicology entitled *Chishtiya Bihishtiya*, had identified as a piece of composition in which Persian and Hindi were combined to create a *raaga* and a *taala*. Whatever the case, the close relationship between poetry and music worked well in developing Rekhta as a medium of poetic expression over the centuries. Mir's preference for Rekhta, which drew upon Khariboli and Brajbhasha with a liberal blending of Perso-Arabic diction, firmly attested to the merit of his poetics. He could well appreciate the integrity of this language, which had developed multilaterally and drawn upon several linguistic registers, including the Sufi and the Yogic. Furthermore, it had been written in various scripts already, including Persian, Gurmukhi, Kaithi and Nagri, by Muslim, Sikh and Hindu authors and saints from different traditions. It had also seen the Nirgun saints, the Krishna devotees, the authors of Guru Nanak's *Janamsakhis*, and the court poets of Rajasthan using it as the preferred medium for both secular and religious expression.

Mir, the poet of the people at large, and Rekhta, their language at best, thus became unanimous in their support of each other and complemented each other's tone and tenor in life and poetry. His Rekhta echoed the lexical connotations, semantic structures, phonological overtones and morphological implications of Hindavi, Hindi, Dehlavi, Gujari and Deccani in the grand hall of linguistic amalgamations and reverberations. He harked back to its glorious tradition, initiated by the iconic poet Amir Khusrau (1253–1325) and validated by its first significant practitioner, Vali Deccani (1667–1707), who blended Persian and Hindavi, setting a model for Delhi poets to practise it with greater confidence. For Mir, Rekhta became a serious aesthetic engagement. He deliberated upon Rekhta more seriously in the eighteenth century and used it, self-confessedly, as the language of his poetic compositions. Towards the end of *Nukat-us Shu'araa*, he even theorized upon Rekhta. He classified it into six categories and prescribed that Rekhta verses should (a) have one line in Persian, another in Hindi (b) have half a line in Persian, another half in Hindi (c) use Farsi words and verbs, although they may be deterring (d) use Farsi turns of phrase if it suited the temperament of Rekhta, which Mir chose for himself (e) use *iihaam*, that is, where the keyword should have a double entendre and (f) insist on *andaaz* that characterized a poetic phrase with eloquence, precision, style and thought—a quality that also drew him to the verses of Khwaja Mir Dard. Mir enriched Rekhta with a more extensive vocabulary; he refined it to discover his diction, which came to be recognized as the Urdu language only towards the end of the eighteenth century.

Rekhta served as a language and a source of diction for Mir; it also gave him a style, a way of speaking, and a tone of voice. This helped him practise poetry as natural speech, drawing upon common idioms and exploit its spontaneity, empowering it with rich ambiguities and multilayered suggestiveness. The trimness of his verses, their eloquence and impulsiveness, conversational ease and dialogic harmony come from his ingenious use of Rekhta. It helped him create rich nebulousness of meaning through wordplay, evolve an atmosphere from slight and solemn discourses, and develop drama through the invocation of moods. Mir's verses are both radiant and mute, private and public; they offer company, they cajole and persuade. They equally impart the pleasures of reading to both ordinary and informed readers. He wished to establish his dialogue with ordinary people rather than the elite, which largely determined his diction and modes of speech. His metres create conditions of ease both for reading and listening.

It is crucial to note here that over time, Rekhta acquired superiority over Farsi as a language as well as its poetic tradition. It also contributed to the development of new parameters in literary sociology, with its domesticity serving as a prominent feature of art; finding its finest expression in Mir, who held a mirror to himself and his times the best.

Epilogue

As a person who grew richer because of his sensitivities to his times and as a poet who matured by mastering the ways of words, Mir became a canon-maker during his lifetime and has remained so ever since. Today, he appears to us as one of our own; he speaks in a language we understand, with gestures we recognize, and of experiences we have grown with. Rilke wrote that birds fly quietly through us, and inside, the tree grows, suggesting that there is only one omnipresent space that encompasses all beings. Mir is our all-inclusive space—terrestrial and extra-terrestrial—he decodes that space for us, and with us, in a language that is his, as much as ours.

Towards the concluding part of *Zikr-e Mir*, there are fifty-five witty tales. The nineteenth tale is about an adolescent boy who visits a calligrapher and seeks his advice on writing the word '*nafs*' (man's baser self). The artist writes the word for him and asks him in turn to write it the same way, but the adolescent wonders if he has written it any differently. The playful calligrapher says he does not question the beauty of his *nafs* but only that it is too impulsive and daunting. Mir probably registered his own choice for genuine simplicity in life and art by narrating this tale. Although he acquired his identity as a person of elemental passions, pride and irreverence, he was also a philosopher of love, markedly divine and yet earthly. Today, he stands as one who defined afresh poetry and poetics, language and diction, mysticism and metaphysics and the philosophy of life and living itself.

The tale of the young calligrapher also complements a moving will that Mir left to his son. He said that he had nothing for him to leave behind, no treasures or worldly possessions that could sustain his son through an uncertain future. He asserted that his only proud possession was his language and its discipline; that was the foundation stone of his life and honour and that this indeed had lifted him from the ignominies of this earth to the high skies of renown and reputation. In bequeathing his language to his son, the story of his life comes full circle. We can attest that his canon lives on; the legacy of his language survives, his style endures and his worldview remains acutely contemporary, even after two centuries of his passing. This legacy has served as a test for poets of every age, to measure their own skills against Mir and compare if theirs can hold a candle to the God of poetry's. More often than not, Mir proved to be inimitable. In fact, the imitating poets often found themselves in a labyrinth of idioms and words. They could neither replicate his ideas nor his style. Life is asymmetrical and defies order; it is a halo of misty luminosities and subdued radiances. Mir's life exemplifies this. A poet who lived a life of myriad dissonances and held a mirror to poetry, breathed his last in Lucknow. He was buried in Akhara Bheem graveyard, where railway lines are now laid out. A thousand whipping wheels run over his breast, causing raucous clatters each day and night. What a prophetic verse Mir wrote, and how he wished his mark to stay on, on the face of this earth after him, but he remained unheeded in death as he was in life:

mat turbat-e Mir ko hataao
rehne do Ghariib kaa nishaa.n to

Don't remove the tomb of Mir from here
Let the poor man's sign remain, but here.

Mir Taqi Mir:
A BRIEF TIMELINE

Early 1600s: Mir Taqi Mir's ancestors arrive in India from the Hijaz in the Arabian Peninsula. Family members settle in Ahmedabad and Agra.

1671–72: Mir's father, Mir Mohammad Ali, alias Ali Muttaqi, is born in Agra.

1703-04: Mir's elder stepbrother, Mohammad Hasan, is born.

1717-18: Second marriage of Mir's father.

1723 (August/September): Mir is born in Agra to his father's second wife and receives his early education there.

1724-25: Mir's younger brother, Mir Mohammad Razi, is born.

1729-1730: Arrival of Amanullah, a resident of Bayana, in Agra. He becomes a disciple of Mir's father, Ali Muttaqi. He brings up Mir with great care, keeps him close to himself and teaches him the Qur'an. Mir addresses him as an uncle.

1733 (18 December): Mir's father's death at sixty-four. Mir is around eleven years old at this time.

1734-35: Mir's first visit to Delhi. He approaches a noble, Khvaja Mohammad Asim, popularly known as Samsam-ud Daula (the sword of the state) through his father's friend, Khvaja Mohammad Basit. Samsam-ud Daula fixes a stipend of one rupee a day for Mir.

1739: Mir's stipend of a rupee a day is withdrawn because of the death of Samsam-ud Daula; who died fighting against the army of Nadir Shah on 30 January 1739. Left helpless, Mir returns to Agra.

1740: Returns to Delhi and stays with Sirajuddin Ali Khan Arzu (popularly known as Khan-e Arzu), the brother of Mir's stepmother and a well-known Persian poet, linguist and lexicographer. Jobless and disappointed, Mir becomes a victim of lunacy.

1740-1741: Mir remains in a state of lunacy for about four months. Begum Fakhruddin Khan, a devotee of Mir's father, invests in his treatment back to normalcy.

1741-1742: Mir begins educating himself with the assistance of Khan-e Arzu. Mir Jafar, a student from Azimabad (Patna) helps him in his pursuit. With his command of language, he begins writing verses in Rekhta at the behest of Mir Saadat Ali. Within the next five years, he comes to be acknowledged as a poet of great worth.

1747: Mir meets Riyaet Ali Khan, an emir, with the assistance of Mir Alimullah. Khan was already appreciative of Mir's talent as a poet and had wished to meet him for long. He takes him under his patronage instantly.

1748-49: Mir's son, Mir Faiz Ali, is born in Delhi.

1750-51: Heartbroken, Mir takes a retreat and spends his time reading and teaching Arabi textbooks. The Nawab continues to give him a stipend.

1751-52: Compiles his first Urdu *diivaan* in Delhi.

1752: Completes writing *Nukaat-us Shu'araa*, a Persian account of early poets writing in Urdu.

1752-53: A period of acute financial strains; struggles for a few years and later shifts to the haveli of Amir Anjam Khan and stays there from 1759 to 1760.

1756-57: Mir's daughter, Begum, is born in Delhi. She also wrote poetry.

1761-62: Mir writes *Faiz-e Mir*, a journal containing the stories of Sufis, to help his son, Mir Faiz Ali, develop his moral and mental education.

1770-71: Utterly disappointed due to personal deprivations, Mir leaves the fourteen-year-old services to Raja Nagar Mal, returns to Delhi—leaving his wife and children in an inn—meets Rai Bahadur Singh, Raja Nagar Mal's eldest son, and apprises him of all the events in his life. Mir's wife dies.

1772/1773: He remains largely unemployed and writes *Zikr-e Mir*, his reminiscences, in Persian. He continues revising it until 1788.

1775-1776: Compiles the second Urdu *diivaan* and also his Persian poetry collection.

1780-1781: He continues living without any employment.

1782: Arrives in Lucknow via Farukkhabad at the invitation of Asaf-ud-Daula, the Nawab of Awadh (r. 1775–1797). Enrolls as a poet of his court, among others. He marries again around this time in Lucknow.

1785: Compiles his third Urdu *diivaan* in Lucknow.

1786-1787: Birth of his son, Mir Hasan Askari, from the wife hailing from Lucknow. Later, he came to be known as Mir Kallu 'Arsh' as a poet.

1794: Compiles his fourth Urdu *diivaan* in Lucknow.

1797: Death of Nawab Asaf-ud-Daula. Mir's stipend is withdrawn, once again leaving him financially crippled.

1797-98: Compiles his fifth Urdu *diivaan* in Lucknow.

1807: Death of Begum, Mir's daughter.

1807-08: Compiles his sixth and last Urdu *diivaan* in Lucknow.

1808: Death of Mir's first son, Faiz Ali, a minor poet.

1809: Death of Mir's second wife.

1810: Dies in Lucknow on the twentieth day of September. Buried in Akhara Bheem, Lucknow. Approximately four hundred admirers attend his funeral. Later, clusters of people say their prayers for the dead in absentia.

1811: The College of Fort William, Calcutta, publishes his *Kulliyaat* (Collected Poems) in Urdu.

VERSES AND COMMENTARIES

DIIVAAN 1

Ghazal 1 | Verse 1

1

تھا مستعار حسن سے اس کے جو نور تھا
خورشید میں بھی اس ہی کا ذرہ ظہور تھا

था मुस्तआर हुस्न से उस के जो नूर था
ख़ुर्शीद में भी उस ही का ज़र्रा ज़ुहूर था

thaa must'aar husn se us ke jo nuur thaa
KHurshiid mei.n bhii us hii kaa zarra zuhuur thaa

(*musta'aar*—borrowed, lent;
nuur—radiance, light;
KHurshiid—sun;
zarra—particle, speck;
zuhuur—manifestation, appearance)

The radiance that showed up was borrowed
but only from His beauty;
Even the sun showed a speck of the same light,
borrowed from His beauty

This opening verse of Mir's first *diivaan* is, appropriately enough, his metaphysical paean to God. He builds his essential argument by positing that the radiance of this universe is borrowed only from God, and even the sun manifests that divine glory with each of its rays. As such, this verse posits that God's glory is all-pervasive from the earth to the sky and may be read as an article of the poet's faith and of all the others', who believe in divine power and glory.

A keener reading brings out the following aspects of the verse: (a) the world is a reflection of an invisible God incarnated as both luminous and beautiful (b) even the particles of the earth borrow their beauty and brightness from God (c) the particles, represented here by the rays of the sun, are like atoms and configure as the nucleus of power in scientific terms to configure the sun as a ball of fire that keeps the world animated (d) God's absolute radiance and glory, which is different from the fake glories of the world, is well reflected in religious texts, for example: 'God is the light of the heavens and the earth.' (Qur'an, 24:35) 'Surely, the Lord our God has shown His glory and His greatness, and we have heard His voice from the midst of the fire.' (Deuteronomy, 5:24) 'He makes his angels winds /and his ministers a flame of fire.' (Hebrews 1:7) (e) the verse clearly echoes a voice of assertion from the poet and reaches out to the listeners with natural ease, leading them to a moment of serious reflection.

Mir's choice of diction imparts the verse its ratiocinative appeal. *Husn* (beauty), *nuur* (radiance), and *KHurshiid* (sun) are homogenous words that act as visual images embodying divine glory. Two other words—*musta'aar* (borrowed) and *zuhuur* (manifestation)—complement each other as a cause and effect combo of poetic expression. Apart from acting as agents of light, spread out as divine manifestations, the rhyming words—*nuur* (radiance) and *zuhuur* (manifestation)—also create a rhythmic design for the verse and develop a calm auditory condition. By inverting the usual turn of phrase from *us kaa hii* (only his) to *us hii kaa* (his only), Mir shifts the degree of emphasis to underline the all-pervasive supremacy of God's glory. With this, Mir also takes us to another verse that reflects keenly on this one: *us ke faroGh-e husn se jhamke hai sab mei.n nuur / sham-'e haram ho yaa ho diyaa Somnath kaa.* Interestingly, this mystical verse reminds us of Mir's close contemporary, the English mystic poet William Blake's opening lines of 'Auguries of Innocence': 'To see a world in a grain of sand/And a heaven in a wild flower.'

Ghazal 2 | Verse 1

2

کیا میں بھی پریشانیٔ خاطر سے قریں تھا
آنکھیں تو کہیں تھیں دلِ غم دیدہ کہیں تھا

क्या मैं भी परेशानी-ए ख़ातिर से क़रीं था
आँखें तो कहीं थीं दिल-ए ग़म दीदा कहीं था

kyaa mai.n bhii pareshaanii-i KHaatir se qarii.n thaa
aankhei.n to kahii.n thii.n dil-e Gham-diida kahii.n thaa

(*pareshaanii-i KHaatir*—ruffled/bewildered state of being;
qarii.n—close, conjoined, contiguous;
Gham-diida—saddened)

Was I too, too close to my ruffled state,
my other;
My gaze lingered at one end, my grievous heart
at another

Man's existence is subject to the whims of time and destiny. The speaker in this verse is portrayed as one who has been in a state of turmoil and has lost control over emotional and physical states. He expresses his despair in personal terms but also seems to make a more extensive comment on the essential human predicament.

There are layers of implication in this verse that may be marked as follows: (a) the speaker is bewildered at his lot, and his voice is marked by mixed tones of wonder, interrogation and lament, as he did not expect any misery to touch him (b) he is, in fact, in a state of disbelief and wonders if he, too, would fall prey to misery (c) pathetically enough, both his wild, roving eyes and sad, stagnant heart are housed in the same body which he finds challenging to negotiate but are also scattered in different places (e) it may well be posited that his sense of despair is not entirely personal as he represents the archetypal human condition characterized by suffering which endorses the existentialist philosophy that suffering is the ultimate reality of life, and pleasure only an illusion.

The phrase—*pareshaanii-i KHaatir* (ruffled state of being)—is the crucial expression in this verse, the nucleus of its meaning, and appears as a generic expression of suffering in life. The phrase—*mai.n bhiii* (I, too)—distinguishes the sufferer as one of all others who also suffer. *Aa.nkhein* (eyes) and *dil* (heart) are configured as metaphors for suffering. The phrase—*kahii.n* (somewhere)—used twice to represent the scattered state of existence, adds an element of gestural drama of sorrow. The vital expression—*Gham-diida* (saddened)—configures the sufferer vividly. Mir appropriates this idea in yet another verse thus: *kyaa dilkash hai bazm jahaa.n kii jaate yaa.n se jise dekho / vo Gham-diida ranj-kashidaa aah saraapaa hasrat hai.* Another representation of this state may be marked in a verse of his junior contemporary poet, Khwaja Haider Ali Atish*: dil kahii.n jaan kahii.n chashm kahii.n gosh kahii.n / apne majmu'e kaa har ek varaq barham hai.*

Ghazal 3 | Verse 4

3

درہمی حال کی ہے سارے مرے دیواں میں
سیر کر تو بھی یہ مجموعہ پریشانی کا

दरहमी हाल की है सारे मिरे दीवाँ में
सैर कर तू भी ये मजमूआ' परेशानी का

darhamii haal kii hai saare mire diivaa.n mei.n
sair kar tuu bhii ye majmu'a pareshaanii kaa

(*darhamii*—disorder, chaos, distress;
majmuu'a—collection, anthology, assemblage)

All over my *diivaan*, the chaos of time present
is writ large;
You, too, should stroll through this anthology
of chaos, writ large

No life is free from distress and disorder. Poets perceive this adage with greater sensitivity than others, especially when it concerns their own state of affairs. This is one of many verses in which Mir expresses his disappointments. He considers life to be the site of all his miseries and invites his readers to observe it.

This seemingly simple verse carries layers of meaning that may be read in these terms: (a) writing is an act of confession, and the most precious confession is about one's own dishevelled state, which a poet makes for himself for his readers to witness it (b) in this respect, Mir's *diivaan* is an extended poetic account of his personal predicament which he shares with us (c) both his life and his *diivaan* reflect upon each other, as both embody suffering in life (d) as such, looking at his *diivaan* is looking at the chaos of his times and vice versa (e) his asking for the readers' attention to watch his state is not an act of self-pity on his part, but it underlines the larger human need to share the pain with fellow human beings to seek relief for themselves (f) as a universal experience, the expression of sorrow and suffering finds its corresponding expression in the opening lines of American poet, Emily Dickinson's poem: 'After great pain, a formal feeling comes/the nerve sits ceremonious, like Tombs.'

The key word in this verse is *darhamii* (disorder), which calls four other words—*haal, saare, sair* and *majmuu'a*—to its service to enlarge the essential meaning of the verse. The duality of meaning in *haal* (encompassing both a human condition and contemporary times) and *majmuu'a* (implying a collection of anything and an anthology of verses) impregnates this verse with a richness of meaning. Mir charges a commonplace word—*saare* (all)—with great energy to underline the grandeur of suffering. The expression—*sair* (stroll through)—is a remarkable example of Mir appropriating this word from the domain of travel to imbue it with layers of irony and impart a rich ambiguity to the verse. Mir takes this state of chaos to a greater height in yet another verse, entirely different in manner, which would be worth quoting here: *mastii se darhamii hai mirii guftuguu ke biich / Jo chaaho tum bhii mujh ko kaho main nashe mein huu.n.* Another verse by Mir's junior contemporary, Ghulam Hamadani Mushafi, echoes Mir's sentiment: *dekhe jo koii Ghaur se diivaa.n mire to haa.n / har bait hai zamaane ke ahvaal kii kitaab.*

Ghazal 3 | Verse 8

4

اس کا منہ دیکھ رہا ہوں سو وہی دیکھوں ہوں
نقش کا سا ہے سماں میری بھی حیرانی کا

उस का मुँह देख रहा हूँ सो वही देखूँ हूँ
नक़्श का सा है समाँ मेरी भी हैरानी का

us kaa mu.nh dekh rahaa huu.n so vahii dekhuu.n huu.n
naqsh kaa saa hai samaa.n merii bhii hairaanii kaa

(*naqsh*—image, portrait;
samaa.n—condition, scene)

I look at her face, so I keep on looking at her face,
nothing else;
My astonishment, too, looks like an image carved,
nothing else

A lover's watching a beloved is more than mere watching. This verse portrays such a scene and unfolds what his watching truly means. The beloved's astonishing beauty mesmerizes him, so much so that he cannot take his eyes away from her. Mir has rendered this simple experience so unassumingly that it naturally becomes an experience worthy of the readers' critical attention.

This verse may be read as a piece of dramatic representation with the following features easily marked: (a) there are only two persons here—the lover as the onlooker, and the beloved as the one being looked at, without anyone else around (b) in looking at the beloved's face continuously, the lover is both mesmerized and stunned by her striking beauty (c) in this act of looking at her, he has turned into a picture of amazement himself, which imparts the verse its real merit (d) this is Mir's way of praising the beloved by idealizing her on the one hand and remaining her subject on the other (e) this very act of watching the beloved also turns the lover himself into a picture of amazement where he watches the beloved's portrait, as if, on a wall (f) thus, he becomes a picture within a picture whom other onlookers may also observe, immersed in amazement and admiration.

The idea of looking intently is well conveyed by the simplest of phrases—*vahii dekhuu.n huu.n* (look at that, and that only). The simple word *naqsh*, which means both an image and a mood, is further qualified by *hairaanii*, which describes a state of being both stunned and entranced. Both these states are reflected in the onlooker's countenance. The most remarkable expression, however, is *samaa.n* (condition/scene), which represents yet another scene within a scene. With this verse, Mir automatically reminds us of his two other verses, which represent an amazing variation on this scene: *darvaaze pe khaRa huu.n kaii din se yaar ke / hairat ne husn kii mujhe diivaar kar diyaa* and *rahe hai.n dekh jo tasviir se tire mun.h ko / hamaarii aa.nkh se zaahir hai ye ke hairaa.n hai.n.*

Ghazal 6 | Verse 2

5

کہا میں نے کتنا ہے گل کا ثبات
کلی نے یہ سن کر تبسم کیا

कहा मैंने कितना है गुल का सबात
कली ने ये सुन कर तबस्सुम किया

kahaa mai.n ne kitnaa hai gul ka sabaat
kalii ne ye sun kar tabassum kiyaa

(*sabaat*—durability, continuance, endurance; *tabassum*—smile)

How long would the bloom last,
I asked;
The bud only smiled at what
I asked

Transitoriness qualifies and characterizes both—human life and the life of nature. Here is Mir's ultimate comment on life and life's temporality. Mir's speaker asks the bud: 'How long would the bloom last?' Hearing this, the blooming bud only gives a smile. By raising a question about the durability of a blossom, the speaker makes a subtle comment on the fragility of all life on this earth. He does not directly comment on the impermanent nature of a bud's life but indirectly suggests the answer through its ironic smile.

There are many layers of meaning in this ostensibly simple verse: (a) first, instead of addressing the season of bloom, Mir's speaker artfully addresses the bud herself that would soon blossom on its own (b) second, he implies that the bud knows well what her fate would be like the very next day, and yet she smiles helplessly, with a certain dignity (c) third, he suggests that the bud's facial gesture is more eloquent than words (d) fourth, he does not address the flower as she has already outlived her span of life and cannot speak any longer, but can only overhear what is being asked, and finally, (e) the cycle of life is visualized in terms of a bud becoming a blossom and a blossom turning into a withering non-being.

The merit of the verse lies in its overpowering simplicity that is imbued with deep irony. This irony is well contained in the word *kitnaa* (how long), which together enfolds a question, a wonder and a monologue. Mir develops a central discourse on the idea of *sabaat* (durability) in this verse through the seminal metaphors of *kalii* (bud) and *gul* (blossom). With these, he weaves his pattern of meaning to deftly suggest that all creations upon this earth are beautiful. Still, all are only essentially transitory. Mir draws upon the idea of life's transitoriness in several of his verses. One good example is: *le saa.ns bhii aahista ke naazuk hai bahut kaam / aafaaq kii is kaar-gah*-e *shiishagarii kaa.*

Ghazal 7 | Verse 8

6

شیخ جو ہے مسجد میں ننگا رات کو تھا مے خانے میں
جبہ خرقہ کرتا ٹوپی مستی میں انعام کیا

शैख़ जो है मस्जिद में नंगा रात को था मय-ख़ाने में
जुब्बा ख़िर्क़ा कुर्ता टोपी मस्ती में इनआ'म किया

sheiKH jo hai masjid mei.n nanga raat ko thaa mai-KHane mei.n
jubba KHirqa kurtaa topii mastii mei.n in'aam kiyaa

(*sheiKH*—preacher, saint, prelate;
jubba—gown, cloak;
KHirqa—ragged/gruffy/patched garment of a devotee or mendicant)

The *sheiKH* who is naked in the mosque,
was in the tavern last night;
In his ecstasy, he gifted his gown,
gruffy garment, *kurta* cap, last night

Inscrutable are the ways of human behaviour; they also become enigmatic, but only to be negotiated with in surprising ways. Mir's speaker makes a caustic comment in the first line on the atypical *sheiKH*, whose ways appear entirely quizzical. He is presented as one who finds himself naked in the mosque, the house of God, because he was in the tavern last night, where he drank to the brim and lost his sense of judgement. As such, he discarded his apparel in a state of frenzy and stood nude without any awareness of what he had done.

This deceptively straightforward verse has specific in-depth suggestions to make: (a) the much-maligned figure of the *sheiKH* as projected in the Urdu ghazal gets an entirely novel representation here as Mir redefines his veiled and unveiled states of appearance in this verse (b) his sinful act of giving away his sacrosanct apparel is his way of reinventing himself and rewarding the curious onlookers who are yet to reach the higher levels of realization of the ultimate reality of one's being and merger with the divine (c) his inebriated state does not represent him as one drunk on the worldly wine, but as one drunk on the divine concoction that has finally helped him see the divine light and glory (d) his outrageous behaviour is surprising on the one hand, but it also receives quiet admiration from the critically conscious onlooker (e) the verse is a stark comment on a notion as received, and a reality as experienced, which underlines the philosophical point that what appears is not real and what is real, does not appear so.

Mir works with a set of analogous Islamic images of the *sheiKH*'s apparel—*jubba* (gown), *KHarqa* (gruffy garment), *kurtaa* (a long shirt) and *topii* (cap)—to configure him in stereotypical terms. He is also characterized by a set of words representing a mental condition—*mastii* (ecstasy) and *in'aam* (reward)—which characterize his act. While 'ecstasy' reflects a state of total absorption, 'reward' points towards a spiritual act of sharing. Mir finds a different way to express this in another verse: *maiKHaana vo manzar hai ke har subh'a jahaa.n sheiKH / diivaar pe KHurshiid kaa mastii se sar aave.*

Ghazal 10 | Verse 7

7

نے خون ہو آنکھوں سے بہا ٹک نہ ہوا داغ
اپنا تو یہ دل میرؔ کسو کام نہ آیا

नै ख़ून हो आँखों से बहा टुक न हुआ दाग़
अपना तो ये दिल 'मीर' किसू काम न आया

ney KHuun ho aa.nkho.n se bahaa tuk na huaa daaGh
apnaa to ye dil Mir kisuu kaam na aayaa

It neither fell from the eyes as blood,
nor turned into a blot;
My heart proved no good to me, Mir,
nor could she improve my lot

A suffering or defeated heart is a more significant subject for a poet than one filled with celebratory passion. In this verse, the speaker laments the heart's inability to bring relief to the sufferer, presumably a lover. The lover is in anguish since his heart has proved of no good use to him in his condition and this has left him lost and disappointed.

A closer reading would call for keeping these points in mind: (a) four central images of blood, eyes, blot and heart appear in the two lines of this verse and for the construction of meaning, blood and eyes go together, as do blot and heart, since they complement each other (b) although the heart occupies a central position in the human body and blood runs through its chambers to help it beat, in this context both have become too helpless as neither can fulfil its role (c) love's misery is writ large in the idiomatic expression of the eyes shedding blood rather than tears, which implies that neither the blood flowing through eyes could drop from the lover's eyes to announce its demise nor the heart appear like a blot to declare its decay (d) as the heart lost its vitality to either seek love from the beloved or share his love with her, it amounted to the loss of its life and also the spirit which it symbolized (e) the height of love could be realized only if the heart could drop like blood from the eyes or become a blot, but with neither happening, the heart's failure to seek or receive love is more than asserted and this makes a way for reading this verse as an elegy on the heart's demise.

The tone of bereavement is evident in this verse. The placement of *KHuun* (blood) and *daaGh (blot)* together underscores the futility of the heart in surviving in any possible manner. The suggestion that tears did not drop like blood from the eyes immediately evokes the idiomatic expression of shedding tears of blood, which further enriches the verse. Asadullah Khan Ghalib seems to draw upon Mir in his verse: *rago.n mein dauRte phirne ke ham nahii.n qaael / jo aa.nk hii se na tapkaa to phir luhuu kyaa hai.*

Ghazal 11 | Verse 6

8

اپنی تو جہاں آنکھ لڑی پھر وہیں دیکھو
آئینے کو لپکا ہے پریشاں نظری کا

अपनी तो जहाँ आँख लड़ी फिर वहीं देखो
आईने को लपका है परेशाँ-नज़री का

apnii to jahaa.n aa.nkh ladii phir vahii.n dekho
aaiine ko lapkaa hai pareshaa.n nazarii kaa

(*lapkaa*—a move forward to snatch something,
quick movement;
pareshaa.n nazarii—distressed eyes)

Wherever my eyes find their aim,
they fix their gaze;
This mirror is ever lured to bring
itself to its raze

The world is full of grand manifestations, but the eyes are naturally attracted to their chosen objects of seeing. Drawing upon this idea, the speaker proudly asserts that he is so enchanted and enticed by his object of seeing that he cannot keep his eyes away. Thus, he does not care if his deep fascination with that object tempts him to his possible distress.

The implied levels of meaning in this verse may be marked as follows: (a) the eyes referred to here are those of a lover, and they are like mirrors that reflect the beloved's tempting face (b) that reflection of the beloved's tempting face in the lover's eyes remains an illusion at best which turns him into a tireless, but failed quester of love (c) as the eyes of the beloved disapprove of the lover's doting looks, the questing lover faces one distress after another (d) this implies that in the saga of love, temptation impels the lover to crave for a loving look and the craving for a loving look leads him to his suffering (e) the lover as such, emerges at best as a failed protagonist of love and the beloved as only a ceaseless temptress who vanquishes her suitor.

Two idiomatic expressions—*lapkaa* (at temptation) and *parashah.n nazarii* (distressed eyes or looking with distress)—are closely interlinked as one leads to the other. Being refreshingly creative, they impart this verse an acute literary value. In yet another verse, Mir draws upon this idea thus: *aaiine kii mashhur pareshaa.n nazarii hai / tuu saada hai aiso.n ko na diidaar diyaa kar*. Shah Naseer, a close contemporary of Mir, known for his deft handling of diction, drew upon him rather closely to create his own verse with distinction: *aaiine ko hai parashah.n nazarii kaa lapkaa / aur hoti hai miyaa.n chashm-e muravvat dekho*. In all three verses, *pareshaa.n nazarii* emerges as the essential expression that holds the real import of the verse and characterizes the lover's distress.

Ghazal 11 | Verse 10

9

لے سانس بھی آہستہ کہ نازک ہے بہت کام
آفاق کی اس کارگہ شیشہ گری کا

ले साँस भी आहिस्ता कि नाज़ुक है बहुत काम
आफ़ाक़ की इस कारगह-ए शीशागरी का

le saa.ns bhii aahista ke naazuk hai bahut kaam
aafaaq kii is kaargah-e shiisha-garii kaa

(*aafaaq*—horizon, quarters of the heaven/world;
kaar-gah-e shiisha-garii—the craft of carving glasses)

Breathe easy; it's too delicate to touch for a go
It's the craft of carving glasses to make for a glow

Actions as simple as one may imagine can sometimes become much more demanding than they appear to be. Breathing is one such act that is as natural as it can be. This verse seemingly suggests that breathing is a sign of being alive, but breathing and being alive make separate demands. Mir develops a discourse on life in this universe, regarding an individual's effort to navigate life and how it may be lived here.

This verse draws our attention to these finer points embedded into it: (a) the metaphorical halo around the verse can be appreciated in terms of how the act of a careful blowing in a tube results in the making of a glass of different shapes, which is akin to blowing life into a human being (b) just as a careless or harsh blowing into the tube to produce glassware breaks the glass, so does a careless nursing of a life spoils a life, which suggests that life is as brittle and delicate as glass (c) both glass and life are examples of carved beauty and both are produced with careful breathing of life into them (d) both allure the attention of observers as works of art—one created by God's design and another by human skill (e) in literal terms, easy breathing makes life easy while breathing fitfully and erratically disrupts the pace of physical existence (e) life is delicate, and it calls for a delicate and cautious treatment (f) the universe is composed and constituted of human beings and the two together create a synchronous relationship (g) this synchronous relationship between the two rests on how man engages with the world and survives along with it, which opens yet another layer of mystical meaning.

The key phrase in this verse—*kaar-gah-e shiisha-garii* (the craft of carving glasses) is a fine analogy for leading a life. It brings out the brittleness of glass, which will break too quickly with a bit of carelessness, just as the universe will go awry with minor mistreatment. In another verse, Mir executes this idea with an added shade of meaning: *har dam qadam ko apne rakh ihtiyaat se yaa.n / ye kaargaah saarii dukkaan-e shiisha-gar hai.* Mir's close contemporary, Qaim Chandpuri also draws upon this idea in his verse—*Ghafil qadam ko rakhiyo apne sambhaal ke yaa.n / har sang rah-guzar kaa dukkaan shisha-gar kaa.*

Ghazal 12 | Verse 1

10

منھ تکا ہی کرے ہے جس تس کا
حیرتی ہے یہ آئینہ کس کا

मुँह तका ही करे है जिस तिस का
हैरती है ये आईना किस का

mu.nh takaa hii kare hai jis tis kaa
hairatii hai ye aaiina kis kaa

(*hairatii*—one who is amazed/astonished)

It stares blankly at random faces—
in wonder;
The mirror looks askance; it wanders—
in wonder

The mundane and the momentous punctuate the moments of life. But they bring much more in their wake to draw human attention. Mir's speaker acts here as an observer who interrogates what a mirror does and how it remains wonder-struck when looking at human faces. He tries to unravel a mirror's mysterious relationship with its onlooker and the onlooker's snooping relationship with the mirror.

Several implications of meanings may be located in this verse: (a) Mir's speaker assumes a larger persona here representing all those who look into the mirror to find themselves (b) there is an interchanging of roles here as it is not the face that looks at the mirror, but the mirror that looks at the face; which turns the mirror into the seer rather than the seen (c) the silent mirror is curiously looking for that mesmerizing face it had seen once and yearns to see yet again, but without success (d) the mirror is too ordinary to do anything extraordinary like recognizing the actual face in the multitude of faces that inhabit God's great kingdom (e) the answer is not proposed or even suggested, since the mirror does not have a tongue, but speaks in silence to the onlookers while reflecting their faces (f) from a metaphysical angle, the mirror in this verse may well be interpreted as the human heart itself that has seen the divine and remained stupefied ever since.

The expression—*aaiina* (mirror) works here as the keyword and matures into a quest metaphor. Mir appropriates the idiomatic expression of *mu.nh taaknaa* (staring at faces) but imparts it a literary value, which turned out to be one of his significant contributions to authenticating Rekhta as a literary language. This is followed by another idiomatic expression—*jis tis* (all and sundry): the one who brings the mirror to a state of amazement and metamorphoses it into a *hairatii* (amazed entity). Mir finds a different angle to this experience in another verse thus: *aaiine ko bhii dekho per tuk idhar bhii dekho / hairaan chashm-e 'aashiq damke hai jaise hiiraa.*

Ghazal 12 | Verse 2

11

شام سے کچھ بجھا سا رہتا ہوں
دل ہوا ہے چراغ مفلس کا

शाम से कुछ बुझा सा रहता हूँ
दिल हुआ है चराग़ मुफ़्लिस का

shaam se kuchh bujhaa saa rahtaa huu.n
dil huaa hai charaGh muflis kaa

(*muflis*—poor, pauper, destitute)

Since evening, I find myself snuffed out
This heart is but a pauper's lamp, snuffed out

Sadness has many faces; it manifests itself in various phases of our lives and somehow teaches us how life may be sustained despite gloomy conditions. Speaking in the first person, Mir spells out his miserable situation, which could well be anyone else's. He is a subject of profound desolation and represents himself as one who has been feeling extinguished or snuffed out since evening, insinuating that a long night of darkness awaits him.

There are various implied meanings in this seemingly simple verse. They may be marked as follows: (a) both the poor man's lamp and the sufferer's heart are alike, as the poor man's lamp does not have enough oil to last through the night and the sufferer's heart no spirit to see through the gloom of life (b) the sufferer is confessional in his tone but does not seek any sympathy (c) being put out since evening forebodes a gloomy night which is akin to a gloomy life itself (d) the gloominess of the heart also suggests that it has been devoid of desire or hope ever since (e) this confessional verse may also be read in psychoanalytical terms to unravel the melancholic nature of the sufferer's mind.

With four keywords—*shaam* (evening), *dil* (heart), *charaaGh* (lamp), and *muflis* (destitute)—Mir creates a condition of utter despondency in this verse. Typically associated with sadness, *shaam* serves as a powerful simile of suffering, *dil* as a metaphor for pain, poor man's *charaaGh* as a symbol of hopelessness and *muflis* as a stock figure of suffering. The striking echoes of Mir's powerful verse may be heard in two other verses by his contemporaries, Ghulam Hamadani Mushafi and Qaim Chandpuri. While Mushafi comes the closest to Mir in *shaam se hii bujhaa saa rahtaa hai / dil hai goyaa charaaGh muflis kaa*, Qaim stays closer still to him in *tab hii Qaim bujhaa saa rahtaa huu.n / kis tahii-dast kaa charaaGh huu.n mai.n.*

Ghazal 14 | Verse 7

12

لیتے ہی نام اس کا سوتے سے چونک اٹھے ہو
ہے خیر میرؔ صاحب کچھ تم نے خواب دیکھا

लेते ही नाम उस का सोते से चौंक उठे हो
है ख़ैर 'मीर' साहिब कुछ तुम ने ख़्वाब देखा

lete hi naam us kaa sote se chaun.k uThe ho
hai KHair Mir sahib kuchh tum ne KHvaab dekhaa

(*KHair*—welfare, well-being)

You woke up with a startle,
you hissed her name in sleep;
Are you fine Mir sahib,
was that a dream in your sleep?

Dreams unravel the subconscious and reflect upon the dreamer's desires. The dreams of lovers have had a mythic reputation in all poetic traditions. Interestingly, Mir makes himself a subject here to state how he is like others in dreaming and waking up from dreams. The beauty of the verse lies in the drama it creates in someone asking him if he is alright because he woke up startled from his sleep.

There are fascinating layers of meaning here: (a) since dreams are the arenas of wish fulfilment, this dreamer, too, had a dream that startled him and woke him up from his sleep with a jerk (b) the ambiguity embedded in the verse whether there was a good foreboding in the dream or it had a message of misfortune, makes the verse doubly meaningful (c) there is yet another enriching ambiguity whether this was he who hissed her name in sleep or was that someone else who named her and he woke up with a start hearing her name (d) the dreamer is thus a subject of two queries—is this he who is really startled, and is this he alone who is asked that question (e) he is speechless and presents a picture of a bewildered lover (f) this bewilderment may be both—a sign of unexpected pleasure or utter disappointment (g) being asked if he had a dream is a query of disbelief and turns the dreamer into a pathetic figure.

This verse is an exemplary dramatic representation of a lover's condition. The element of drama in this verse is well represented by the word *chau.nk* (startle). However, the element of irony is best depicted with gestural expression marked by exclamation and questioning in each word of the second line: *kuchh tum ne KHvaab dekhaa* (well, did you have a dream!). It should be interesting to note that Mir also reminds us of the early seventeenth-century English metaphysical poet John Donne's poem 'The Dream', where desire, fantasy and reality balance against each other to portray a lover who is stunned to find his beloved by his side when he wakes up from his dream.

Ghazal 15 | Verse 1

13

دل بہم پہنچا بدن میں تب سے سارا تن جلا
آ پڑی یہ ایسی چنگاری کہ پیراہن جلا

दिल बहम पहुँचा बदन में तब से सारा तन जला
आ पड़ी ये ऐसी चिंगारी कि पैराहन जला

dil baham pahu.nchaa badan mei.n tab se saaraa tan jalaa
aa padii ye aisii chingaarii ke pairaahan jalaa

(*baham*—reach, grasp;
pairaahan—dress, apparel)

My heart found a home in my body;
my whole body has burnt ever since;
Such an ember found its way, it has
burnt all my raiments ever since

Heartbeats keep us alive, but the same heartbeats may echo different pleasures and pains. The speaker in this verse is at odds with his heart and affirms that his heart has burnt him ever since it found its place in his body. Further still, he asserts that it did not burn his body alone; it also burnt his clothes to ashes. This is yet another variation on Mir's representation of the heart as the cause of man's downfall.

There are interesting suggestions in this verse: (a) the heart has been gifted to the human body to help it thrive with life, and as such holds a prime position in the body (b) this is undoubtedly a lover's heart that bears the onslaughts of loving and is vanquished by love itself (c) heart and spark act together as agents of fire and consume all (d) body is the apparel or veil of heart and heart a treasure of body in philosophical terms, but both are ephemeral (e) heart is the substance of which the body is the garment, and they are complementary and equally important to each other, and most importantly (f) the heart represents passion and it stands out as a metaphor of vitality, but it has unfortunately burnt the lover.

Four interrelated images—*dil* (heart), *tan* (body), *chingaarii* (spark) and *pairaahan* (apparel)—compose the plot of this verse and work with logical synchrony to construct the suffering of the lover. The word *tab* (then) in the first line underlines the sequence of events, but it is also a *tap* (heat) that has burnt the body. With this, an extra layer of meaning is added to the verse. Mir represents this suffering with a fantastic variation in this verse: *ab to badan mei.n saare ik phu.nk rahii hai aatish / vo mah gale na lagtaa to yuu.n jigar na jaltaa.* In another verse he says: *aatish sii phu.nk rahii hai saare badan mei.n mere / dil mei.n ajab tarah kii chingaarii aa paRii hai.* In Ghulam Hamadani Mushafi this idea finds yet another variation: *tan to kahaa.n hai sh'ola-i faanuus kii tarah / ik aag sii bharii hai mire pairhan ke biich.*

Ghazal 17 | Verse 1

14

جب جنوں سے ہمیں توسل تھا
اپنی زنجیر پا ہی کا غل تھا

जब जुनूँ से हमें तवस्सुल था
अपनी ज़ंजीर-ए पा ही का गुल था

jab junuu.n se hamei.n tavassul thaa
apnii zanjiir-e paa hii kaa Ghul thaa

(*junuu.n*—craziness, madness;
tavassul—union, companionship;
Ghul—noise, din, clamour)

When I was friends with my madness,
all abound;
The clangour of my feet's chain
was all around

Lovers are known to go crazy and become wild in love. The verse suggests that when this lover lost control over his senses, he was bound in chains, to keep him in check. Despite that, he did not stop running amok. Thus, the chains on his feet created a clatter and declared his madness even louder.

The suggestions that this verse makes are fascinating to note: (a) in poetry, madness is a condition of romantic psychosis even though it is a condition of concern in psychiatry and medicine (b) as such, madness in love is a prominent mark of lovers who are sick with love and not ill with it (c) in fact, there would be no lover around if there were no madness in love (d) this mad lover takes pride in his frenzy and announces this with a sense of superiority over other lovers (e) he personifies madness and asserts his friendship with it (f) clatter, in this case, is the music of his love and announces freedom even in a state of enchainment, and at the ultimate stage, this madness in love defies its stereotypical reception and becomes the norm in love and loving.

This wild lover speaks to a supposed listener and asserts his obsession with himself with two interdependent expressions—*hamei.n* (me) and *apnii* (mine). They also suggest his sense of assumed superiority. Another expression—*Ghul* (clatter)—creates a note that reverberates through the space and announces his proud presence as one who had his *tavassul* (companionship) with madness. One of the finest expressions of *junuu.n* in Urdu ghazal is found in Mir's contemporary Siraj Aurangabadi's iconic verse: *KHabar-e tahayyur-e 'ishq sun na junuu.n rahaa na parii rahii / na to tuu raha ana to mai.n rahaa jo rahii so be-KHabarii rahii.*

Ghazal 19 | Verse 1

15

فرہاد ہاتھ تیشے پہ ٹک رہ کے ڈالتا
پتھر تلے کا ہاتھ ہی اپنا نکالتا

फ़रहाद हाथ तेशे पे टुक रह के डालता
पत्थर तले का हाथ ही अपना निकालता

Farhaad haath teshe pe tuk rah ke daaltaa
patthar tale kaa haath hii apnaa nikaaltaa

(*tesha*—axe, hatchet, adze;
tale—beneath, under)

Farhad could have put his hand on his axe—
but with a pause;
He could draw out his hand from under the rocks—
but with a pause

The human passion for pursuing a much-desired goal knows of no conditions or constraints. The verse alludes to the tragic story of Farhad, the stone cutter, and Shirin, the princess of Persian Armenia. Farhad had to meet the crazy condition of cutting the stones and drawing a milk channel for Shirin's bath if he wished for his union with her to be realized. To meet this unreasonable condition, Farhad himself turned to madness and started cutting the stones until his destiny brought him to his death when the false news of Shirin's demise reached him while he was cutting stone. This verse suggests that Farhad could have paused a while and drawn out his already-strained hands for a while rather than madly pursuing his frenzy and meeting his tragic death, trying to do the impossible.

This verse offers more profound insights into the madness involved in love: (a) the speaker in the verse who is sympathetic to Farhad suggests that he could not have cut the stone if his hand was too hard-pressed or crushed under the stone (b) so he could have drawn it out first, but his stubborn will and urgency did not allow him to do so (c) this implies that love seals senses and leads lovers to disaster as it led Farhad to his (d) passion characterized by frenzy brought Farhad to his tragic end but imparted him a mythic status, which is a greater reward than the reward of the union in love (e) although love demands frenzied persuasion of the goal, all frenzied persuasions do not necessarily bring success.

Human hands hard-pressed or crushed under a stone is a macabre idea that has also found its way as a proverbial expression. The pain it creates for the bearer is not too hard to imagine. This idea of pain can be appreciated by remembering that a hand made of brittle bones, lean flesh and flowing blood is juxtaposed against the hardest objects—*tesha* (axe) and *pathhar* (stone). This idea is also ably poeticized by Mir's contemporaries, Khwaja Mir Dard and Qalandar Bakhsh Jurat. Dard almost echoed Mir: *pathhar tale kaa hath hai Ghafalt ke haath dil / sang-e garaa.n huaa hai ye KHvaab-e giraa.n mujhe.* Jurat also remains too close to Mir: *dil mira us sang-dil ke saath hai / kyaa karuu.n pathhar tale kaa haath hai.* Mir's eminent successor, Asadullah Khan Ghalib's most urbanized execution of this experience is equally remarkable: *majbuurii-o-d'ava-i giraftari-i ulfat / dast-e tah-e sang aamdaa paimaan-vafaa hai.* In Persian, *dast-e tah-e sang* translates into hands under the stone, which means to be defeated. When this phrase entered Urdu, it took the meaning of duress and helplessness, which Mir appropriated for himself in both senses.

Ghazal 21 | Verse 2

16

پیدا ہے کہ پنہاں تھی آتش نفسی میری
میں ضبط نہ کرتا تو سب شہر یہ جل جاتا

पैदा है कि पिन्हाँ थी आतिश-नफ़्सी मेरी
मैं ज़ब्त न करता तो सब शहर ये जल जाता

paidaa hai ke pinhaa.n thii aatish-nafasii merii
mai.n zabt na kartaa to sab shahr hii jal jaataa

(*paidaa*—revealed, manifest;
pinhaa.n—concealed, hidden;
aatish-nafasii—fiery, fire-natured;
zabt—restraint, forbearance)

Was it revealed or concealed—
this nature of mine, bearing the rage of fire
Had I spared my forbearance
this entire city would have been consumed by fire

Man is a reservoir of passion, and passion is symbolized by fire. This verse represents man in a glorious frame. His nature is fiery, but he is also endowed with the quality of forbearance that enables him to maintain equilibrium. The world would have burnt to ashes had he not been blessed with this saving grace of endurance and fortitude.

The implied meanings in this characteristically philosophical verse may be noted as: (a) man's nature is composed of the elements, and one of them is the element of fire (b) another element of nature is water that quenches the fire (c) human existence is conditioned and balanced by an interplay of both fire and water (d) in a larger context, the earth, too, is balanced by the interplay of water and fire, but it acquires greater power and velocity with wind (e) in sum, the four elements of air, earth, water and fire sustain the existence of man and nature (f) the Arabic word *nafs* (self), appears two hundred ninety-five times in the Qur'an and its baser manifestation has been frequently referred to as one that overpowers man by anger, pride and such sordid passions.

Two expressions—*aatish-nafasii* (fire-natured) in the first line and *jal jaataa* (would have burnt in fire) in the second line work sequentially and lay out the plot of the verse about man's fiery nature. Two other expressions—*paidaa* and *pinhaa.n*—used in the sense of revealed and concealed rather than born and hidden, spell out the essentially mutable nature of man, which is qualified further by another expression, *zabt* (forbearance). Asadulah Khan Ghalib's verse would be worth consideration in this context as well: *Dhu.nde hai us muGhannii-i aatish-nafas ko jii / jis kii sadaa ho jalva-i barq-e fanaa mujhe.*

Ghazal 28 | Verse 5

17

دل سے مرے لگا نہ ترا دل ہزار حیف
یہ شیشہ ایک عمر سے مشتاق سنگ تھا

दिल से मिरे लगा न तिरा दिल हज़ार हैफ़
ये शीशा एक उम्र से मुश्ताक़-ए संग था

dil se mire lagaa na tira dil hazaar haif
ye shisha ek 'umr se mushtaq-e sang thaa

(*haif*—alas, pity;
mushtaaq-e sang—craving for a stone)

Your heart didn't beat with mine—
alas, a thousand times, alas!
For ages, this glass had
yearned for a stone, alas!

Lovers are known for their unusual thoughts about their beloveds. Here is one such lover who mildly but sorrowfully complains to the beloved that her heart did not strike a chord with his heart, although he had ever been willing to accept all her incursions.

The curious sentiments expressed in this verse make pointed suggestions: (a) lovers turn helpless in matters of love and yearn for acceptance (b) they should also expect miseries in love and not only the pleasures of loving (c) a lingering sense of disappointment accompanies the lover, but he does not disengage from his yearning for union with the beloved (d) the pleasures of union and joys of love are best craved for than realized as fulfilment of love takes all the sheen out of the idea of love (e) the more profound implication lies in the lover saying that his heart is clear and reflective like a glass but the object of its affection is like an unemotional stone (f) even in this metaphorical comparison of glass and stone, as the devoted lover remains committed to the possibility of a change in heart of the cruel beloved, the lover also betrays his bitterness in the end.

Mir has built the central idea of this verse with two opposing materials—*shiisha* (glass) and *sang* (stone)—to explicate the notion of disappointment and heartbreak in love. While glass works as a metaphor for the lover's heart, the stone appears both as a metaphor for the onslaughts in love and a cruel or unemotional beloved. The mood of the aspiring lover is reflected in the word *haif* (alas!), which also demonstrates the irony of the lover's lot. The idiomatic expression of *lagaa*, implying *dil lagnaa* (to fall in love), underlines that the beloved's heart did not find a friend in the lover or fall in love with the lover. This sense of loss and longing, as reflected in Mir, is represented with equal artistic finesse in Haider Ali Atish: *diivaana hai dil yaar tirii jalva-garii kaa / mushtaaq nihaayat hii ye shiisha hai parii kaa.*

Ghazal 31 | Verse 1

18

گل کو محبوب ہم قیاس کیا
فرق نکلا بہت جو باس کیا

गुल को महबूब हम-क़्यास किया
फ़र्क़ निकला बहुत जो बास किया

gul ko mehbuub ham-qiyaas kiyaa
farq niklaa bahut jo baas kiyaa

(*ham-qiyaas*—of close conjecture/reasoning/ratiocination;
baas—smell, odour, fragrance)

I took the sweet blossom to be love's scent
It was nothing compared to my beloved's scent

Lovers never tire of finding similes and metaphors for their beloveds and their charming countenance. The lover in this verse, too, has configured his beloved in terms of a blossom, but when he draws closer to her, he finds his metaphor failing, as her countenance defies any comparison.

The verse makes the following suggestions of meanings: (a) the speaker seems to think that blossoms and beloveds are traditionally akin to each other, concerning their beauty and appeal (b) even while one represents the beauty of nature and the other the loveliness of human face and figure, they are different, which is signified here by their fragrance (c) this implies, that even if they are the manifestations of God's effulgence, the beloved's fragrance is distinctly different from the flower's fragrance (d) obviously enough, the beloved's fragrance is better than the flower's fragrance for the beloved (e) it is suggested, as such, that the web of appearance and reality keeps man preoccupied towards exploring and distinguishing one reality from another (f) the difference in perception of the two—the beloved and nature—enables the lover to appreciate God's beauty in the beauty of his beloved.

Two expressions—*ham-qiyaas* (close conjecture) and *farq* (difference)—provide the logical complements in this verse and underline the complexity of deciphering one from the other. Another sensitive point is driven home with the expression *jo baas kiyaa* (when I smelt), which exposes the limits of viewing as a predominant sensory experience. In a verse by Qalandar Bakhsh Jurat we may mark yet another way of poeticizing this experience: *kahaa.n hai gul mei.n safaaii tire badan kii sii / bharii suhaag kii tis per ye buu dulhan kii sii.*

Ghazal 31 | Verse 2

19

دل نے ہم کو مثال آئینہ
ایک عالم کا روشناس کیا

दिल ने हम को मिसाल-ए आईना
एक आलम का रू-शनास किया

dil ne ham ko misaal-e aaiina
ek 'aalam kaa ruu-shanaas kiyaa

(*misaal*—similitude, likeness;
ruu-shanaas—acquaintance)

Like a mirror, my heart brought me to perceive
All the world's images for me to conceive

The bounties of God are plenty, but only the sensitive eyes and the doting minds can perceive them. This verse is a delicate paean to the heart's extraordinary prowess in helping man see and appreciate these bounties. Being the most sensitive part of the human body, the heart can bring the beholder to witness the world in all its manifestations.

Various levels of meanings of the verse emerge: (a) heart is clear and limpid like a mirror which reflects all manifestations of this world that pass before it one after another (b) but such a heart must be of a mystic or a lover that reflects, like mirrors, images even beyond the obvious (c) reaching out to the world of myriad manifestations is like entering an unending quest where the heart can be a better guide than the mind (d) man's superiority lies in paying heed to the heart and allowing it to be a guide (e) there is a sense of benediction for the heart which is encapsulated in this discourse of seeing.

Mir executes three images of *dil* (the heart), *aaiina* (mirror) and *'aalam* (the world) to construct a design of meaning in this verse. More than presenting the heart as a simile for the mirror, he puts a premium on the heart that keeps man alive to the world's myriad manifestations. The phrase—*ek 'aalam* (one world)—suggests more worlds than one and imparts extraordinary thematic strength to the verse. Asadullah Khan Ghalib develops a philosophical discourse around Mir's proposition with his mark of complexity: *jalva az bas ke taqaazaa-i nigah kartaa hai / jauhar-e aaiina bhii chaahe hai mizgaa.n honaa.*

Ghazal 31 | Verse 6

20

صبح تک شمع سر کو دھنتی رہی
کیا پتنگے نے التماس کیا

सुब्ह तक शम्अ' सर को धुनती रही
क्या पतिंगे ने इल्तिमास किया

sub'ha tak sham'a sar ko dhuntii rahii
kyaa patenge ne iltimaas kiyaa

(*iltimaas*—request, implore)

The lamp kept beating its head
till the dawn's break;
What did the moth implore,
indeed, to partake?

Visuals of seemingly lesser significance may sometimes carry many more layers of meaning for a discerning reader to dwell upon. Mir portrays a visual condition in this verse where the lamp keeps beating its head all night about something the moth implored for. Despite this, no answer comes from the lamp, the moth, or even the poet, who constructs this dramatic condition. This leaves the reader curious to explore the real intent of the verse.

The verse seems to make several suggestions: (a) the moth probably asked the lamp for a longer life of her own, but sadly enough, the lamp was helpless to oblige (b) the image of the lamp's beating its head all night underlines its intense sympathy for the moth, but ironically the moth has nowhere else to die except at the feet of the lamp (c) the lamp's helplessness drives the poet to ponder upon the hiatus between the lamp's desire and her inability to fulfil the desire (d) the unsaid in the destiny ever remains unsaid, and the ultimate reality can be deduced only silently and helplessly.

The moth is a stock symbol in the classical Urdu ghazal for the lover, and a lamp for the beloved. Mir uses these two symbols but in an entirely new frame, which is dramatic on the one hand and allegorical on the other. The expression—*kyaa* (what)—carries a sense of interrogation, which adds an extra layer of meaning to the verse. *Iltimaas* (imploring) is another expression imbued with a sense of pathos, which typifies the moth in relation to the lamp. The impact of an ordinary idiomatic expression—*sar dhun'naa*—(to beat one's head)—is creatively heightened with the help of the context that Mir creates to convey the sense of the moth's grief. Despite this, the beauty of the verse lies in its ambiguity regarding what the moth's imploring was all about. Mir leaves it to the reader's imagination at best. In another verse, Mir uses the same idiom to construct a rich variation on this idea: *qissa tamaam Mir kaa shab ko sunaa kiyaa / be-dard sar bhii subh'a talak sar dhunaa kiyaa.*

Ghazal 35 | Verse 3

21

گر کوئی پیر مغاں مجھ کو کرے تو دیکھے پھر
میکدہ سارے کا سارا صرف ہے اللہ کا

गर कोई पीर-ए मुग़ाँ मुझ को करे तो देखे फिर
मै-कदा सारे का सारा सिर्फ़ है अल्लाह का

gar koii piir-e muGhaa.n mujh ko kare to dekhe phir
maikada saare kaa saaraa sirf hai Allah kaa

(*piir-e muGhaa.n*—superior priest, mystic master;
maikada—tavern, bar)

Let someone make me the mystic master—
I'll show him in and out;
This tavern is but of Allah—
only of Allah, in and out

Audacity may also be a virtue when it is blended with a certain humility. Here is an ostensibly bold, even daring claim from Mir's speaker that God alone is the master of the tavern. Even more audacious is the speaker's claim that if he is made a superior priest or a mystic master, he will assert that the tavern is owned by no one else, but God alone. This makes us explore the verse further for its implications.

The real intent of the verse lies in these aspects: (a) God is the supreme commander of all that is here upon this earth and up there in the heavens, which implies that all that is here and there is of God, and God alone (The Quran, 42:11 and The Holy Bible (Genesis 2: 15-22) (b) the world, too, is a larger tavern of two kinds; one where men get drunk audaciously and lose their way, and the other where men get drunk humbly on the love of the divine (c) the wine that intoxicates is inferior to the metaphoric wine that transports man to a realization of the ultimate truth (d) the verse opens ways for a liberal understanding of man, world and God (e) the idea of tavern in this verse is characteristically different from the much-celebrated notion of the tavern in Omar Khayyam, who considers the actual tavern of this world as a source of celebrating epicureanism as well as mystical transcendence.

The expression—*piir-e muGha.n* (mystic master) distinguishes one priest from all other priests who alone can offer the proper resolution. He offers a challenge, as if, with the phrase—*to dekhe phir* (let him see then). He adds further assurance with his proclamation that comes out emphatically in the second line. Asadullah Khan Ghalib develops a much larger and secular view in his verse: *jab maikada chhuta to phir ab kyaa jagah kii qaid / masjid ho maikada ho koii KHaanqaah ho.*

Ghazal 40 | Verse 3

22

ملا ہے خاک میں کس کس طرح کا عالم یاں
نکل کے شہر سے ٹک سیر کر مزاروں کا

मिला है ख़ाक में किस किस तरह का आलम याँ
निकल के शहर से टुक सैर कर मज़ारों का

milaa hai KHaak mei.n kis kis tarah kaa 'aalam yaa.n
nikal ke shahr se tuk sair mazaaro.n kaa

(*'aalam*—the world, people, time, state of being;
mazaar—tomb, shrine, grave)

Eras of splendour have sunk
into the ground;
Come out of the town, stroll down
the tombs all around

Does anyone go for a stroll in the graveyards and remain in the silent companionship of the dead ones buried there? This unusual idea becomes the subject of this verse, where Mir makes a queer but significant proposition. Plainly enough, he invites us to stroll down the graves, probably because that is where men who lived in glory upon this earth once are lying under the earth's surface. There is, however, much more to the proposition he makes to his addressees.

In asking us to visit the graveyards, Mir makes several suggestions: (a) cities that are agog with life's activities are fanciful and temporal, just as man's existence with all its glamour on this earth is temporal (b) this implies that the eternal human habitat is in the skies, but before reaching there, graves are the repositories for the dead till the doomsday (c) this also reminds us of the Qur'anic verse: 'out of the dust We have created you, to it We shall return you' (20:55) and Biblical verse about Adam: 'for dust you are and to dust you shall return' (Genesis 3:19) (d) it also reminds us of a tradition of the Prophet Mohammad, the last prophet of Islam: 'Visit the graves; for visiting them becomes the cause of remembering the next world' (*Sunan Ibn-e Maaja*, V. 1, p. 113) (e) putting city and shrine against each other, Mir unravels both: life as unreal and afterlife as real.

The most striking phrase in the verse is *sair* (stroll), which suggests an easy and relaxed walk. This implies that such a walk is better than running helter-skelter after the world's temptations. Two other phrases in the first line—*KHaak (*dust) and *'aalam* (world)—underline the world's transitoriness and foreground the advice to stroll among graves in the second line. This idea has again engrossed Mir's attention in another verse: *kiyaa hai 'ishq-e 'aalam-kash ne kyaa suthraao logo.n kaa / nikal chal shahr se baahar nazar kar tuk mazaaro.n kaa.* Imam Bakhsh Nasikh, another junior contemporary of Mir, also engages with this idea in his verse: *kar chuke aqliim-e vahshat mei.n bahut josh-o KHarosh / chand muddat 'aalam-e shahr-e KHamoshaa.n dekhiye.*

Ghazal 52 | Verse 1

23

دل جو تھا اک آبلہ پھوٹا گیا
رات کو سینہ بہت کوٹا گیا

दिल जो था इक आबला फूटा गया
रात को सीना बहुत कूटा गया

dil jo thaa ik aabla phuutaa gayaa
raat ko siina bahut kuutaa gayaa

(*aabla*—blister)

The heart was a blister,
it burst open;
It was badly battered last night,
badly broken

Miseries in love can be terrible sometimes. Here is a lover who presents an awful image of himself. In a confessional way, he tells how he pounded his breast last night, which burst his blisters and caused him immense suffering.

The internal suggestions of this verse bring these interpretations to the fore: (a) the heart contains blood and thrives because of its movement in its chambers, but the lover's heart and body is riddled with blisters—marking an overexertion (b) the suffering of the lover has weakened his heart and body, his figurative wounds threaten to fester c) as such, his heart is no heart but only for namesake (d) it is rather outrageous that a lover should inflict pain upon himself and not upon the beloved who has brought all miseries to him (e) one wonders if the lover is revengeful against himself in loving an unsympathetic lady, and is a sadist in doing what he does to himself in the verse (f) one also wonders if he is seeking sympathy by narrating his chilling tale and if at all he has a listener (g) the visual image of such a lover is close to that of a bewildered being for whom the line between sanity and insanity is blurred.

The artless art of this verse strikes us the most. Mir's choice of the blister as a symbol for the heart is striking. The pathos of the lover comes out in the two *qaafias* of the verse—*phuutaa* (broke) and *kuutaa* (pounded) that bear out the acts of infliction and suffering. Mir's detached tone, quaint diction and graphic representation are the other qualities that make the verse impeccable and much too appealing. In his characteristic style, Asadulah Khan Ghalib also engages with this experience thus: *phir kuchh ik dil ko be-qaraarii hai / siina joyaa-i zaKHm kaarii hai.*

Ghazal 53 | Verse 2

24

اتنی گزری جو ترے ہجر میں سو اس کے سبب
صبر مرحوم عجب مونس تنہائی تھا

इतनी गुज़री जो तिरे हिज्र में सो उस के सबब
सब्र मरहूम अजब मूनिस-ए तन्हाई था

itnii guzrii jo tire hijr mei.n so us ke sabab
sabr marhuum 'ajab muunis-e tanhaaii thaa

(*hijr*—the state of being in separation/parting;
marhuum—late, deceased, departed;
muunis—consoler, empathizer)

So much I suffered in parting from you,
but I also found my patience in that parting;
Poor patience gone for good, was a kind consort
in my solitude after that parting

The two inevitable conditions in love are suffering caused by separation from the beloved and the endurance to bear that and continue to live despite separation. As such, suffering and union are the two conditions in love. One brings pain, the other brings bliss. The only panacea that makes parting bearable is fortitude. After some time, that pain also becomes a thing of the past and is remembered with gratitude as a sympathetic sustainer and a friend.

In their relationship with each other, parting and patience reveal still more: (a) when lovers unite in love, they are predestined to suffer in parting (b) it is in separation from the beloved that the value of union is appreciated (c) patience sustains even as it makes its demands upon the lover (d) when recollected in a moment of tranquillity later, the cycle of union, parting and patience are appreciated in a larger philosophical context (e) the speaker in this verse complains of his misery but also turns reconciliatory considering that love is not always either all pleasure or all pain.

The word *guzrii*—which implies the passing of time or a condition—also carries an ironic implication of bearing the onslaughts of time that pass slowly and painfully. Another word, *sabr* (patience), has a more significant connotation, similar to the word *muunis* (sympathetic friend), which personifies patience and helps the lover sustain his lot in love. This patience is further personified as a friend with an exclamatory expression—*'ajab* (strange/unique)—which does not imply strangeness but intimacy, enriching the verse. Asadullah Khan Ghalib has developed this experience in a sibling of a verse: *ranj se KHuugar huaa insaa.n to mit jaataa hai ranj / mushkilei.n mujh per paRii.en itnii ke aasaa.n ho gaei.n.*

Ghazal 58 | Verse 3

25

یہ توہم کا کارخانہ ہے
یاں وہی ہے جو اعتبار کیا

ये तवहहुम का कारख़ाना है
याँ वही है जो ए'तिबार किया

ye tavahhum kaa karKHaana hai
yaa.n vahii hai jo 'itebaar kiyaa

(*tavahhum*—imagination, fancy, conjecture;
'itebaar—confidence, trust, reliance)

This is the house of illusions we live in
What is seen here is what we believe in

Illusion and reality have been perennial issues of philosophical discourse across literatures. This verse presents the world as a workshop of illusions, but these illusions are like realities that must be believed in—or we are compelled to believe in.

Such a proposition opens up a larger discourse on the world and life itself: (a) the world is a phenomenon of God's gigantic imagination that has led men to discover fanciful images within it (b) those images are essentially illusions within the world that entangle men as webs entangle objects (c) thus the phenomenon known as the world and the God's gift known as life are mere illusions or shadows of something that exists in the heavens as per the Neoplatonic philosophy (d) the world is an enormous workshop where reality appears as fancy and fancy as reality and this paradox opens ways to engage with philosophical questions concerning perception, representation and actual phenomenon, as well as the building and unbuilding of images without ever arriving at any kind of finality (e) images so variously constructed indeed remain illusions at the core, but they appear to be real and have to be believed in (f) man who is precariously placed between illusion and reality has to live with them without being disillusioned (g) this brings man to a broader realization of mystical knowledge about reality and illusion.

Two phrases—*tavahhum* (illusion) and *'itebaar (*belief) are central to the verse and bear the metaphysical burden of the verse as they balance against each other in the well-conceived structure of the two lines of the verse. Another phrase— *kaarKHaana* (workshop)—emerges as a metaphor for the world where things endlessly remain in states of mutation. The verse maintains a calm tone, defying any sense of joy or sorrow, and exudes a remarkable kind of clinical detachment. Asadullah Khan Ghalib's engagement with this philosophical issue can be considered comparatively in this context: *juz naam nahii.n suurat-e 'aalam mujhe manzuur / juz vahm nahii.n hastii-i ashiyaa mere aage.*

Ghazal 58 | Verse 6

26

ہم فقیروں سے بے ادائی کیا
آن بیٹھے جو تم نے پیار کیا

हम फ़क़ीरों से बे-अदाई क्या
आन बैठे जो तुम ने प्यार किया

ham faqiiro.n se be-adaaii kyaa
aan baiThe jo tum ne pyaar kiyaa

(*be-adaaii*—incivility, rudeness)

Why neglect *faqiirs* like me
I'd love you—if you, too, loved me

There are innumerable ways for human beings to interact with other human beings. They live in harmony or disharmony with their fellow beings, but the *faqiirs* do not figure in their ways of life and living. Here is a *faqiir* speaking in the first person to any addressee who would choose to listen to him, and he wonders why one should neglect him since he is the one who would lend himself with love if he was treated with love.

This verse engages essentially with the institution of *faqiir* where the following points emerge well: (a) a *faqiir* mentioned here is not a street beggar who collects alms but more of a wandering monk or ascetic as found in the Middle Eastern and South Asian cultures (b) he is a holy man who follows the Islamic faith, is mystically charged, magically endowed—a self-sufficient human oblivious to worldly possessions and believes in blessing others rather than receiving favours (c) far from being poor in lexical terms, *faqiirs* are rich human beings who endow spiritual riches upon the impoverished worldly men (d) in a humane and friendly tone the *faqiir* in the verse thus addresses these beings and kindly conveys to them not to neglect him as he would reciprocate their love with his own and reward them richly (e) as he seeks their company, he teaches them humility and kindness and emerges as one who is far more empowered than them although he lives wrapped in rags.

The verse reads like a *faqiir*'s kind and courteous address and stands out for its warmth and appeal. Notes of simplicity and intimacy mark his address prominently. The tone is intimate, as expected of a *faqiir*, a mystic, a sage, a soft-spoken mendicant, or all rolled into one as an emblem of humility. Mir brings a different aspect to this iconic figure of the faqiir in another verse: *ham to faqiir hai.n KHaak baraabar aa baiThe to lutf kiyaa / nang jahaa.n lagtaa ho un ko vaa.n se vaisii 'aar karei.n.*

Ghazal 58 | Verse 7

27

سخت کافر تھا جن نے پہلے میرؔ
مذہب عشق اختیار کیا

सख़्त काफ़िर था जिन ने पहले 'मीर'
मज़हब-ए इश्क़ इख़्तियार किया

saKHt kaafir thaa jin ne pehle Mir
mazhab-e 'ishq iKHtiyaar kiyaa

(*kaafir*—infidel, disbelieving, unbeliever;
mazhab—canon, belief, creed;
iKHtiyaar—choice, preference, option)

He was indeed an infidel, Mir, who
of all others,
chose to embrace the faith of love
of all others

Is love a religion? Or is it a faith? Are both of them the same? Is there a God— formless or incarnate—in them for man to worship? What kind of love is being referred to here—romantic or divine? Whatever may be the answer to these questions, this verse prioritizes the importance of love most liberally. It appears as a paean to one who adopts love as a mode of life, which is no less than adopting a religious school of thought. Mir broaches several issues, not necessarily in doctrinal terms but in terms of man's close attachment to a being—human or divine.

There are deeper meanings to the verse still: (a) religion is a system of man's faith and worship that shows his devotion to something real or imagined (b) faith is a matter of man's inner belief, which shows his trust in an object or things seen or unseen (c) love in itself is both a religion and a faith in terms of devotion as well as trust that it inspires and demands, respectively, and this may be both romantic and divine (d) in saying that the first person who adopted the religion or faith of love was an infidel, Mir indeed suggests the opposite by creating an in-built paradox; this man thus became the first prophet of this religion or faith and acquired far greater a status than can be imagined (e) by juxtaposing faith and non-faith, Mir assigns a high status to love as a religion and a faith, and institutionalizes it since all Western and Eastern religions and faiths believe in love (f) one who embraces this religion or faith emerges as the high priest of love in this world.

The verse reads like a statement, but it appeals as an intense exposition of man's conviction in love. Mir plays upon the juxtaposition of the two words—*kaafir* (infidel) and *mazhab* (faith)—and expands their meaning beyond the typically received ones. To intensify the significance of this newly-defined infidel, Mir executes the adjective *saKHt* (hard/ intense). The in-built dichotomy in this verse concerning this infidel who embraced the faith of love makes the verse doubly edged. In addition, the expression *iKHtiyaar kiyaa* (chose to embrace/adopt) drives home the idea that the lover made an informed choice, portraying him as an archetypal protagonist or agent of love. Mir's discourse on love that mirrors this verse deserves attention: *kyaa haqiiqat kahuu.n ke kyaa hai 'ishq / haq-shanaaso.n ke haa.n KHudaa hai 'ishq.*

Ghazal 60 | Verse 3

28

باہم ہوا کریں ہیں دن رات نیچے اوپر
یہ نرم شانے لونڈے ہیں مخمل دو خوابا

बाहम हुआ करें हैं दिन-रात नीचे ऊपर
ये नर्म-शाने लौंडे हैं मख़मल-ए दो-ख़्वाबा

baaham huaa kare hai.n din raat niche uuper
ye narm-shaane launde hai.n maKHmal-e do-KHvaaba

(*narm-shaane*—soft-shouldered;
launde—lads, boys, brats;
maKHmal-e do-KHvaaba—fine quality velvet lined
with the fabric on either side)

They keep tossing up and down,
night and day—together,
These soft-shouldered lads are
the velvety ones—together

Same-sex love, and in this case, between two men or boys, is not a prohibited idea or experience to address in Urdu poetry. Mir has several verses that belong to this category. This verse eulogizes the young lads who are playful with each other in bed and seek pleasure of a different kind compared with the more common male-female relationship and their love-making.

There are certain exciting aspects in this verse to explore: (a) the choice for same-sex, or male-male love is neither concealed nor underestimated in this verse, which underlines Mir's courage for uninhibited expression (b) for him, this love is worth talking about without any shame attached to it since this expresses essential human libido, howsoever disapproved of it might be morally, socially, or even religiously (c) the act of this love-game is presented as pleasurable, but with restrained sensitivity rather than as a way of seeking sheer voyeuristic pleasure (d) even the boy in this love-game plays his role day and night by changing his position and seeks appreciation from his lover for doing so and also for being so soft-shouldered and supple-bodied (e) the element of sensuality comes out prominently with the tactile sensation the lover receives by feeling the soft shoulders of the beloved and finding them velvety.

The diction of the verse calls for our keener attention. The expression—*baaham* (together)—projects two actors on the scene, *uuper-niiche* (above and under) represents the young boy's posture in the love game, and *din-raat* (day and night) brings out a favoured obsession pursued by the two actors in love, and *narm-shaana launde* (soft-shouldered lads) works as phrase of appreciation for their bodies. The most striking literary merit of the verse may best be noticed in the simile that Mir finds for the lad by calling him *maKHmal-e do-KHvaaba* (fine quality velvet lined with the fabric on either side). This is an elegant example of Mir's imaginative vitality, which suddenly takes the verse to a remarkable artistic height. Mir's other verse of this category is equally worth noticing for the same frankness of expression: *Mir chhuu sakte bhii nahii.n hai.n ham lipte baal us ke / hai.n shaana-gar se jo ye ladke narm-shaana.*

Ghazal 63 | Verse 6

29

نمود کر کے وہیں بحر غم میں بیٹھ گیا
کہے تو میرؔ بھی اک بلبلا تھا پانی کا

नुमूद कर के वहीं बहर-ए ग़म में बैठ गया
कहे तो 'मीर' भी इक बुलबुला था पानी का

numuud kar ke vahii.n bahr-e Gham mei.n baiTH gayaa
kahe to Mir bhii ik bulbula thaa paanii kaa

(*numuud*—appearance, visibleness;
bahr-e Gham—ocean of pain)

He showed up and sat down—
in the ocean of pain
Mir, too, I say, was a bubble
of water, in vain

Pain is an essential condition of life, but it also has a way of easing in its own in time. This verse develops a unique angle of vision to negotiate with pain that is a part of man's predicament. The remarkable point is that like pain, the sufferer, too, dissolves and disappears just like the water bubble in the womb of the water body.

The settling down of the sufferer and the bubble of water makes further suggestions: (a) howsoever intense, pain is temporal and makes the sufferer either used to it or turns him insensitive to it (b) there is a reconciliatory relationship between suffering and sufferer just as there is a relationship between the ocean and the bubble of water (c) pain is like an ocean itself in which the sufferer disappears just as a drop of water disappears into it (d) there is also an intimate relationship between external nature and human nature that spells out the balance of living, on a broader level.

The word *numuud*—appearance—and the speaker's sinking in the water after his brief surfacing at first creates a picturesque condition. This applies to both the drop and the sufferer, further reinforcing the idea that man, too, has a temporal appearance like a water bubble. The metaphoric value that this verse embodies makes for its more profound appeal. A verse from Imdad Ali Bahr, an early nineteenth-century poet, may be quoted as a variation on Mir: *mujh ko rone to do dikhaa duungaa / bulbula hai ye asmaan nahii.n.*

Ghazal 69 | Verse 7

30

ہیں مشت خاک لیکن جو کچھ ہیں میرؔ ہم ہیں
مقدور سے زیادہ مقدور ہے ہمارا

हैं मुश्त-ए ख़ाक लेकिन जो कुछ हैं 'मीर' हम हैं
मक़्दूर से ज़ियादा मक़्दूर है हमारा

hai.n musht-e KHaak lekin jo kuchh hai.n Mir ham hai.n
maqduur se ziyaada maqduur hai hamaaraa

(*musht-e KHaak*—a fistful of soil;
maqduur—capability, means, resource)

A fistful of dust, but I am for—
what all I am;
More than my reach, I reach out—
for what all I am

Man is known for his infinite capabilities. This verse acknowledges this truism, which is widely represented in different literary traditions and texts. With his extraordinary intellectual and physical prowess, man can turn the tides even though he may appear fragile.

The aspects involved in reading this verse may be explored as such: (a) created out of clay (The Qur'an, 15:26) and out of dust (The Holy Bible, Genesis, 2:7), man has turned out to be the epitome of reason, faculty, form, action, and apprehension (b) his being the quintessence of dust is writ large on the face of this verse which typifies Mir here, as in many other verses (c) man is aware that he is only a handful of dust, yet he is too proud of himself that he alone is what he is (c) suggesting that there is no one else like him, he asserts that his capability excels the limits of capability itself (d) philosophically speaking, Mir reposes faith in man's earthen existence which is the ultimate repository of infinite strength (e) as a fine example of self-glorification, this verse forcefully asserts an individual's potential as a nucleus of power before the entire creation (f) Mir asserts himself to represent all human beings in the plural rather than singular term.

The expression—*musht-e KHaak* (handful of dust)—stands out as the archetypal configuration of man. This configuration's vitality and vibrancy are carried out precisely in the first line, especially with the compound phrase—*jo kuchh hai.n Mir ham hai.n* (I am for what all I am). This is reinforced by the word—*maqduur* (capacity)—which is multiplied by *maqduur* yet again to reach the apex of all capacities. The equational structure of the lines of this verse adds to its meaning and appeal. Mir reminds us of a monologue by Hamlet in Shakespeare's *Hamlet*, where man is represented as infinite in faculty, admirable in form and moving, a god in apprehension, the beauty of the world, and finally, the paragon of animals. Mir has developed this idea further in another verse with equal conviction: *'ijz-o niyaaz apnaa apnii taraf hai saaraa / is musht-e KHaak ko ham masjuud jaante hai.n.*

Ghazal 71 | Verse 4

31

یے نشان عشق ہیں جاتے نہیں
داغ چھاتی کے عبث دھوتا ہے کیا

ये निशान-ए इश्क़ हैं जाते नहीं
दाग़ छाती के अबस धोता है क्या

ye nishaan-e 'ishq hai.n jaate nahii.n
daaGh chhaatii ke 'abas dhotaa hai kyaa

('*abas*—for no reason)

These are the marks of love;
they wouldn't go;
Why wash the blots on your chest;
they wouldn't go

Love brings pleasure but also leaves scars that cannot be erased. This verse explains this idea in plain terms. The speaker advises the lover that there is no reason why he should wash the blots of love from his chest because they are there to stay and not to be erased. Like several other verses, this one also makes us ponder over the complicated levels of meaning.

The points that Mir makes in this verse may be surmised in these terms: (a) there is an implicit suggestion by the speaker that love has been a source of suffering for the lover, but he shares this reality with a sense of admonition (b) the lover is thus advised not to try and wash the blots off his chest since they are there to remind him constantly of his pitiable lot (c) thinking of love as a mark on the chest could be a positive sign, but considering it as a blot presents love in negative terms (d) the romantic love referred to here is contrasted with the divine love where no one would like to erase the marks over the chest, rather preserve it as a matter of pride and as a memento for all life (e) an interesting aspect is that these marks of love are created both by the lover himself as also the beloved.

The speaker in this verse chooses a conversational and persuasive tone, but he does not get any response from the lover's side, who only remains a mute listener. In this monologic advice from the speaker, what is referred to as *nishaan* (mark) in the first line is presented as a *daaGh* (blot) in the second line, and paradoxically enough, both appear as marks of pride. In the second line—*'abas* (for no reason)—is a very suggestive expression that underlines the futility of getting rid of the blot impressed on the lover's chest. The expression *dhotaa hai kyaa* (why do you wash) refers to the dressing of wounds done by surgeons over the ages. Mir adds another aspect to this sentiment in a different verse: *zaKHm jhele daaGh bhii khaae bahut / dil lagaa ke ham to pachhtaaye bahut.*

Ghazal 74 | Verse 11

32

ہیں چاروں طرف خیمے کھڑے گرد باد کے
کیا جانیے جنوں نے ارادہ کدھر کیا

हैं चारों तरफ़ ख़ेमे खड़े गर्द-बाद के
क्या जानिए जुनूँ ने इरादा किधर किया

hai.n chaaro.n tarf KHeme khade gard-baad ke
kyaa jaaniye junuu.n ne iraada kidhar kiyaa

(*gard-baad*—whirlwind, dust storm, devil, demon;
junuu.n—wildness)

The domes of dust are spread all around
Who knows whither my wild passion is bound

Mir portrays a physical condition in which one can see the tents of dust stalled all over, and it is in this condition that he finds a wild being preparing to set out. This is a curious and worrying matter because nothing can be said about what will happen the next moment.

As usual, this verse asks for further exploration of its implied meanings: (a) both the tent of dust and the wild passion are akin to each other as they both forebode a dreadful condition (b) wild passion is personified here as it seems to set out in highly rough weather, but it does not know which direction it would take (c) by bringing together the rough weather and the wild passion, a suggestion is made that both nature and man are out of their average bearings and are prepared to create a disastrous situation, (d) as nature and man are known to create havoc, there is a profound apprehension of the unseeable that could indeed be disastrous (e) since the phenomenon is destined to be ruined sooner or later, the ultimate reality of creation and destruction, appearing in cycles like a whirlwind, is driven home.

The verse has two phrases—*gard-baad* (whirlwind/dust storm) and *junnu.n* (wild passion) that are strikingly visual. Together, they create a catastrophic condition marked by madness in this verse in imagist terms and help realize the physicality of the condition with great precision. Mir has appropriated the image of the whirlwind in different ways. A verse that strikes for its awful potential may be marked in this verse: *mar gayaa aavaara ho kar mai.n to jaise gard-baad / per jise ye vaaqea pahu.nchaa use vahshat huii.*

Ghazal 77 | Verse 10

33

زمیں گیر ہو عجز سے تو کہ اک دن
یہ دیوار کا سایہ دیوار ہوگا

ज़मींगीर हो इज्ज़ से तू कि इक दिन
ये दीवार का साया दीवार होगा

zamiin giir ho 'ijz se tuu ke ik din
ye diivaar kaa saaya diivaar hogaa

(*zamii.n giir*—stuck to the earth;
'ijz—modesty, humility)

Be stuck to the earth in modesty—
as one day,
The wall's shadow will be the wall,
surely, one day

The central idea of this verse is the significance of humility. Humility distinguishes human beings and makes them worthy as individuals and as units of a larger social order. The idea behind the verse is not directly stated but suggested only in a metaphoric framework, as can be seen below.

This extremely suggestive verse may be interpreted in philosophical terms: (a) the speaker is a humble being, but his addressee is not, and hence needs to be taught the lesson of humility (b) as such, he is advised to learn the virtue of humility, which alone will sustain him in times to come (c) being sadly oblivious of that, man subjects himself carelessly to impending misery (d) there are two lives that a man lives, that is, the life here and the life hereafter; and the first life is that of action and the second is that of bearing the consequences of the action (e) the wall has a double entendre here—one, it will save man from the impending punishment due to him and second, it will prevent the divine grace from reaching him (f) in yet another interpretation, the wall that offers protection to man in the precincts of the house is only temporal, but the shadow of the same wall will assume significant proportions and offer him protection in the grave till the doomsday.

The verse bears the tone of a kind counsel. The most compelling images that constitute the kernel of the verse are those of the wall and the shadow of the wall, which represent both literal and metaphoric layers of meaning. The essence of the kind counsellor's message lies richly embedded in a single phrase— *zamii.n giir* (stuck to the earth). This acquires greater meaning if we consider that it also conveys that both in life and death, earth offers him a home in this world and the world hereafter. In a self-reflexive mood, Mir develops the central idea of humility with a certain degree of difference in another verse: *naala-i 'ijz nuqs-e ulfat hai / ranj-o mehnat kamaal-e raahat hai.*

Ghazal 78 | Verse 7

34

دور بیٹھا غبار میرؔ اس سے
عشق بن یہ ادب نہیں آتا

दूर बैठा ग़ुबार-ए 'मीर' उस से
इश्क़ बिन ये अदब नहीं आता

duur baiTha Ghubaar-e Mir us se
'ishq bin ye adab nahii.n aataa

(*Ghubaar*—dust, haze)

Mir's dusty being sat removed—
from the beloved;
Such manners don't come without—
falling for the beloved

Love is an institution that lays down its paths for lovers to follow. It also calls for respecting both love and the person loved as institutions. For a lover, suffering is not a deterrent, and it does not keep him from loving. This is how he considers love an adorable experience and the beloved as an incarnation of love. It is in this manner that the dignity of love can be maintained with self-discipline.

This verse develops an entirely fresh perspective on romantic love. It suggests: (a) the romance of love lies both in maintaining and respecting its sanctity (b) the lover is one entity, and the suffering he bears is another, and the two sit apart (c) sitting apart is a way of expressing respect for each other (d) suffering is a condition of love, and also a state of being immersed in it with forbearance (d) loving is persevering, learning, submitting and achieving a state higher than merely physical or lustful (e) experiencing and representing love in these terms accounts for observing the hallowed manners of the institution of love (e) after the lover turns to dust, he becomes a dust-cloud and wanders all over, seeking the beloved.

Two expressions—*ghubaar* (haze) and *adab* (discipline)—hold the central intent of the verse. While one represents the suffering experienced in love, the other signifies the manner of absorbing that suffering with a clinical detachment from it. This indicates that love must also find an objective correlative for suffering in love, which may not be more than the pain brought to the lover. In figurative terms, the dust cloud, sitting apart, implies that it may settle down and reach a state of equilibrium. Harking back to Mir, Vali Aasi, a modernist poet, responded in a lighter vein: *'ishq bin jiine ke aadaab nahii.n aate hai.n / Mir sahib ne kahaa hai ke miyaa.n 'ishq karo.*

Ghazal 97 | Verse 2

35

کن نیندوں اب تو سوتی ہے اے چشم گریہ ناک
مژگاں تو کھول شہر کو سیلاب لے گیا

किन नींदों अब तू सोती है ऐ चश्म-ए गिर्या-नाक
मिज़्गाँ तो खोल शहर को सैलाब ले गया

kin niindo.n ab tuu sotii hai ai chashm-e girya-naak
mizhgaa.n to khol shahr ko sailaab le gayaa

(*chashm-e girya-naak*—weeping eyes, tear-afflicted eyes;
mizhgaa.n—eyebrows)

How can you sleep, weeping eyes—
heedless of the day;
Lift your eyebrows, a flood has swept—
the town away

The common folks' insensitivity to social, communal miseries has irked poets, and they have drawn upon such experiences with great sensitivity to censure this inability. Here is one example: the speaker addresses those people who are insensitive and remain oblivious to all that has happened around them. As such, they stand robbed of their possessions and are left tragically dispossessed. The causes for such disasters could be personal, social, or even other than these. This verse makes an apparent reference to the upheavals that history brought, which Mir has referred to countless times in his autobiographical tract and poetry.

This verse allows for reading it in a much larger context too: (a) human beings are subject to the calamities of time, but they remain helpless to bring about any change in their lot (b) this is equally true of the calamities that the human beings have borne through the history of their existence on this earth (c) human survival on this earth is thus a story of precarious existence and perilous survival (d) the lone call for realizing the state of affairs comes as forebodings to the human beings, and it writes the other side of human history (e) because of weeping heavily as detailed in this verse, the sufferers' eyelids cannot open now even though he is urged to do so (f) with the eyes closed in sleep, the sufferer denies the sights of disaster, but he is urged to forsake sleep, open his eyes, and see the city swept away in metaphorical terms.

There are two remarkable metaphors—*chashm-e girya-naak* (weeping eyes) and *sailaab* (flood)—in the two lines of the verse. The weeping eyes represent the sufferers, but the flood has a double meaning here: it could be the flood caused by the weeping eyes, or it could also be the flood of the disaster of time and history that has swept the entire city away. As the verse addresses a listener or a group of listeners, it emits a sense of sadness and a gesture of disapproval for their insensitivity, which comes out in the first line. It should be interesting to note how Qaim Chandpuri portrays this condition: *ab chashm-e girya-paimaa sarfa hai kyaa jahaa.n kaa / sailaab-e Khuu.n se tere jal-thal to bhar chukaa hai.* Mirza Mohamad Rafi Sauda's verse too is of equal importance here: *us chashm-e girya-naak ne 'aalam dubo diyaa / jiidhar gaii udhar ko ye tuufaan le gaii.*

Ghazal 101 | Verse 1

36

دیر و حرم سے گزرے اب دل ہے گھر ہمارا
ہے ختم اس آبلے پر سیر و سفر ہمارا

दैर-ओ-हरम से गुज़रे अब दिल है घर हमारा
है ख़त्म उस आबले पर सैर-ओ-सफ़र हमारा

dair-o harem se guzre ab dil hai ghar hamaaraa
Hai KHatm us aable per sair-o safar hamaaraa

(*dair-o harem*—temple and *K'aba*;
aabla—blister)

My heart is my home now—
the mosque and temple paths; I've trodden all;
Now, with my blisters come to an end—
All my journeys, my ambles all

Once again, the human heart is the subject of this verse. This time, it is presented as the most precious possession that man may be proud of at the end of the long journey of life. The heart here is not necessarily, and not even traditionally, the heart of a lover, but it is represented in the most glorious terms as the finest human possession.

The following meanings may be derived from this verse: (a) temple, mosque and heart are equated as the three most sacred spaces but the heart is ultimately prioritized (b) religious sites are sacred for the faiths they represent, but the heart, being a secular space, defies all faiths and, at the same time, incorporates the values that various faiths represent (c) the idea of home as a heart brings forth the idea of a final destination which provides man with his paramount home (d) long travels across religious sites brought blisters to the poetic persona's soles, but arrival in the heart's domain has brought relief, and a final release from the travails of journeys (e) all travels undertaken so far were only exploratory, but arriving in the heart's domain conveys the sense of quintessential arrival.

One particular expression—*guzre* (passed through)—underlines the explorer's sense of observation and presents him as a quester who is not enamoured by the destinations he chooses one after another. This sense is well borne out by—*ab* (now)—which imparts a sense of the termination of his journey, which had only brought him suffering in terms of—*aabla* (blisters) on his soles. The phrase—*sair-o safar* (excursion and journey)—bears tragic and ironic overtones that enrich the verse immensely. Ghalib enhances the image of the blister by turning it into a metaphor and adds a rich perspective on Mir's verse: *asar-e aabla se jaada-i sahraa-i junuu.n / suurat-e rishta-i gauhar hai charaaGha.n honaa.*

Ghazal 102 | Verse 3

37

دل نہ پہنچا گوشۂ داماں تلک
قطرۂ خوں تھا مژہ پر جم رہا

दिल न पहुँचा गोशा-ए दामाँ तलक
क़तरा-ए ख़ूँ था मिज़ा पर जम रहा

dil na pahu.nchaa gosha-i daamaa.n talak
qatra-i KHuu.n thaa mizha pe jam rahaa

(*gosha*—corners/crannies/edges;
daamaa.n—hem of a shirt;
mizha—eyebrow)

My heart did not even reach
the hems of my raiment;
That was a drop of blood that congealed
on my eyebrow bent

Here is a verse that eulogizes the pain of the lover, destined to shed tears of blood. He is so unfortunate that his tears cannot even reach and show up on the hem of his attire. Instead, his pain appeared like a drop of tear in the form of blood, and in the process of shedding it, it congealed on his eyelashes.

This is a picturesque representation of a lover who has much more to suggest: (a) suffering is a part of loving, and lovers are destined to suffer and shed tears perennially (b) tears of blood intensify their suffering and symbolize their predicament (c) with congealing, the tears live on; they neither disappear nor are wasted (d) the lover's hem of the shirt bears all marks, but tragically enough, this pain does not even trickle down in the form of a tear to the hem of his attire but gets congealed near the eyes and acquires a life of its own there (e) although the heart aspires for the beloved's reciprocation, it is deprived of that and turns, in its defeat, into a drop of blood that makes the situation macabre.

The image of blood drops congealing on the eyelashes imparts a unique visual appeal to this verse. It also adds a distinctive layer of meaning to it. Other images that carry the meaning of this verse—*dil* (heart), *gosha-i daamaa.n* (corners of hem), *qatra-i KHuu.n* (drop of blood) and *mizha* (eyelashes)—add to the vividness of this ocular verse. Consider Qaim Chandpuri's verse for a comparative reading of this condition—*na dil bhartaa hai na ab nam rahaa hai aa.nkho.n mei.n / kabhii jo roe the Khu.n jam rahaa hai aa.nkho.n mei.n*

Ghazal 104 | Verse 2

38

آیا جو واقعے میں درپیش عالم مرگ
یہ جاگنا ہمارا دیکھا تو خواب نکلا

आया जो वाक़िए में दरपेश आलम-ए मर्ग
ये जागना हमारा देखा तो ख़्वाब निकला

aayaa jo vaaqae mei.n darpesh 'aalam-e marg
ye jaagnaa hamaaraa dekhaa to KHvaab nilkaa

(*vaaqeya*—event, occurrence, incident;
darpesh—in front, confront, before)

When in the chain of events appeared
a death gleaming;
I saw my waking up was but
a state of dreaming

To uncover the complex realities of life and death have been the predominant issues in philosophy and literature. Life is characterized by action, and death by stasis. However, there are lives that are pictures of complete stasis. This is akin to passing through dreams, which signify another kind of stasis or death. These seemingly paradoxical positions open avenues for a deeper understanding of life and death.

We can infer the following meanings from the verse: (a) the moment of death is unknown on its own, but the one thing that is certain is that death will strike at the appointed hour (b) life is a series of events that take place one after another, but it is in the middle of or in between these events that death strikes (c) the state of awakening and dreaming are only illusory as one is often taken for the other (d) this means that life can be taken for death if lived with physical adversity or with spiritual paucity, and death for life if it opens ways for living an eternal life beyond an ephemeral life (e) a life lived in misery creates the illusion of death hovering around and only when death arrives in actuality, the eyes open (f) so, a life lived here is akin to being in an intoxicating spell of dream which is far from reality (g) as such, life is a dream unto itself, and when one dies, one wakes up from that dream.

The phrase—*vaaqaye* (incidents)—is quite comprehensive in terms of meaning in the context of this verse. It suggests that life is an incident as much as death is an incident. The interplay of the two states of *KHvaab* (dream) and *jaagnaa* (staying awake) richly complicates the two acts as they stand individually as much as they complement each other. The mystic and revelatory tones of the verse empower it further in terms of its appeal. Khwaja Mir Dard, a mystic poet, comes to mind: *vaae naadaani ke vaqt-e marg ye saabit huaa / KHvaab tha jo kuchh ke dekhaa jo sunaa afsaana thaa.*

Ghazal 107 | Verse 3

39

سرسری تم جہاں سے گزرے
ورنہ ہر جا جہان دیگر تھا

सरसरी तुम जहान से गुज़रे
वर्ना हर जा जहान-ए दीगर था

sarsarii tum jahaan se guzre
varna har jaa jahaan-e diigar thaa

(*sarsarii*—casually, hurriedly, cursorily; *diigar*—different)

You passed through this world,
but only in passing;
Each spot was a world indeed,
worth watching

This verse reflects upon man and the world together. It posits that since man has passed through this world but only casually, he did not realize that each spot was a different world unto itself, which called for reflection.

We can arrive at the following inferences from this verse: (a) nothing can reveal all its magic unless probed deeply (b) this applies far more pertinently to the phenomenon called the world, which has many facets to it (c) in suggesting that the world has much more to reveal than conceal, a more significant place is assigned to the world than to man, but it is man alone who can unravel the secrets of the world (d) interestingly, he also invokes a Quranic verse which describes the earth as a resting place and sky as a canopy (40:64) for man to discover (e) the world is a place of endless possibilities.

The most remarkable phrase in this verse is *jahaan-e diigar* (another world), which suggests that there are many worlds within this world and that each one is worth witnessing rather than passing by casually. The tone of the verse is one of mild advice rather than a harsh warning, which qualifies the persuasive nature of this verse. Mir expresses this idea in the first person in another verse with similar conviction: *guzre basaan-e sarsar 'aalam mei.n be-ta'ammul / afsos Mir tum ne kyaa sair sarsarii kii.*

Ghazal 107 | Verse 4

40

دل کی کچھ قدر کرتے رہیو تم
یہ ہمارا بھی ناز پرور تھا

दिल की कुछ क़द्र करते रहियो तुम
ये हमारा भी नाज़-परवर था

dil kii kuchh qadr karte rahiyo tum
ye hamaara bhii naaz-parvar thaa

(*qadr*—value, respect, deference;
naaz-parwar—delicately nurtured, nourished by coquetries)

Value this heart,
if you will;
So dearly, I had nursed it
by my will

The human heart needs tending. This is far truer in the context of the lover than in any other context. Here is a piece of precious advice from one person to another who is not necessarily a lover but one who believes in human camaraderie and must appreciate how valuable a heart is and how best it can be cherished and valued.

The implied meanings in this verse may be read alongside its apparent meanings: (a) heart is the most precious possession of a lover—as it is anyone else's too—which needs careful tending (b) all lovers tame the heart just as they tame the beloved who herself is the embodiment of a tender heart (c) the speaker/lover shows a close camaraderie with the listener/lover when he says that he too had nurtured this heart with great care and caution (d) it appears that the speaker/lover is leaving the scene, but before doing that he passes on his heritage of love to another listener/lover (d) in doing this, he assigns a place of prestige to the listener/lover, as also to his heart apart from the beloved's heart, which is too delicate and may break with the most minor of jerks (e) the counsel offered by the speaker/lover amounts to a counsel that one generation passes on to another to see the institution of love stay in bloom forever.

Two phrases—*qadr* (value) and *naaz-parvar* (delicately nurtured)—are analogous expressions and qualify the value and fragility of the human heart. The delicately tended heart also stands here for the delicate beloved whom the speaker/lover has seemingly nurtured with amorous attention and care. Mir Asar develops an interesting variation on this idea of nurturing and loving somewhat playfully: *mujh se le to chale ho dekho per / toRiyo mat magar miyaa.n dil ko.*

Ghazal 108 | Verse 15

41

بنجر زمین دل کی ہے میرؔ ملک اپنی
پر داغ سینہ مہر فرمان ہے ہمارا

बंजर ज़मीन दिल की है 'मीर' मिल्क अपनी
पुर-दाग़ सीना मोहर-ए फ़रमान है हमारा

banjar zamiin dil kii hai Mir milk apnii
pur-daaGh siina mohr-e farmaan hai hamaaraa

(*milk*—property, inheritance, legacy;
mohr-e farmaan—seal of command)

Mir, my heart's barren plane
is my legacy;
This wounded chest, my seal of decree,
my entity

Here is yet another discourse on the heart, but it differs entirely from all other verses in terms of its intent. The poet declares with pride that his heart is an arid plane, but despite that, it is his legacy. More importantly, he proclaims rather defiantly that his wounded chest is full of blots, but those blots, far from being those of shame, are the seals of his decree.

This thought-provoking verse suggests various meanings: (a) heart is distinguished for its expansiveness, but its turning infertile or arid does not minimize its importance (b) heart's decay has shown up in the form of blots on the lover's chest, but that too is no reason for considering it insignificant (c) the blots on the chest could have been caused by disappointments and assaults on his heart, but he does not reveal that in order to save his heart's dignity (d) he considers thus that blots on the chest are no blots, but the seals of his order, command and verdict (d) the positivity of attitude even in adversity puts both the lover and heart in a lofty position.

Expressions like *banjar zamiin* (arid/infertile land) and *milk* (property/legacy) represent a study in contrast but convey a sense of pride as well on the speaker's part. Other expressions that intensify this pride are *pur-daagh siina* (a chest full of blots) and *mohr-e farmaan* (seal of decree). Significantly enough, the speaker speaks in the singular number of *apnii* (mine) in the first line but resorts to the plural form of *hamaaraa* (ours) in the second, which also signifies a commanding tone of ownership associated with emperors rather than commoners. In another verse, Mir takes pride in the blots of the chest: *tamasha kardanii hai daaGh-e siina / ye phuul is takhta mei.n taaza khilaa hai.* This pride is also shared by Siraj Aurangabadi: *siina-i daaGh daaGh mei.n mere / sehn-e gulzaar kaa tamaasha hai.*

Ghazal 109 | Verse 2

42

آدم خاکی سے عالم کو جلا ہے ورنہ
آئینہ تھا یہ ولے قابل دیدار نہ تھا

आदम-ए ख़ाकी से आलम को जिला है वर्ना
आईना था ये वले क़ाबिल-ए दीदार न था

aadam-e KHaakii se 'aalam ko jilaa hai varna
aaiina thaa ye vale qaabil-e diidaar na thaa

(*KHaakii*—of the dust, earthly;
jilaa—splendour, polish, lustre)

The world endures as Adam of its soil
helped it to endure
This was a mirror for sure, but not
worth a look, for sure

According to Christianity and Islam, Adam was the first of God's human creations out of the soil. He has been the subject of innumerable literary constructions. This verse praises him—whose progeny all human beings are and since the beginning of time, they have constructed this world as they have wished, but the verse undercuts that power by implying that this world is not worthy of a look despite that.

As a discourse on Adam, his progeny, and the world, this verse opens up different avenues of interpretation: (a) this universe would not have been created had Adam not been created by God and sent upon this earth (b) so all praise be to Adam for being the prototype of human beings (c) the world endures because Adam was there first and *banii Adam* (Adam's progeny) who followed, crafted the world and lived and prospered here as they wished (d) it is immensely significant that Adam was created out of the soil but he became the prototype of concrete worldly images (e) the world that the progeny of Adam created is like a mirror, but it turned into a dusty mirror and reflected only ugliness and defied the image of the ideal world (f) as such, Adam himself is defied even though he is the one who is the cause of all that was manifested subsequently.

Some of the qualifying phrases in this verse deserve our attention. Adam is qualified as *KHaakii* (made of soil), but his configuration in soil is more potent than the rest of the world. So, appropriately enough, he is the source of the world's *jilaa* (sustenance). Further, there is a suggestive correspondence between *aaiina* (mirror) that truthfully reflects the image(s) and *KHaakii* (earthly image) that blurs the mirror. There are innumerable representations of Adam in poetry across languages, but here is Mir's perception concerning Adam, his progeny and the world worthy of attention. A verse by Firaq Gorakhpuri may be referred to in this context: *ba-faiz-e Adam-e KHaakii zamii.n sonaa ugaltii hai / isii zarre ne daur-e mehr-o maah-o mushtarii badlaa.*

Ghazal 121 | Verse 2

43

کیسا چمن کہ ہم سے اسیروں کو منع ہے
چاکِ قفس سے باغ کی دیوار دیکھنا

कैसा चमन कि हम से असीरों को मना है
चाक-ए क़फ़स से बाग़ की दीवार देखना

kaisaa chaman ke ham se asiiro.n ko man'a hai
chaak-e qafas se baaGh kii diivaar dekhnaa

(*asiir*—imprisoned, restrained, trapped;
chaak-e qafas—slats in the cage)

What a garden is this—the captive ones
are kept from seeing;
The garden walls from the slats of the cage
that allows an allusion of seeing

Garden, a stock motif of Urdu ghazal, is represented here as a space where, instead of the availability of rejuvenation and freedom, there is a denial of the same. The speaker wonders with dismay and displeasure that even from the slats of the cage, there is no permission to look beyond it.

There are several suggested meanings in this verse that call for further probing: (a) cages represent both imprisonment and a warped sense of liberty, insofar as they limit the ambit of movement but also define it, which could be confused as a form of freedom, hence they are paradoxical (b) the inability to see the garden wall from the slats of the cage underlines almost no access to even a momentary pleasure (c) the politics of life and living centres around the oppressive acts of denial and imprisonment (d) desire and fulfillment mark the dynamics of existence and man has a role in playing up these against nature.

The speaker's gestures reflect the spirit of questioning, helplessness, perplexity and disdain in this verse. This is expressed through the stock symbols of *chaman* (garden), symbolizing pleasure; *asiir* (captive), symbolizing the oppressed figure; *qafas* (cage), symbolizing the onslaughts of imprisonment; and *baaGh* (garden), symbolizing the physical phenomenon called the world at large. Mir capitalizes upon this idea in another verse again: *kyaa Mir asiiro.n ko dar-e baaGh jo vaa ho / hai rang-e havaa dekhne ko chaak-e qafas bas.* This stock subject of Urdu ghazal finds its expression in Mirza Mohammad Rafi Sauda as well: *KHaamosh apne kulba-i ahzaa.n mei.n roz-o shab / tanhaa paRe hue dar-o diivaar dekhnaa.*

Ghazal 124 | Verse 2

44

ترے اس خاک اڑانے کی دھمک سے اے مری وحشت
کلیجا ریگ صحرا کا بھی دس دس گز تھلکتا تھا

तिरे उस ख़ाक उड़ाने की धमक से ऐ मरी वहशत
कलेजा रेग-ए सहरा का भी दस दस गज़ थिलक्ता था

tire us KHaak uRaane kii dhamak se ai mirii vahshat
kalejaa reg-e sahra kaa bhii das das gaz thilaktaa thaa

(*vahshat*—wild state;
thilaknaa—thumping, trembling, throbbing)

You raised such dust clouds,
such terrifying clamour;
Even the heart of the desert
thumped scores of yards in terror

Human beings can also turn wild in the frenzy of love and raise dust in symbolic terms. They create a clamour when they do so. In such a situation, even the deserts tremble.

Further implications of this verse may be marked as follows: (a) a wild lover knows of no worldly constraints and makes his own choices for himself (b) a wild lover and untamed nature are akin to each other in specific ways, although for different reasons (c) a wild lover can also be as furious as wild nature, and he too can infuse fear and terror in the onlookers (d) in a state of his sanity or insanity, he can severely shake the desert which is kept and controlled only by the divine power.

The lover is personified here as *vahshat* (wild state) incarnate, whom the speaker addresses directly. The impact of the lover's wild behaviour is aptly reflected in two comparable expressions—*dhamak* (bumping) and *thalak* (thumping)—that create an auditory condition in this verse and add to expanding the area of meaning. In his verse, Ghalib develops the metaphor of *sahra* (desert) as a fistful of dust and imparts yet another facet to it: *sar per hujuum-e dard Ghariibii se daaliye / vo ek musht-e KHaak ke sahra kahei.n jise.*

Ghazal 144 | Verse 7

45

آوارگان عشق کا پوچھا جو میں نشاں
مشت غبار لے کے صبا نے اڑا دیا

आवारगान-ए इश्क़ का पूछा जो मैं निशाँ
मुश्त-ए ग़ुबार ले के सबा ने उड़ा दिया

aavaargaan 'ishq kaa puuchha jo mai.n nishaa.n
musht-e Ghubaar le ke saba ne uRaa diyaa

(*aavaaragaan-e 'ishq*—wanderers in love;
musht-e Ghubaar—handful of dust;
sabaa—breeze)

When I asked where
the wandering lovers were;
The breeze held a handful of dust
and blew it in the air

Lovers are known to be wanderers and aimless vagrants. They cannot be located in one place or even at one time. They are ubiquitous too, and too elusive. Being such an entity, the figure of the lover is best compared with a handful of dust that can wander anywhere without ever reaching the desired destination, or in this case, the beloved's threshold.

A closer look will help spell the undertones of this verse: (a) wanderers are oblivious to their destination, and those in love are all the more so (b) metaphorically, they are themselves like a handful of dust, and just as dust wanders and knows not where it would settle, the lovers too are unaware of where they are destined to be (c) rather than allowing the speaker to say this, the wind has been personified and made to say so which makes the verse much more layered (d) lovers are wanderers, as much as they are the oblivious and the possessed one, endowed with higher consciousness (e) like the wind, they are traceless and unaware of their destination themselves which indeed is the beloved's door.

We might wonder if the lovers are the *avaaragaa.n* (the wandering beings), but even if they are, being a wanderer in love is a virtue rather than a vice. A more remarkable phrase, however, is *musht-e Ghubaar* (handful of dust), which underlines the lover's way of wandering much more prominently. Mir has expressed this idea again in another verse: *intihaa shauq kii dil ke jo sabaa se puuchhii / ik kaf-e KHaak ko le un ne pareshaan kiyaa*. This idea also finds its expression in Qalandar Bakhsh Jurat: *kyaa dushmanii thii tujh ko sabaa us galii se jo / aksar miraa Ghubaar bhii tuu ne uRaa diyaa.*

Ghazal 178 | Verse 3

46

موند رکھنا چشم کا ہستی میں عین دید ہے
کچھ نہیں آتا نظر جب آنکھ کھولے ہے حباب

मूँद रखना चश्म का हस्ती में ऐन-ए दीद है
कुछ नहीं आता नज़र जब आँख खोले है हबाब

muu.nd rakhnaa chashm kaa hastii mei.n 'ain-e diid hai
kucch nahii.n aataa nazar jab aa.nkh khole hai habaab

(*'ain*—eye, sight;
diid—seeing,
habaab—bubble)

Keeping one's eyes closed
is just an act of seeing the being;
Nothing is seen when
the bubble opens its eyes for seeing

Literary texts that propose a discourse also create grounds for further philosophical explorations. Here is a verse that unveils the dichotomy between the act of seeing and what it yields or does not yield to the seer.

We can read the verse in the following manner: (a) what appears is essentially relative and does not necessitate the opening of eyes to enable seeing (b) what remains invisible may indeed be visible through heightened human faculty, which suggests that not seeing is indeed the act of seeing (c) when the eyes open, reality eludes man quite often which underlines his limitations despite all his hidden and manifest abilities (d) the seeming contradiction between the ability to see through closed eyes and the inability to see with open eyes suggests that man can exercise spiritualist power to enable himself to see the reality (e) and most remarkably, with the opening of the bubble, its very existence comes to an end.

The verse is constructed on the principle of antinomy, as the act of closing one's eyes enables man to see, and opening it divests him of the power to see. The visual of *habaab* (bubble) configures the image of an eye that is too fragile to retain its life in the waves of water. This ultimately suggests that reality can be achieved in seemingly contradictory ways. Creatively, the bubble is used as a simile for the eye. Mir executes this idea with a different metaphor in another verse: *is mauj-KHez dahr mei.n tuu hai habaab saa / aankhei.n khulei.n tiri to ye 'aalam hai KHvaab saa.*

Ghazal 190 | Verse 3

47

چشم ہو تو آئینہ خانہ ہے دہر
منہ نظر آتا ہے دیواروں کے بیچ

चश्म हो तो आईना-ख़ाना है दह्र
मुँह नज़र आता है दीवारों के बीच

chashm ho to aaiina-KHaana hai dahr
mun.h nazar aataa hai diivaaro.n ke biich

(*chashm*—eye;
aaiina-KHaana—house of mirrors;
dahr—world)

If you can see, the world is a house of mirrors
Faces show up between the walls, not in mirrors

Mir projects his mystical intent by saying that the world is a house of mirrors and considers the wall a mirror of mirrors. On the face of it, this verse conveys the idea that if a man is endowed with the superior skills of a discerning vision, the world is a house of mirrors, and faces can be seen between the walls or even within the walls.

There are multiple meanings implied here: (a) first, walls do not have ears alone as it is said proverbially; they also are mirrors that reflect the images around (b) second, the mirror is clean of heart, so is the wall which reflects images just as they are (c) third, walls are the bearers of images but only the seeing eyes can see them (d) Mir valorizes man's infinite capacity to explore both the obvious and the hidden objects (e) a layer of mystical meaning could be marked well if one considers that the capacitated eyes could have the vision to perceive the world as a house of mirrors where the right could well be distinguished from the wrong.

The tone of the verse is one of sharing a secret in a sermonizing mode. The idiom—*mu.nh nazar aana* (seeing the face)—carries far greater weight than just suggesting the idea of seeing a face. More remarkable phrases that constitute an imagistic pattern in this verse, however, are *chashm* (eye), *aaiina-KHaana* (house of mirrors), *dahr* (world), *mun.nh* (face), and *diivaar* (wall). They suggest far greater layers of meanings than they usually embody and acquire metaphoric value about the seer, the seen, and the objects of seeing. They also underline the realities of the images that life presents before man. *Dahr* has been a frequent reference in poetry and has been perceived differently. Mir found another perspective on this in this verse: *haasil hai kyaa sivaae taraaii ke dahr mein mei.n / uTh aasmaa.n tale se ke shabnam bahut hai yaa.n.*

Ghazal 203 | Verse 1

48

میرے سنگ مزار پر فرہاد
رکھ کے تیشہ کہے ہے یا استاد

मेरे संग-ए मज़ार पर फ़रहाद
रख के तेशा कहे है या उस्ताद

mere sang-e mazaar per Farhaad
rakh ke tesha kahe hai yaa ustad

(*sang-e mazaar*—tombstone;
Farhad—a legendry lover;
tesha—axe)

To my tombstone, there comes
Farhad to disaster;
He puts down his axe and calls out—
Master! My master!

In this verse of extraordinary merit and appeal, Mir draws upon the example of Farhad, the archetypal lover, who ultimately came to Mir's tombstone and submitted to him in complete resignation. The verse suggests that Farhad failed in accomplishing his task, and now he looks up to Mir, his master, to seek his consolation. It also indicates that he needs blessings to continue his task and achieve union with Shirin, his life's aspiration.

More than what appears on the surface, the verse carries much more in terms of its suggestive meanings: (a) both Farhad and Mir had extraordinary skills in their arts as stone-carvers and word-carvers, respectively, and both were extraordinary lovers of their kind (b) Farhad's coming to Mir suggests that he considers him a master who could sympathize with him or enthuse him to accomplish his task as a master does (c) conversely, Farhad's gesture could also symbolize his feeling towards Mir as a rival (d) in this respect, he could stand only as a secondary figure compared with Mir, which he would not accept.

Farhad is projected here as a primordial figure—a symbol of a true romantic lover—who accepted the challenge of cutting the stones of a mountain to carve a milk channel to achieve his union with Shirin. *Tesha* (axe) is used here both as a symbol of power, which Farhad mustered as a stone carver, and as a symbol of his failure since cutting through the stones of a mountain with his axe proved too demanding to bear. The phrase—*yaa ustaad* (O, my master) suggests that he pays his obeisance to Mir, who excelled in the arts of love and art. The element of drama makes the verse extremely fascinating. Mir laments the loss of Farhad in this verse with a sense of pathos: *Majnuu.n na dasht mei.n hai na Farhad koh mei.n / thaa jis se lutf-e zindagii ve yaar mar gae.*

Ghazal 210 | Verse 4

49

ہوا ہے ہاتھ گلدستہ ہمارا
کہ داغ خوں بہت ہے آستیں پر

हुआ है हाथ गुलदस्ता हमारा
कि दाग़-ए ख़ूँ बहुत है आस्तीं पर

huaa hai haath guldasta hamaara
ke daaGh-e KHuu.n bahut hai aastii.n per

(*aastii.n*—sleeves)

These are my hands; they have turned
into a vase of flowers;
The hems of my raiment are blotted
with blood that looks like flowers

Loving is putting up with penance, and penance manifests itself in myriad ways. Mir's lover has suffered too much, and idiomatically speaking, he has shed enough blood, which now shows up as blots on his sleeves. In pride, however, he says that his hands have ultimately turned into a vase brimming as if with red flowers.

Built up as a sad saga of love, the verse is enlivened with certain moving propositions: (a) love calls for suffering and sacrifice, and it leads to the shedding of blood in turn (b) the lover's hands have become his urn or vase, and they are decorated with the blots of blood that look like blossoms (c) the blossoms of blood showing up on his sleeve suggest that he is himself both the assassin and the assassinated in love (d) this brings him a sense of pride and he stands apart in the company of lovers for the understanding he nourishes towards love.

Mir appropriates a common idiom of *daaGh-e KHuu.n* (blots of blood) and its appearance on the *aastii.n* (sleeve) to his advantage and imparts a touch of poetic excellence to the verse. The clause—*bahut hai aastii.n per* (there are too many on the sleeve)—reflects the lover's pride in his suffering in love. In sum, he takes greater pride in his hands becoming an urn/vase and the sleeve bearing many a blot of blood. Mir appropriates this image in another excellent verse: *dil go ke daaGh-o KHuu.n hai rahtii hai laag tujh se / insaaf kar ke jaa kar dikhlaavei.n phir kise dil.*

Ghazal 213 | Verse 2

50

دل وہ نگر نہیں کہ پھر آباد ہو سکے
پچھتاؤ گے سنو ہو یہ بستی اجاڑ کر

दिल वो नगर नहीं कि फिर आबाद हो सके
पछताओगे सुनो हो ये बस्ती उजाड़ कर

dil von agar nahii.n ke phir aabaad ho sake
pachhtaaoge suno ho ye bastii ujaaR kar

The heart is not a habitat
to be made alive again;
You would repent, do you listen
turning it to ruin again

Mir's speaker compares a derelict heart with a ruined habitation and admonishes his supposed addressee that just as a habitation deserted once cannot ever be brought back to life, a desolate heart, too, cannot ever be drawn to love again.

In this metaphor, Mir (a) underlines the value of a habitation that thrives only with the populace (b) this is also true of a heart that throbs only with love (c) as he values both, he respects life that is agog only with activity and heart that is enlivened only with emotions (d) this verse may also be read as a reflection on the personal predicament, as also the historical upheavals of which Mir was a sore witness (e) in this respect, the heart emerges here as a city that has fallen and stands forsaken by history and the people it swore by.

The tone of this verse is decidedly one of admonition, and this comes out quite clearly in the second line. However, comparing the heart with a habitat is unique, as both thrive only when inhabited and nourished actively.

Ghazal 223 | Verse 3

51

مرگ اک ماندگی کا وقفہ ہے
یعنی آگے چلیں گے دم لے کر

मर्ग इक माँदगी का वक़्फ़ा है
या'नी आगे चलेंगे दम ले कर

marg ik maa.ndgii kaa vaqfa hai
yaanii aage challenge dam le kar

(*marg*—death;
maa.ndgii—fatigue, tiredness;
vaqfa—a shred of time/period)

Death is but only a moment of fatigue
I'll move; let me catch my breath, shed my fatigue

Apart from being an eternal reality, death emerges here as a philosophical subject. Mir's speaker defines death in this verse and develops the idea that it is only a stopover on the long road of existence and that even though death is inevitable for all of us, but we might yet take another stride after death.

The speaker unveils different layers of meaning here: (a) death is equated to a moment of fatigue, which implies that one can resume one's journey after recovering from the fatigue of a journey that is life (b) fatigue accumulates with years, it can be warded off with rest which is what happens in the journey of life (c) as such, death is negated by life and life is an eternally rejuvenating force that does not terminate at any point (d) in this manner, life moves in a cycle and takes the past, the present and future in its wake and underlines the concept of life and time as flux, and philosophically speaking (e) this flux of life and time is equally true of the cycle of creation which acquires a new life after every period of fatigue.

Two expressions—*marg* (death) and *vaqfa* (a shred of time/period) together stress upon the transitoriness of life as opposed to the phrase—*dam le kar* (after collecting one's breath), which underscores the idea that another life starts subsequently. This is strengthened by the optimism carried forward in the second line—*yaani aage chale.nge dam le kar* (that is, I will fare forward after collecting myself). As opposed to Mir, Ghalib considers death as a terminator, which opens another perspective on this eternal subject: *Gham-e hastii kaa Asad kis se ho juz marg 'ilaaj / sham'a har rang mei.n jaltii hai sahar hote tak.*

Ghazal 240 | Verse 2

52

پان تو لیتا جا فقیروں کے
برگ سبز است تحفۂ درویش

पान तो लेता जा फ़क़ीरों के
बर्ग-ए सब्ज़ अस्त तोहफ़ा-ए दर्वेश

paan to leta jaa faqiro.n ke
barg-e sabz ast tohfa-i darvesh

(*paan*—betel leaves;
barge-e sabz—green leaves)

Come, receive the betel leaves
from the *faqiirs;*
These green leaves are gifts
from the *faqiirs*

Here is an unusual, somewhat raw feeling that is amazingly poeticized. We come across a *faqiir* who possibly meets a wayfarer and to whom he makes a kind offer of betel leaves as his parting gift. He offers this as he has nothing else that he may offer as a token of his love for him, but what he has to offer has a special significance and testifies to the warmth in his heart.

This pleasant gesture of the *faqiir* carries forth more profound messages than can be apprehended on the surface: (a) green betel leaves, when prepared with other condiments for chewing, turn the chewer's mouth and lips red and impart them a pleasant look (b) betel leaves that represent a cultural sign are symbolic of the warmth of one who offers it and the courtesy of another who accepts it (c) betel leaves cost little but pay more to both—the one who offers it and the other who accepts it (d) the one who offers it is doubly qualified as both *faqiir* and *darvesh* which puts him many a pedestal higher than the one to whom it is offered and whom he wishes to bless liberally with his unique gift.

The tone of endearment comes straight from the first line, although it also creates the impression that the addressee is not quite willing to stay on and accept the *faqiir's* offer. The second line in simple Persian appears too appropriate and befitting, coming from the lips of a *faqiir* who embodies blessings to everyone who comes his way. Nazir Akbarabadi, the pioneer of modern Urdu nazm, writes about the offering of *paan* in one of his poems, 'Dar-ul Makaafaat', as such: *jo aur kisii kaa maan rakhe to us ko bhii armaan mile / jo paan khilaave paan mile, jo rotii de to naan mile.*

Ghazal 277 | Verse 8

53

ہو عاشقوں میں اس کے تو آؤ میرؔ صاحب
گردن کو اپنی مو سے باریک تر کرو تم

हो आशिक़ों में उस के तो आओ 'मीर' साहिब
गर्दन को अपनी मू से बारीक-तर करो तुम

ho 'aashiqo.n mei.n us ke to aao Mir sahib
gardan ko apnii muu se baariik-tar karo tum

(*muu*—hair;
baariik-tar—thinner than the thin)

If you're one of her lovers, Mir Sahib,
come on here;
Just make your neck thinner, yes, thinner
than your hair

The figure of the archetypal lover is akin to one who has grown thin and looks emaciated in separation from the beloved. Here is a call to the lover that if he is a true lover, he should make no pretence and appear before the beloved as he is and prove his loyalty.

The unusual image of the lover also carries unusual connotations: (a) the lover should appear compliant; he should have no arrogance, defy egotism, and have a metaphorically thin neck representing submission (b) such a neck would naturally deny conceit and make him bow easily before the beloved (c) this neck would also be a kind of kin to the beloved's proverbial thin waist (d) it is only after reducing his neck thinner than a hair that he may be accepted as a suitable companion to his beloved.

Gardan az muu baariik tar—neck thinner than hair—is an idiomatic expression in Persian that implies the acceptance of an order without distaste or denial. This verse uses this idiom of thinning the hair creatively. Making the thin hair thinner still means shedding all pride and being acquiescent. This is the speaker's advice to the lover, which would put both the lover and the beloved in good stead if followed in the right spirit. The informal and conversational style of the verse makes it appealing. Mir appropriates this idea in another verse with different metaphors: *gardan-kushii kyaa haasil maanind bagule kii / is dasht mei.n sar gaaRe juu.n sail chale jaanaa.*

Ghazal 290 | Verse 10

54

یہ سنا تھا میرؔ ہم نے کہ فسانہ خواب لا ہے
تری سرگذشت سن کر گئے اور خواب یاراں

ये सुना था 'मीर' हम ने कि फ़साना ख़्वाब ला है
तिरी सर-गुज़श्त सुन कर गए और ख़्वाब याराँ

ye sunaa thaa Mir ham ne ke fasaana KHvaab laa hai
tiri sarguzasht sun kar gae aur KHvaab yaaraa.n

(*KHvaab-laa*—sleep-inducing;
sarguzasht—one's own tale)

I'd heard that the tale was dream-inducing, Mir,
and induced dreams;
Listening to your tale,
all other dreams vanished as false dreams

Sleep and dream tell the stories of dreamers and those who visit the dreamers in dreams. As some stories are too fascinating, they please the dreamers, but the unpleasant ones haunt them. When narrated to others, they create curious conditions in the hearts and minds of listeners.

We can read this verse in the light of these inferences: (a) the narrator says that he had only heard that the story was fascinating, but when narrated to other persons, it robbed the listeners of their sleep (b) the dream-story was either false and unbelievable, or it was a sleep snatcher being too fascinating (c) what appears as a sleep-inducing story, turned ultimately into a macabre dream (d) the realization of the difference between what was heard and what happened underlines the difference between dream as romance, and reality as outraging of romance (e) in Freudian terms, all dreams being the dreams of love and sex, also turn the listeners wary of dreams that vanish as nightmare or fantasy.

It should be noted that in the first line, *KHvaab* means sleep, but in the second line, it refers to sleep loss. The expression *KHvaab-laa* (sleep-inducing) is Mir's coinage, developed from *KHvaab-aavar*, which also means 'sleep-inducer'. Mir's coinage fascinates auditorily, as does the idea that this sleep-inducing story turns terrible for the listener, and they lose their sleep. The following verse by Mir may also be read in conjunction with this verse: *sar rafta sun na Mir kaa gar qasd-e KHvaab hai / niindei.n uchaTtiyaa.n hai.n sune ye kahaaniyaa.n.*

Ghazal 291 | Verse 2

55

متصل روتے ہی رہیے تو بجھے آتش دل
ایک دو آنسو تو اور آگ لگا جاتے ہیں

मुत्तसिल रोते ही रहिए तो बुझे आतिश-ए दिल
एक दो आँसू तो और आग लगा जाते हैं

muttasil rote hii rahiye to bujhe aatish-e dil
ek do aa.nsuu to aur aag lagaa jaate hai.n

(*muttasil*—aligned, regular;
aatish—fire)

Keep shedding incessant tears
to quench the heart's fire;
A drop or two only add
fuel to this fire

Tears and laughter punctuate man's life. Mir's speaker emphasizes the importance of tears that assuage man. This sounds paradoxical on the surface, but he asserts further that the more a person sheds tears, the better his chances of achieving tranquillity. This verse, like many others, develops a discourse on pain and suffering and helps appreciate how man may negotiate with dismay in his life.

The implied suggestions of this verse may be inferred as: (a) shedding tears is no sign of being vanquished as it may be an enriching experience of achieving equilibrium through purgation (b) tears need to align with the fire that burns the heart, and the heart's raging fire is akin to the flow of tears that may quench it as water quenches any other fire (c) fire and water, being the two elements, also regulate life and bear testimony to the divine design of existential balance (d) the idea of shedding tears to achieve equilibrium harks back to Aristotle's theory where pity and fear lead to catharsis.

The parallel placement of *aatish* (fire) and *aa.nsuu* (tears) maintains the verse's thematic balance. The key word in the verse, however, is *muttasil* (aligned/regular), which also keeps the shedding of tears aligned well with the heart's raging fire. It is in these balancing acts that Mir strikes the chord of meaning. The second line of the verse also refers to a common proverbial expression. A modernist poet, Mohammad Alvi, puts it in a pungent way: *roz achhe nahii.n lagte aa.nsuu / KHaas mauqo.n pe mazaa dete hai.n.*

Ghazal 292 | Verse 9

56

فرصت خواب نہیں ذکر بتاں میں ہم کو
رات دن رام کہانی سی کہا کرتے ہیں

फ़ुर्सत-ए ख़्वाब नहीं ज़िक्र-ए बुताँ में हम को
रात दिन राम कहानी सी कहा करते हैं

fursat-e KHvaab nahii.n zikr-e butaa.n mei.n ham ko
raat din raam kahaanii sii kahaa karte hai.n

(*zikr-e butaa.n*—speaking about the beloved)

I have no time to dream; I only speak;
speak only about my love;
Day and night, I tell an epic tale
to myself, about my love

The lover in this verse makes a confessional statement, as lovers generally do, in a state of self-absorption. He is so given to praising the beloved that he does not even have the time to dream about her. Obsessed with her, he speaks of her and her alone. Interestingly, only he is the speaker here, and all others are mere listeners.

A keener analysis reveals more stimulating ideas behind this verse: (a) lovers dream and have pleasant visions of their beloveds, but dreams, as such, are reflections of their romantic desires (b) while speaking about the beloved, he turns his desire into a reality (c) the beloved dwells between dreams and reality, but the lover seeks her actual companionship and cares little about his wishful dreams about her (d) the lover's proximity with her makes him tell her tale, which indeed is more of his tale than her tale (d) the two together constitute a world of their own in which the lover is physically present, but the beloved is present in her conspicuous absence.

This verse's most remarkable counter of expression is *zikr* (description), which has a Sufistic connotation and transports the beloved to a higher status. Another phrase that imparts an amazing beauty to this verse is *raam kahaanii* (story of one's self), which also gives the lover an other-worldly status. With this chiselled diction, Mir weaves a pattern of meaning that transforms lovers and beloveds into icons rather than human beings. The remarkable blending of *zikr* and *Raam kahaanii* and the mixing of two traditions of Sufistic and Hindu retelling of Ram's story imparts a truly secular nature to the verse. It should be befitting to consider the following verse of Mir that reflects on this tradition of telling tales: *uThh gai per mire takiye ko kahenge yaa.n Mir / dard-e dil baiThe kahaanii sii kahaa karte the.*

Ghazal 294 | Verse 4

57

سہل اس قدر نہیں ہے مشکل پسندی میری
جو تجھ کو دیکھتے ہیں مجھ کو سراہتے ہیں

सहल इस क़दर नहीं है मुश्किल-पसंदी मेरी
जो तुझ को देखते हैं मुझ को सराहते हैं

sehl is qadar nahii.n hai mushkil-pasandii merii
jo tujh ko dekhte hai.n mujh ko saraahte hai.n

(*sahl*—easy;
mushkil-pasandii—choice/liking for difficulty)

My choice for the difficult things
is not so easy;
Those who look at you, praise me
for finding it so easy

The lover–beloved relationship often takes a curious turn. This is one such verse where the lover considers the task of considering his beloved to be a difficult one. This has led others to wonder and praise him for making the most of a beloved who has been so challenging to negotiate with.

The delicate angles of interpretation may be marked thus: (a) the lover praises himself for his choice, but he does not disparage the beloved as she remains his beloved despite all constraints (b) those who look at him praise him, but they are indeed critical of him for his choice (c) the beloved is present on the scene, but she is mute and is addressed by the lover who sounds self-deprecating (d) there is no ideal love, but genuineness in love demands understanding from both sides which also includes the kindness to let things go that are not as pleasant as they could be.

The structure of meaning is built in the first line with the placement of two conflicting phrases—*sahl* (easy) and *muskhil* (difficult)—which characterize the unique nature of the lover. Similarly, another web of a curious relationship of the lover and beloved is brought forth with two words—*tujh* (you) and *mujh* (me) who are both—compatible and incompatible—yet proudly together. Haider Ali Atish draws upon this dichotomy and resolves it through rapprochement: *'ishq kii mushkil pasandii se huaa ye aashkaar / KHuubsuurat ko Ghuruur-e husn thoRaa chahiye.*

Ghazal 297 | Verse 2

58

چہرے پہ جیسے زخم ہے ناخن کا ہر خراش
اب دیدنی ہوئی ہیں مری دستکاریاں

चेहरे पे जैसे ज़ख़्म है नाख़ुन का हर ख़राश
अब दीदनी हुई हैं मिरी दस्त-कारियाँ

chehre pe jaise zaKHm hai naaKHun kaa har KHaraash
ab diidanii huii hai.n mirii dast-kaariyaa.n

(*KHaraash—scratch, graze;*
diidanii—worth seeing;
dast-kaariyaa.n—handicraft, embroideries)

Each scratch of my nail is like
a wound on my face;
Now, my embroideries are worth
a look on my face

Lovers are known for going wild and taking pride in their uneven behaviour. Here, the lover has scratched his face, and the scratches caused by his nails have turned into wounds. He takes pride in his wild behaviour and asserts that they look like embroideries on his face, which presents a sight worth looking at.

The implied connotations may be marked as follows: (a) wild acts defy all norms and evolve their behavioural patterns, which may be socially outrageous (b) instead of harming others, the wild lover harms himself and takes pride in doing so (c) he projects himself as an ideal lover who shows his wounds as mementos of love (d) taking pride in madness is unique and peculiar of lovers (e) not resorting to self-pity is another mark of such a crazy lover (f) by calling his act an act of craftsmanship, he projects himself as an artist and finds himself duly fulfilled.

The verse has three velar fricative sounds in particular—*zaKHm* (wound), *naaKHun* (nail), *and KHaraash* (scratch)—that work like agents or causes of suffering willingly caused and borne by the lover. As opposed to these, there are two more nouns—*chehra* (face) and *dastakaarii* (embroidery)—that portray a pleasant picture born out of pain. Mir's artistry is remarkable for being natural and acutely appealing. The portrayal of the lover as a craftsman is a unique example of Mir's craftsmanship as a poet of great imaginative vitality. Consider this verse by Mir where he recreates the image of scratches on the forehead with equal poetic excellence: *har KHaraash-e jabii.n jaraahat hai / naaKHun-e shauq kaa hunar dekho.*

Ghazal 302 | Verse 3

59

مت سہل ہمیں جانو پھرتا ہے فلک برسوں
تب خاک کے پردے سے انسان نکلتے ہیں

मत सह्ल हमें जानो फिरता है फ़लक बरसों
तब ख़ाक के पर्दे से इंसान निकलते हैं

mat sahl hamei.n jaano phirtaa hai falak barso.n
tab KHaak ke parde se insaan nikalte hai.n

(*sahl*—easy;
falak—sphere, sky)

Don't take me to be easy, the firmament
moves on and on for years;
Then emerges a man from
the veil of dust after so many years

Born as the best of God's creations, man is celebrated across all faiths and knowledge systems. This verse celebrates man in a poetic frame. It asserts that the sky keeps rotating for years before man takes his birth from the veil of soil to constitute its vital part and adorn this world subsequently.

More profound meanings that enrich this verse in multiple ways are as follows: (a) there is a unique relationship in the constituents of nature as the movement of the sky and that of the cycle of man's birth are interrelated (b) the birth of man from behind the veil of the earth suggests that man is made of soil and he goes back to the soil, which is also registered in religious texts (c) there is a distinction between man as an ordinary creature shorn of values and man as an embodiment of excellence and identified as superman (d) the sky also travels and explores for years for the birth of such a man endowed with superior power both physically and intellectually (e) thus comes out the distinction between man and human being, as well as human being and superman.

The verse has a mixed tone of both advice and warning. It addresses anyone who would care to listen to the message of human creation. The first line is a statement of fact composed of two parts—*mat sahl hamei.n jaano* (don't take me to be easy) and *phirtaa hai falak barso.n* (the sky moves for years), just as the second line comprises two statements—*tab KHaak ke parde se* (then from the veil of dust/soil) and *insaan nikalte hai.n* (human beings take their birth). These four clauses contain four ideas and are inextricably blended together to create a larger discourse on man's extraordinary status. Mir draws upon this idea with great ease and creates a closely corresponding verse: *mat sahl hamei.n samjho pahunche the baham tab ham / barso.n taii.n garduu.n ne jab KHaak ko chhana thaa.* Ghalib also engages with this idea in an admirably quizzical manner: *bas-ke dushvaar hai har kaam kaa aasaa.n hona / aadmii ko bhi mayassar nahii.n insaa.n honaa.*

Ghazal 307 | Verse 5

60

اپنی ہی سیر کرنے ہم جلوہ گر ہوئے تھے
اس رمز کو ولیکن معدود جانتے ہیں

अपनी ही सैर करने हम जल्वा-गर हुए थे
इस रम्ज़ को व-लेकिन मादूद जानते हैं

apnii hii sair karne ham jalva-gar hue the
is ramz ko va-lekin m'aaduud jaante hai.n

(*jalva-gar*—to show up, manifest, appear;
ramz—secret, sign, enigma;
m'aduud—precious few, limited)

I had appeared only to enjoy
my stroll;
But only a few know the secret of
my stroll

This verse reflects upon the purpose of man's existence at large. Man considers that he was manifested in this world only to admire his movements, but this is one of those secrets that only a few know.

With such a proposition made in simple terms, Mir opens avenues for further speculation about the secrets of man's existence: (a) man is surrounded by the proverbial God's plenty all around him, but he considers himself superior to all others (b) despite being enlightened enough to know himself and the world around, man knows the world and himself but only partially (c) although he is at the centre of all that happens around him, he does not realize his prowess and falls short of expectations associated with him (d) although born in all glory, only a few actualize their potential as Adam did and whose progeny all human beings are (e) humans, thus, emerge as the mirror of the creator, in which He sees Himself.

Three key expressions—*sair* (stroll), *jalva-gar* (manifested), and *m'aduud* (precious few)—embody the central intent of the verse. All these expressions put man on the highest pedestal and distinguish him from the host of others born as men but those who lack self-awareness and remain sadly impoverished. In another verse of this very ghazal, Mir finds a different way to broaden this idea: *suurat paziir ham bin hargiz nahii.n ve maane / ahl-e nazar hamii.n ko m'abuud jaante hai.n.*

Ghazal 314 | Verse 6

61

شہاں کہ کحل جواہر تھی خاک پا جن کی
انہیں کی آنکھوں میں پھرتے سلائیاں دیکھیں

शहाँ कि कोहल-ए जवाहर थी ख़ाक-ए पा जिन की
उन्हीं की आँखों में फिरते सलाइयाँ देखीं

shahaa.n ke kuhl-e javaahar thii KHaak-e paa jin kii
unhii.n kii aa.nkho.n mei.n phirte salaaiyaa.n dekhii.n

(*kuhl-e javaahar*—expensive collyrium in which pearls
and jewels are mixed;
KHaak-e paa—dust of feet)

The treasure troves of jewels were the dust
of the emperor's feet once;
In the same emperor's eyes, I witnessed,
the sharp needles being pierced once

Literary texts sometimes write history, and they make history alive when they do. This is one such verse in which the tragic lot of Mughal emperors is represented. They had commanded vast empires and had all the possessions at their feet once, but they fell prey to the onslaughts of time as history took a turn for the worse. The reference here is apparently to the blinding of Ahmad Shah, who was dethroned and blinded by his vazir Imad-ul Mulk.

This verse imparts multiple messages: (a) history, as it is said, has many cunning passages, and it turns a man into a victim, irrespective of the status he enjoys (b) man has neither control over his destiny; nor his worldly possessions can keep him in good stead forever (c) even while man knows that blessings and punishments are parts of divine dispensation, he cannot save himself from meeting his awful destiny at the appointed hour (d) it is much too ironic that the riches that lay at his feet once ultimately turn useless and that he cannot help prevent the awful punishment being meted out to him (e) the tragic aspect of this matter comes through the fact that in the past, needles dipped in poison were used to blind the accused ones, and now the same needles are used to pierce the eyes of the emperor.

Irony is the hallmark of this verse, operating at both the situational and verbal levels. *Kuhl-e javaahir* (treasure trove of jewels) and *KHaak-e paa* (dust of feet) stand apart, contradict each other, and create an ironic paradigm of meaning, as does the relationship between *paa* (feet) and *aankhei.n* (eyes) that add to the tragic fate of the sufferer. Further, the image of *salaaiyaa.n* (pins/needles) acts here as a cause of oppression and a reminder of punishment imparted through cruel methods. With the use of *unhii.n* (they alone), Mir particularizes the sufferer and adds a bitter edge to the verse. This awful predicament probably led Mir to put a premium on the dust of feet than on riches: *falak ai kaash ham ko KHaak hii rakhtaa ke is mei.n ham / Ghubaar-e raah hote ya kisuu kii KHaak-e paa hote.* In a variation on this theme, Ghalib asserts in defiance: *tere javaahir-e tarf-e kulah ko kyaa dekhei.n / ham auj-e t'aala-e l'al-o guhar ko dekhte hai.n.*

Ghazal 316 | Verse 6

62

خاک آدم ہی ہے تمام زمیں
پاؤں کو ہم سنبھال رکھتے ہیں

ख़ाक-ए आदम ही है तमाम ज़मीं
पाँव को हम सँभाल रखते हैं

KHaak-e Aadam hii hai tamaam zamii.n
paao.n ko ham sanbhaal rakhte hai.n

(*KHaak*—dust)

All this earth is the dust of Adam's feet
With caution, on this earth, I put my feet

Mir's speaker develops a unique perspective here by proposing that this earth is the dust of Adam's feet, and one is thus obliged to put one's feet on this planet carefully and cautiously.

This easy and statement-like verse suggests further avenues of meaning: (a) man is inextricably related and perennially indebted to earth as the mother that sustains with food and provides its lap for an abode (b) Adam, being the first human on the earth, walked through its colossal length and breadth not in pride, but in pure humility (c) losing the heavens after being driven away from there by God, Adam had to duly respect his new haven (d) the heirs of Adam can only draw their lessons from him and treat the earth with respect as he did (e) both earth and Adam are presented as subjects of great esteem and they reinforce each other's existence and legacy.

The first line of this verse is hugely emphatic, and it is well asserted with two words—*hii* (only) and *tamaam* (all). Similarly, the placement of two words—*KHaak* (dust) and *zamii.n* (earth)—in the same line is worth noticing. Dust materializes as earth, even though it has lesser significance than the earth. Still, by considering it the dust of Adam's feet, it acquires far greater importance in the verse. The sense of caution reflected in the phrase—*sambhaal rakhte hain* (put with caution)—further strengthens the idea of respect for the specks of dust that compose the entire earth. The word *ham* (we) represents humanity, further enhancing the idea of respect for the earth. Earth is well adored by the modernist poet Irfan Siddiqui thus: *vo marhala hai ke ab sail-e Khuu.n pe razii hai.n / tere zamiin ko shaadaab dekhne ke liye.* A mystical representation of earth's sanctity may well be discovered in William Blake's 'Introduction' and 'Earth's Answer' in his *Songs of Innocence and of Experience.*

Ghazal 318 | Verse 7

63

پھروں میرؔ عریاں نہ دامن کا غم ہو
نہ باقی رہے خار خار گریباں

फिरूँ 'मीर' उर्यां न दामन का ग़म हो
न बाक़ी रहे ख़ार-ख़ार-ए गरेबाँ

phiruu.n Mir 'uryaa.n na daaman kaa Gham ho
na baaqii rahe KHaar-KHaar-e garebaa.n

(*'uryaa.n*—naked, nude, bare;
KHaar-KHaar—anxiety, perplexity, disquietude)

May I walk naked, Mir, carefree,
unaware of my clothes lapping in the air;
May there be no lament for my
shredded collars and hems anywhere

Strange, even unbecoming ideas may sometimes be the staple material for poetic upsurge. Here is an idea where the speaker expresses a desire of this kind: he wishes to walk naked without ever bothering if his shirt hems are intact or torn into pieces.

While wondering what Mir's speaker wishes to say, one comes across these ideas: (a) the difference between two physical appearances of being dressed or undressed is only relative as one who is dressed may indeed be naked, and vice-versa (b) the one in a state of undress may have achieved a higher state of consciousness, while the other who is well-kept externally may be preoccupied only with falsities of life and living (c) this brings one to appreciate the real meaning of appearance and reality as one is often taken for the other (d) in walking naked, there would be no care either for the attire or for the collar that completes the attire (e) the hem and the collar, being parts of the attire, complement each other, but in getting a release from the attire, none of them would matter.

The speaker appears careless, but he is indeed too careful about realizing the existentialist meaning of life. The repetitive word—*na* (no)—underlines the speaker's mood. This is borne out by his two desires to walk naked in the first line and to be utterly oblivious of his shredded collar in the second line, which may pinch like thorns and keep him restless. The expression—*KHaar-KHaar*—has two connotations of desire and perplexity and defines the speaker together. In addition, they enhance the inferential meaning of the verse. Momin Khan Momin comes to mind here with reference to the double use of this word: *KHaar-KHaar-e Gham aashkaara huaa / misl-e dil jaama paara paara huaa.* Mir's verse aptly reminds here of W. B. Yeats's poem 'A Coat', which ends with these lines: 'For there is more enterprise / In walking naked.'

Ghazal 321 | Verse 2

64

لایا ہے مرا شوق مجھے پردے سے باہر
میں ورنہ وہی خلوتیِ رازِ نہاں ہوں

लाया है मिरा शौक़ मुझे पर्दे से बाहर
मैं वर्ना वही ख़ल्वती-ए राज़-ए निहाँ हूँ

laayaa hai miraa shauq mujhe parde se baahar
mai.n varna vahii KHalvatii-i raaz-e nihaa.n huu.n

(*KHalvatii*—a hermit, confidant;
raaz-e nihaa.n—hidden secrets)

Only my curiosity has brought me
out of my veil;
Else, I'm the lonely keeper of secrets
kept in a veil

The superior beings among the ordinary men are intellectually and mystically charged. A person of this potential speaks through this verse in a confessional mode, asserting that he has cultivated himself as a confidant of the unveiled secrets, and his ardor for this has brought him out of his hallowed precincts.

The philosophical intents of this verse are worth noting: (a) this confidant derives his strength from his seclusion, which is a state of developing a deeper dialogue with oneself (b) it is close to the Islamic concept of achieving *vilaayat* (authority/dominion), the Christian concept of achieving hermitage and the Hindu and Buddhist concept of achieving *samadhi* (union with the divine) (c) his well-qualified solitariness from the physical world affords him a philosophical status and imparts a spiritualist halo to his personality to help unveil the secrets of existence (d) as he is metaphysically drawn towards this, he has come out of his fold to unravel the secrets of the phenomenon.

Mir adds the simplest of the words—*vahii* (he alone)—with extraordinary potential and identifies him in two ways—one that he was earlier and the other that he is now. This verse takes us back to another verse of Mir privileging the same idea: *apnii hii sair karne ham jalvagar hue the / is ramz ko valekin m'aduud jaante hai.n.* Ghulam Hamadani Mushafi also unveils this reality as such: *maKHluuq huu.n yaa KHaaliq-e maKHluuq-numaa huu.n / m'aluum nahii.n mujh ko ke mai.n kaun huu.n kyaa huu.n.*

Ghazal 328 | Verse 4

65

مری نمود نے مجھ کو کیا برابر خاک
میں نقش پا کی طرح پائمال اپنا ہوں

मिरी नुमूद ने मुझ को किया बराबर ख़ाक
मैं नक़्श-ए पा की तरह पाएमाल अपना हूँ

miri numuud ne mujh ko kiyaa baraabar KHaak
mai.n naqsh-e paa kii tarah paaemaal apnaa huu.n

(*numuud*—manifestation, appearance;
naqsh-e paa—footprints;
paaemaal—trodden, trampled, crushed)

My emergence on its own
has turned me into dust now;
I have trampled upon myself
with my own footprints now

To what extent has the purpose of human existence been fulfilled, and how does humanity respond to its predicament? This is a matter of philosophical concern. The speaker ponders over his larger lot and considers that his appearance on the face of the earth has only been a cause of disappointment for him. Thus, he is a picture of his defeat, much like his footprints, which convey no message.

There are other philosophical derivations: (a) created in the image of God, as proclaimed in The Bible (Genesis, 1:27), man has not met the aim[s] he was created for (b) man's defeat accounts for his failures and not for God's failure who made him as his vicegerent on the earth (Al-Baqara, 2:30, Genesis, 1: 26-27) (c) man's failure thus deprives the earth and makes it poorer (d) the imbalance between God's intention and man's achievement or failure spells out the balance or imbalance between God's intention behind the creation and man's inability or inadequacy to justify his existence (e) man is thus the picture of failure which is reflected by his footprints to suggest that he has walked, but only to arrive nowhere.

Two interrelated expressions—*KHaak* (dust) and *naqsh-e paa* (footprint)—create a complex array of meanings relating to man's futile cruising through time. The second line marks the pivotal point, where failure has been mythicized. With his mystical-cum-philosophical leanings, Mir Dard expresses this idea thus: *huu.n fitaada ba rang-e naqsh-e qadam / raftagaa.n kaa magar suraaGh huu.n mai.n.*

Ghazal 336 | Verse 2

66

گوشِ دیوار تک تو جا نالے
اس میں گل کو بھی کان ہوتے ہیں

गोश-ए दीवार तक तू जा नाले
उस में गुल को भी कान होते हैं

gosh-e diivaar tak tuu jaa naale
us mei.n gul ko bhii kaan hote hai.n

(*gosh*—ear;
naala—entreating)

I make a plea, I say—
reach up the walls', ears;
Listen! even the blossoms have
their ears here

No existence is all joy or all enjoyment. Human beings, thus, make their plea and seek their release from the feelings of loss and suffering. One way for the sufferer is to reach the wall, which is proverbially known for having ears. The speaker suggests that the wall's sympathetic ears may listen to the sufferer and offer him relief.

Drawing upon a proverb that walls, too, have ears, this verse makes diverse suggestions: (a) walls are seemingly passive objects, but they have ears (b) ears that listen can also be moved and bear the wailer's pain, simply by the act of listening (c) a silent bearer of pain is like a wall that is also silent, but like the sufferer, full of pain too (d) there is a desire to restore the sufferer from his misery but pain being a condition of life is a reality and has to be endured (e) the verse reflects on the existential angst that human beings are born with.

The essential tone of the verse is one of beseeching. The speaker entreats the sufferer to bring their prayer to the wall. This is borne out by the first line, especially in the clause—*tuu jaa* (reach out). The second line offers hope for relief and redemption from suffering. *Kaan honaa* (to have ears) is an idiom and aptly translates into English as 'to be all ears'. Mir glosses over the idea of hearing in a different framework of images like cage, encaged, wall and bud in another verse: *shor nahii.n yaa.n suntaa koii Mir qafas ke asiiro.n kaa / gosh nahii.n diivaar-e chaman ke gul ke shaaed kaan nahii.n.*

Ghazal 348 | Verse 3

67

مجلس میں تیری ہم کو کب غیر خوش لگے ہے
ہم بیچ اپنے اس کے دیوار کھینچتے ہیں

मज्लिस में तेरी हम को कब ग़ैर ख़ुश लगे है
हम बीच अपने उस के दीवार खींचते हैं

majlis mei.n teri ham ko kab Ghair KHush lage hai
ham biich apne us ke diivaar khainchte hai.n

(*majlis*—assembly, gathering;
Ghair—the other)

In your assembly, how can I appreciate
the presence of another;
I draw a line between him and me,
to keep him away and us together

Between the lover and the beloved, the figure of the 'other' has always been a cause for serious concern. This verse draws upon this theme as the speaker shows no hesitation in asserting that he never likes the presence of the other in an assembly. Unable to deter him from being there, he draws a wall between himself and the other to live in peace.

As is often the case, there is more to the verse than what appears at first: (a) lovers are perennially possessive and characteristically conscious of the beloved, and jealous of other happy lovers (b) lovers are distinguished and made conspicuous by their their appearance and demeanour in any assembly (c) love is an institution to be valued and preserved by lovers themselves, (d) even while being in the company of the other, the lover does not care if he is marked for his hatred for him and possessiveness of the beloved.

The idea of drawing a wall is more symbolic than literal in this verse. Drawing a line between the two—the lover and the other—suggests blinding one against the other and denying the existence of the nagging other. The verse acquires its strength by invoking the images of the other characteristically known in the ghazal tradition as a rival who, interestingly enough, strengthens the central intent of all ghazal verses. However, Ghalib offers a fascinating variation on this figure that may be marked for its rich ambiguity: *ham bhii dushman to nahii.n hai.n apne / Ghair ko tujh se mohabbat hi sahii.*

Ghazal 354 | Verse 3

68

سنا جاتا ہے شہر عشق کے گرد
مزاریں ہی مزاریں ہو گئی ہیں

सुना जाता है शहर-ए इश्क़ के गिर्द
मज़ारें ही मज़ारें हो गई हैं

sunaa jaataa hai shahr-e 'ishq ke gird
mazaarei.n hii mazaarei.n ho gaii hai.n

(*mazaar*—grave, tomb)

Around the hamlets of love,
They say—
Only tombs and tombs
and tombs now lay

This verse invokes a poignant image of the cycle of life and death of the lovers and beloveds. It suggests that the lovers have reached their life's end and have ultimately kissed the ground by finding their graves for themselves.

The verse, however, appeals to our imagination by invoking several associated ideas: (a) dying and being allotted a grave is a routine event for humans, but the death of lovers is an extraordinary incident (b) love brings suffering and because of their pain, lovers perish, but their lives are still of more consequence than those who lead ordinary and colourless lives (c) with a more significant number of lovers dying, yet another city of dead lovers and tombs has come into being alongside the city of the living lovers (d) in their lives, as well as in their deaths, the lovers live together to constitute a unique community of their own (e) the dead lovers will ever be remembered and visited by the living ones—in turn keeping the cycles and legacies of love and pain alive.

Instead of stating it directly, the speaker shows his objective detachment in the first line with the phrase *sunaa jaataa hai* (it is heard). This imparts the verse a unique appeal and naturally attracts the supposed listeners. The repetition of *mazaar* (tomb) twice in the second line—*mazaarei.n hii mazaarei.n* (tombs and tombs) with an added counter of expression—*hii* (only)—adds to its immediacy of meaning. Overall, the tone of the verse is one of sobriety and thoughtfulness rather than of making a statement, which accounts for its appeal. It should be interesting to see how Mir develops this idea in another verse, which appears as a variation on this verse: *kyaa zulm hai us KHuuni-i 'aalam kii galii mei.n / jab ham gae do chaar naii dekhii.n mazaarei.n*

Ghazal 429 | Verse 2

69

رات مجلس میں تری ہم بھی کھڑے تھے چپکے
جیسے تصویر لگا دے کوئی دیوار کے ساتھ

रात मज्लिस में तिरी हम भी खड़े थे चुपके
जैसे तस्वीर लगा दे कोई दीवार के साथ

raat majlis mei.n tiri ham bhii khaRe the chupke
jaise tasviir lagaa de koii diivaar ke saath

(*majlis*—assembly, gathering)

Last night, in your assembly
I too stood silently
Like a portrait on a wall,
I was there too, silently

Lovers can be as loquacious as they can be voiceless according to different life situations. We have a lover here who is statuesque in his muteness and is, at best, a worldless spectator of whatever happens around him or to him in the beloved's *mehfil* (gathering).

There are various other avenues of meaning for us to consider critically: (a) a lover is an image of helplessness, and he has no control over the way he is treated in the assembly of people (b) there are agencies of control in a social system that dictate norms and the lover in that order is only a marginal figure (c) the lover is present on the scene but he is merely a spectator of his own self, and is mute and lifeless in literal terms (d) an image can be animated and a painter's portrait can be eloquent, but here the lover is entirely deprived of expression (e) neglected, the lover stands isolated among other suitors (f) as such, he looks like a lifeless picture hung on the wall.

In artistic terms, the verse gains merit in the simile of a mute portrait created for a lover deprived of speech. While *majlis* (assembly) establishes a sense of a congregation abuzz with activity, the words *tasviir* (portrait) and *diivaar* (wall) develop as metaphors of incapacitation, qualified by *chupke* (silently). Consider Mir re-configuring this condition in another verse: *tasviir ke maanind lage dar hii se guzrii / majlis mei.n tiri ham ne kabhuu baar na paayaa.*

Ghazal 451 | Verse 1

70

کچھ موج ہوا پیچاں اے میرؔ نظر آئی
شاید کہ بہار آئی زنجیر نظر آئی

कुछ मौज-ए हवा पेचाँ ऐ 'मीर' नज़र आई
शायद कि बहार आई ज़ंजीर नज़र आई

kuchh mauj-e havaa pechaa.n ai Mir nazar aaii
shaayed ke bahaar aaii zanjiir nazar aaii

(*pechaa.n*—warped, twisted, coiled)

That was the warped blow of wind; I saw, O Mir
I saw chains; I guessed spring had arrived, O Mir

Lovers act and react in unpredictable ways. A lover sometimes appears wild and is apprehensive that he, too, could be fettered and kept in check like other lovers who seem to have lost control over themselves. He senses this when he sees the wind blowing in a warped manner. As such, he foresees that spring is about to arrive; he will go berserk again and chains will be put around his feet that will rattle and announce his movement.

This verse represents the classical image of a lover in Urdu ghazal as follows: (a) lovers are traditionally prone to insanity and they have to be checked to make sure they are not disrupting the social order (b) spring, being the season of merriment, makes the lover merrier with anticipation and eventually insane because of the overwhelming rush of emotions (c) he is aware of his impending fate and as if corresponding with the imminent outburst of spring, he explodes with his own emotions and goes berserk thinking that spring has actually arrived when it has not (d) this testifies to the idea why the typical lover of the ghazal tradition has to be put in chains.

There is an imagistic representation in both *mauj-e havaa-pechaa.n* (warped winds) and *zanjiir* (chain). Between the two the lover is placed who would be enchained when warped winds will blow. The selection of matching images to configure the lover makes the verse worthy of our attention. The warped wind and chain contrast against each other and reflect the protagonist's fate. An extension of this verse may be witnessed in another verse of Mir: *mausam gul kaa shaayed aayaa daaGh junuu.n ke siyaah huve / dil khinchtaa hai jaanib-e sahra jii nahii.n lagtaa ghar mei.n ab.*

Ghazal 451 | Verse 2

71

دلی کے نہ تھے کوچے اوراق مصور تھے
جو شکل نظر آئی تصویر نظر آئی

दिल्ली के न थे कूचे औराक़ मुसव्वर थे
जो शक्ल नज़र आई तस्वीर नज़र आई

Dilli ke na the kuuche auraaq musavvar the
jo shakl nazar aaii tasviir nazar aaii

(*auraaq*—pages, leaves;
musavvar—painted, portrayed)

Those lanes of Dilli—those were—
the painter's canvas painted;
Each face I saw, I only saw
those lanes' portraits painted

This is yet another verse referring to the atrophied cityscape of Delhi, which had a reputation for being a strategically important seat of power and centre of culture at one point in its history. The verse portrays the city as a space that was once luminous in its glory, untouched and seemingly unchangeable as a painting. The beauty of this verse does not necessarily lie in the portrayal of the city's merits but in how it has been portrayed, which has made it a highly quotable verse.

The literary merit of this verse lies in these aspects: (a) the city lanes are compared to the pages portrayed on a larger spatial canvas, which implies that the city was an artist's configuration of sorts with great imaginative vitality (b) the faces that showed up did not appear like faces, but like portraits, which again was a testament to the artists' remarkable acumen (c) it is significant to note further that the pages so portrayed, and faces so configured, represent the city as a work of art (d) every space of which Dilli is a replica is a work of art unto itself, which is indeed an example of outstanding workmanship.

The first line of this verse is generally read as *Dilli ke na the kuuche auraq-e musavvir*, which means that 'they were not the lanes of Dilli, but they were the pages from an artist's work'. This rendering of the line is prompted by the misreading of the phrase as *auraaq-e musavvir* (pages of the artist's work), which utilizes the *izaafat* (a diacritical mark indicating a conjunction) of 'e' with auraaq, resulting in *auraaq-e musavvir*. The verse gains significantly in its scope of meaning if read as *auraaq mussavar* (pages portrayed) rather than *auraaq-e musavvir* (pages of the artist's works), which limits its implications and appeal. This verse is a remarkable example of image-making in poetry in optic terms. One is reminded here of Mushafi's image-making as well: *KHaak-e Dilli ki zaraa sair to kar / ye 'ajab aab-o havaa rakhti hai.* Also close to this is Mir Soze: *hazrat-e Dilli kii kis mu.nh se karuu.n t'aariif mai.n / ek ek us ujRe ghar mei.n 'aalam-e tasviir hai.*

Ghazal 471 | Verse 5

72

پیشہ تو ایک ہی تھا اس کا ہمارا لیکن
مجنوں کے طالعوں نے شہرت میں یاوری کی

पेशा तो एक ही था उस का हमारा लेकिन
मजनूँ के तालेओं ने शोहरत में यावरी की

pesha to ek hii thaa us kaa hamaaraa lekin
majnuu.n ke t'aaleo.n ne shohrat mei.n yaavarii kii

(*t'aaleo.n*—destiny, fortune;
yaavarii—alliance)

Our occupations were indeed
one and the same;
But *Majnuu.n*'s fortune favoured him
to get him fame

The speaker in this verse draws upon the example of the archetypal lover Qais Ibn Al-Malawwah, better known as *Majnuu.n*, to highlight how he achieved a unique identity and unbeatable fame because of his love for Laila. Thinking of his love, the speaker is reminded of *Majnuu.n*, who had been known since the eleventh century in Arabia, but it was Nizami Ganjavi, the major Persian poet of the twelfth century, who immortalized him—as did many other poets in different Indic languages after him.

Through the example of *Majnuu.n*, the speaker drives home that (a) *Majnuu.n* was a benchmark as a devotee of love and his beloved, but the speaker is not any lesser in his own passions, although he did not get the same name and fame as the legendary lover (b) the desire to be remembered alongside *Majnuu.n* is a rueful expression of an unfulfilled desire (c) the regretful tone of the speaker also suggests his inability to measure up to the highest level of sacrifice in love and thereby of his falling short of expectations associated with true love (d) *Majnuu.n* gave up his life when not united with his love, but he remains alive in history, which the speaker mourns as he cannot achieve that same status for himself (e) it is also suggested that luck matters too in love and he was not as lucky as *Majnuu.n* was (f) in the affairs of love, a sense of jealousy with *Majnuu.n* is also marked quite conspicuously.

Two words in the verse—*pesha* (occupation) and *t'aalao.n* (destiny)—are central to the construction of meaning in this verse. In considering love as a favoured occupation, the speaker elevates the status of love, which requires steadfastness and devotion. He assigns his inability to reach the level of *Majnuu.n* to his destiny, which the failed lovers often do to seek their consolation. In many of his verses, Mir has configured *Majnuu.n* as an archetypal lover. Here are two examples where he puts himself vis-a-vis *Majnuu.n*: *kaun letaa thaa naam Majnuu.n kaa / jab ke 'ahd-e junuu.n hamaaraa thaa* and *diivaangii mei.n Majnuu.n mere huzuur kyaa thaa / ladkaa sa un dino.n tha us ko shu'uur kyaa thaa.*

Ghazal 472 | Verse 1

73

دیکھ تو دل کہ جاں سے اٹھتا ہے
یہ دھواں سا کہاں سے اٹھتا ہے

देख तो दिल कि जाँ से उठता है
ये धुआँ सा कहाँ से उठता है

dekh to dil ke jaa.n se uThtaa hai
ye dhuaa.n saa kahaa.n se uThtaa hai

(*jaa.n*—life's breath, soul, self)

From the heart or the soul,
from where does it rise?
This, something like smoke,
from where does it rise?

The speaker in this verse, evidently a disappointed lover, knows that his heart is burning. Still, he is incapable of understanding what burns and where the smoke rises from. This typical image of a lover at a loss only testifies to the image of the archetypal lover who can only seethe without finding a way of redressal for himself.

The following aspects of this verse are worth noting: (a) the speaker in this verse could be either the lover wondering by himself, or asking the beloved, or even an outsider looking at the scene with curiosity (b) the speaker is not sure whether it is the heart that burns or the soul, but he certainly knows that there is smoke, and where there is smoke, there must also be fire (c) as he cannot distinguish from where the smoke rises, his asking someone sympathetic to see what is happening, only underlines his pathetic state of existence (d) he also seems to suggest that this smouldering has been there for some time and he can only bear this perennial state of burning for so long (e) love burns the lover metaphorically, but this burning is made real with the smoke rising from either the heart or the soul.

The verse is characterized by an express tone of wondering imbued with questioning. The first line initiates it by bringing two questions or wonderments to the fore—*dil se uThtaa hai* (rises from the heart) and *jaa.n se uThtaa hai* (rises from the soul). The second line reiterates the same spirit of questioning or wondering in open terms—*ye dhuaa.n saa kahaa.n se uThtaa hai* (from where does this smoke rise). These impart the verse a muted yet firm tone of despair. The significance of *saa* (like) is also worth noting. In another verse of this very ghazal, Mir extends this idea admirably well in a different direction: *gor kis dil jale kii hai ye falak / sh'ola ik sub'ha yaa.n e uThtaa hai.*

Ghazal 472 | Verse 9

74

عشق اک میرؔ بھاری پتھر ہے
کب یہ تجھ ناتواں سے اٹھتا ہے

इश्क़ इक 'मीर' भारी पत्थर है
कब ये तुझ ना-तवाँ से उठता है

'ishq ik Mir bhaarii pathhar hai
kab ye tujh naa-tavaa.n se uThta hai

(*naa-tavaa.n*—feeble, weak, frail)

Love is a heavy stone, Mir,
much too heavy;
How can this feeble one lift this
stone so heavy

Love may be bliss, but love is also demanding. This idea has been expressed variously by poets across ages, but Mir's speaker admits this with a unique certainty. His plain admission, expressed confessionally, also accounts for the verse's appeal.

However, the verse acquires depth in what lies behind what is stated: (a) love is not merely a romantic affair; it entails trials and tribulations more on the part of the lover than on the beloved (b) it involves meeting expectations and calls for fulfilling obligations that prove more challenging than they appear to be (c) love is also a matter of moulding oneself to meet the call or needs of the body, which body, which is yet another call that is not easily met (d) loving is a constant act of precarious balancing between reality and illusion, desire and fulfilment and hope and despair.

The novelty of this verse lies in the metaphor of a heavy stone as a symbol of love and the lover's inability to lift it. It appears to be a mundane metaphor, but its relevance lies in how rationally it is used in the verse. The contrast between *bhaarii pathhar* (heavy stone) and *tujh naa-tavaa.n* (the feeble you) can be well imagined by any observer but is best realized by one who is expected to lift it. Love is one of Mir's most favoured subjects, which he has explored in numerous ways. Consider these two verses that come close to this verse: *Mir marnaa pade hai KHuubaa.n per / 'ishq mat kar ke bad balaa hai 'ishq* and *jin jin ko thaa ye 'ishq kaa aazaar mar gae / aksar hamaare saath ke biimaar mar gae.*

Ghazal 473 | Verse 1

75

کلی کہتے ہیں اس کا سا دہن ہے
سنا کریے کہ یہ بھی اک سخن ہے

कली कहते हैं उस का सा दहन है
सुना करिए कि ये भी इक सुख़न है

kalii kahte hai.n us kaa saa dahan hai
sunaa kariye ke ye bhii ik suKHan hai

(*dahan*—mouth;
suKHan—word, speech, poetry)

A mouth like hers is a bud; it's so said
Listen! That, too, is poetry; it's so said

Of all the parts of the beloved's body, her mouth and lips are of exceptional beauty, deserving the maximum attention and praise. The mouth is compared here to a bud, and one is urged to listen to the bud as that has a word or message stored in it worth listening to.

There are some astounding interpretations that we can draw from this verse: (a) a bud opens to become a blossom, as does the beloved's mouth to address the lover or the onlooker (b) the bud opens up to spread its fragrance, as does the beloved's mouth to spread the fragrance of love (c) the speaker asks the addressee to listen to her word of love which is spoken with love (d) the words, the lips, and the mouth embody the beauty of the bud's language (e) the beauty of speech lies in the speech itself as much as it lies in the beauty of the beloved, her mouth and her lips.

Remarkably, the first line is richly ambiguous and may be read in three different ways: (a) a mouth like hers is a bud (b) her mouth is like a bud (c) a bud has a mouth like hers. The simile of the beloved's mouth and the bud paints a stunning visual and adds beauty to the verse, but the actual beauty of the verse lies in the second line, where the word *suKHan* performs the magic of holding two meanings of 'word' on the one hand and 'poetry' on the other. Mir plays upon this experience with a novel variation in another verse: *ye baatei.n rang rang hamaarii hai.n varna Mir / aa jaatii hai kalii mei.n kabhuu us dahaa.n kii tar'ha.*

Ghazal 475 | Verse 1

76

کب سے نظر لگی تھی دروازۂ حرم سے
پردہ اٹھا تو لڑیاں آنکھیں ہماری ہم سے

कब से नज़र लगी थी दरवाज़ा-ए हरम से
पर्दा उठा तो लड़ियाँ आँखें हमारी हम से

kab se nazar lagii thii darvaaza-i harem se
parda uTha to laDiyaa.n aankhei.n hamaarii ham se

(*harem*—a sacred territory in Mecca)

For so long had my eyes waited, yearning
at the harem's door;
With the curtain raised, my eyes encountered me
at the harem's door

A yearning for the most desired object sometimes takes unexpected turns. The speaker in this verse, who yearned to look at the *harem*, has ultimately arrived there. Standing right in front of the *harem*, he finds himself in a strange situation and feels as if his own eyes have encountered him, not the *harem* he stands facing.

In this remarkable way of portraying his intimate experience, the speaker represents a curious condition of his self: (a) his eyes preserved dreams and when these dreams were realized, his eyes only tried to believe what they saw (b) the idea of seeing as believing was defied when the long-yearned object of seeing turned into a reality (c) another idea of the eyes encountering eyes suggests that the image looked at became the eyes of the seer himself (d) this act of seeing a desired sanctuary turning into a reality obliterates the distinction between a dream and reality (e) this is a situation that brings a shock of recognition to the seer and fills his senses with delight.

The verse contains an element of drama, which is acted upon the seer, who turns into a sight himself to be watched with surprise. The door of the *harem* and the curtain constitute a set of images that comprise the plot of that drama. The idea of an eye encountering an eye imparts a natural touch of genius to the verbal artistry of the verse. The word—*laRiyaa.n* (encountered)—drawn from the common vocabulary with conversational ease adds a novel linguistic appeal to the verse. The idiom—*aa.nkh laRnaa* (eyes meeting eyes)—has generally carried a romantic connotation across ages. Still, it is employed here only to create an impression of a romantic encounter with the object yearned for. This contributes to enriching the meaning and appeal of the verse in two different ways, as mentioned above. This reverence for the *harem* is rendered with a fanciful difference in Faiz Ahmad Faiz: *raqs-e mai tez karo saaz kii lai tez karo / suu-e maiKHaana safiiraan-e harem aate hai.n.*

Ghazal 478 | Verse 2

77

اندوہ وصل و ہجر نے عالم کھپا دیا
ان دو ہی منزلوں میں بہت یار تھک گئے

अंदोह-ए वस्ल-ओ-हिज्र ने आलम खपा दिया
इन दो ही मंज़िलों में बहुत यार थक गए

andoh-e vasl-o hijr ne 'aalam khapaa diyaa
in do hii manzilo.n mei.n bahut yaar thak gae

(*andoh*—pain, agony)

My world succumbed to the agonies of
union and parting;
These two stages alone tired me out:
union and parting

Mir's speaker once again brings us face to face with the reality of love, which is not necessarily and primarily all bliss. This verse, like so many others, reiterates that love brings both pleasures and pains in its stages: union and separation, but interestingly, both tire the lover equally, beyond his power of revival. As such, he sounds tired of love and the acts associated with loving.

We can read the verse more deeply with these points in our mind: (a) love is not all fun, but pain too; in both the cyclical acts of union and separation (b) it is paradoxical, but experientially tangible too that union can be tiresome as separation can be trying (c) love robs the lover of himself and the world he nurses for himself with hope and faith (d) the ultimate effect of love and loving is exhaustion that turns the lover disappointed and in despair.

The expression—*bahut yaar thak gae*—suggests that the lover is exhausted, not just tired on the one hand and also that many of his friends got tired in the act of loving on the other. Another word to read closely in this verse is *manzil*, which also has double implications: 'stage' on the one hand and 'destination' on the other. These double entendres enrich the verse quite substantially. The experience of fatigue in love is well represented in a verse by a modernist poet Munir Niazi: *thakan safar kii badan shal saa kar gaii hai Munir / buraa kiyaa jo safar mei.n qayaam kar baiThaa.*

Ghazal 481 | Verse 1

78

برنگ بوے گل اس باغ کے ہم آشنا ہوتے
کہ ہمراہ صبا ٹک سیر کرتے پھر ہوا ہوتے

ब-रंग-ए बू-ए गुल उस बाग़ के हम आश्ना होते
कि हमराह-ए सबा टुक सैर करते फिर हवा होते

ba-rang-e buu-e gul us baaGh ke ham aashnaa hote
ke hamraah-e sabaa tuk sair karte phir havaa hote

(*aashnaa*—acquainted, familiar)

I wish I were familiar with that garden,
the fragrance of flowers;
Where I could stroll with the breeze now,
now blow as the wind beyond the bowers

Mir's speaker in this verse expresses his intense love for a garden and shows his desire in the most evocative terms. He wishes to be more intimate with it and become a part of the garden's fragrance like the flowers that bloom in it. More than this, he also yearns to blow through the garden as the wind blows through it before finding its way beyond its peripheries. This desire to join nature in all its resplendence distinguishes him distinctly.

In this verse, uniquely endowed with love for nature, some specific points deserve our attention: (a) man is inseparable from nature and constitutes a seminal part of it in pantheistic terms (b) man's life is regulated by the elements, as is nature punctuated by seasons and both reflect the supremacy of nature in a broader sense (c) nature and man are God's two separate manifestations, but they constitute parts of a larger whole called creation (d) the garden could be of various manifestations: the natural garden, the world, and the garden of the human body (e) the speaker yearns to belong to the garden like the wind and the fragrance of its flowers, than languish and disappear for good.

This verse is an artistic representation of the desire for freedom. With a set of two analogous images of concrete and abstract kinds—*buu-e gul* (fragrance of flowers) and *baaGh* (garden)—on the one hand, and—*sabaa* (breeze) and *havaa* (wind)—on the other, Mir's speaker develops a design to underscore their compatibility and mutuality that constitute a cosmos where man finds his space in companionship with nature rather than remaining in isolation. The idiomatic and proverbial use of *havaa hote,* which suggests 'blowing beyond', adds deeper layers of meaning to the desire for unlimited freedom. Mir finds a closer way to annotate this experience in another verse: *ra.ng-e gul-o buu-e gul hote hai.n havaa dono.n / kyaa qaafila jaataa hai jo tuu bhii chalaa chaahe.*

Ghazal 481 | Verse 2

79

سراپا آرزو ہونے نے بندہ کردیا ہم کو
وگرنہ ہم خدا تھے گر دل بے مدعا ہوتے

सरापा आरज़ू होने ने बंदा कर दिया हम को
वगर्ना हम ख़ुदा थे गर दिल-ए बे-मुद्दआ होते

saraapa aarzuu hone ne banda kar diya ham ko
vagarna ham KHudaa the gar dil- be-mudda'aa hote

(*saraapa*—incarnate;
aarzuu—longing, yearning, desire, wish;
be-mudd'aa—without desire)

I was desire incarnate,
so I turned into a man;
I'd be God, otherwise, if shorn
of desires as a man

Man's heart is a province of desires, and thus he stands out as desire personified. In this verse, the speaker develops a discourse that if man had not been so, he would have been as powerful as God. He implies, therefore, that the presence and absence of desire distinguish man from God.

A few other meanings come to light on keener observation: (a) as man is the living image of desire, it implies conversely that God would be a man if he too was driven by desires (b) desire divests man of Godhood while abstinence from it enables him to attain God-like stature (c) since desire is earthly and leads man to pursue vile passions, it cannot be associated with God (d) God's desires are different from man's, as man's desires are wordly whereas God's desire found its manifestation through the creation of this earth that man inhabits.

The verse projects two key entities—*banda* (man) and *KHudaa* (God); one representing *aarzuu* (desire) and the other representing the state of being *be-mudda'aa* (without desire). These two phrases distinguish the two entities, each affirming the other in one way and denying the other in another. The idea of the abundance of desire in man prompts Mir to express himself in a different frame of reference in another verse: *ham jaante to 'ishq na karte kisuu ke saath / le jaate dil ko KHaak mei.n is aarzuu ke saath.*

Ghazal 481 | Verse 4

80

الٰہی کیسے ہوتے ہیں جنھیں ہے بندگی خواہش
ہمیں تو شرم دامن گیر ہوتی ہے خدا ہوتے

इलाही कैसे होते हैं जिन्हें है बंदगी ख़्वाहिश
हमें तो शर्म दामन-गीर होती है ख़ुदा होते

Ilaahii kaise hote hai.n jinhei.n hai bandagii KHvaahish
hamei.n to sharm daamangiir hotii hai KHudaa hote

(*bandagii*—worshipping, act of devotion;
daamagiir—cling, attach)

What kind of men are those who wish
for men to worship men, O God;
I am so ashamed of myself
to be revered as a God

This verse makes a corrosively realistic point. It is a harsh comment on men who wish to be adored and worshipped and assume thereby the status of God on this earth. It further adds that it is also a matter of shame for man to elevate himself to this level and speaks to his overbearing nature in assuming the status of God.

The possible meaning of this verse may be identified in the complex of conflicting intentions: (a) the speaker here is indeed a moral commentator on man driven by the ghastly passion of assuming the high status of being an earthly God (b) the man driven by this idea is truly a man of this pretentious world, itself inhabited by false gods (c) the idea of one God is sacrosanct, but it is sullied by the false notions of godhood created on this earth (d) while man may strive to achieve godhood, God remains the creator and sustainer that man cannot afford to be, despite all the false power he may possess on the earth (e) shame involved in becoming a god has two possible meanings: (i) in the lordliness of the lord countless people are unhappy (ii) our ambition is to attain a rank even loftier than that of the almighty is enough to put man to shame (f) God calls man to serve on him which means that to be at God's service is a matter of pride for man, which reminds one of John Milton's 'On His Blindness' where he, being blind, proclaims in indivual terms: 'they also serve who only stand and wait.'

In this verse, the speaker addresses God and shares his anguish about the aspirations of the earthly gods, which is conveyed effectively in two key phrases: *Ilaahii kaise hote hai.n* (God! What kind of men are those) and *hamei.n to sharm daamangiir hotii hai* (I feel ashamed). The element of irony that heightens the impact of the verse is particularly well-contained in the second line. In another verse, Mir puts this idea in simpler terms: *sar kisuu se faro nahii.n aataa / haif bande huve KHudaa na huve.*

Ghazal 485 | Verse 3

81

چشم دل کھول اس بھی عالم پر
یاں کی اوقات خواب کی سی ہے

चश्म-ए दिल खोल इस भी आलम पर
याँ की औक़ात ख़्वाब की सी है

chashm-e dil khol is bhii 'aalam per
yaa.n kii auqaat KHvaab kii sii hai

(*auqaat*—status, means, ability)

Open your heart's eyes to this world and see
This world is but only a dream if you see

The tension between illusion and reality is often represented in poetical texts but in amazingly diverse and dissimilar ways. Here is a verse that underlines the reality of this world, which the speaker conceives, but only as a dream.

The different suggestions of this verse may be appreciated by looking at the actual nature of this world as it appears: (a) the first line urges one to open the heart's eyes and see what this world is like, but this idea gets a sudden fillip in the second line when the speaker calls this state as one of a dream (b) he suggests that dreams are ephemeral and life itself is a dream, and both the dream and the world it is created in would disappear when one's eyes would open (c) here is a delicate balance of ideas in implicating dream and awakening as the two states of being (d) paradoxically, the poet equates the opening of eyes to death and its closure to life.

The tone of the verse is typically persuasive, which comes out emphatically in the first line itself—*chashm-e dil khol is bhii 'aalam per* (open your heart's eyes to this world and see). A remarkable word—*auqaat*—embodies two distinct meanings of 'status' on the one hand and 'capacity' on the other, which enhances the verse's richness. We may reflect upon this verse in a comparative perspective by recalling another by Mir: *kuchh nahii.n aur dekhei.n hai.n kyaa kyaa / KHvaab kaa saa hai yaa.n kaa 'aalam bhii.*

Ghazal 490 | Verse 2

82

عشق و مے خواری نبھے ہے کوئی درویشی کے بیچ
اس طرح کے خرج لاحاصل کو دولت چاہیے

इश्क़-ओ-मय-ख़्वारी निभे है कोई दरवेशी के बीच
इस तरह के ख़र्ज-ए ला-हासिल को दौलत चाहिए

'ishq-o-mai-KHvaarii nibhe hai koii darveshii ke biich
is tarah ke KHarj-e laahaasil ko daulat chaahiye

(*mai-KHvaarii*—wine drinking;
darveshii—mendicancy;
KHarj—spending;
laa-haasil—fruitless)

How can mendicants afford
love and love of wine;
These fruitless indulgences
need the riches fine

This verse defines the state of mendicancy and how it affects or reduces human beings. It undoes the prevalent notion about mendicancy and posits that loving and drinking do not go with pious practices typically associated with *darveshes*.

The verse works through a method of subversion. It suggests that: (a) love does not necessarily mean love between a man and a woman, and drink does not essentially refer to wine that drives man out of his senses (b) significantly enough, the other aspect of love is spiritual, and drinking also implies being drunk on divine love (c) this mendicancy may thus be achieved both with divine love and divine drinking (d) the devotee would thus require to accumulate enough wealth in terms of divine love and divine drink to realize the vision of the ultimate power (e) divine passion and divine drinking are intertwined, and they also mark the ways of the *darvesh* who aspires to visualize the ultimate power rather than soil himself by immersing into the earthly.

The first line sounds like a note of negation—*nibhii hai koi* (has this ever been sustained)—but the second line shifts and turns the negation into affirmation—*daulat chaahiye* (wealth is required). In this manner, *KHarj-e laa-haasil* (fruitless spending) becomes a source of accumulating *daulat* (wealth) and imparts meaning through the technique of intent inversion rather than a direct statement. The element of irony in fruitless expenditure may not be missed as it adds an artistic edge to the verse. The figure of the drinker is conceived in analogous terms in this verse by Insha Allah Khan: *KHayaal un kaa pare hai 'arsh-e 'aazam se kahii.n saqii / Gharaz kuchh aur dhun mei.n is ghaRii maiKHvaar baiThe hai.n.*

Ghazal 518 | Verse 3

83

ابھی اک عمر رونا ہے نہ کھوؤ اشک آنکھو تم
کرو کچھ سوجھتا اپنا تو بہتر ہے کہ دنیا ہے

अभी इक उम्र रोना है न खोवो अश्क आँखो तुम
करो कुछ सूझता अपना तो बेहतर है कि दुनिया है

abhii ik 'umr ronaa hain na khovo ashk aa.nkho tum
karo kuchh suujhtaa apnaa to behtar hai ke duniyaa hai

(*ashk*—tears)

Don't lose your tears, dear eyes,
you've got to weep for all this life still;
Think about your own benefit for once,
that is the way of the world, what it wills

The trials of life are endless, and the tears to shed, too, are countless. The speaker asks not to shed too many tears, for a long life ahead would ask for more tears. He advises the eyes to look after themselves because life is short, and there are more demands to make than may ever be met, while also suggesting that such is the way of the world, to think selfishly and always about itself.

This seemingly simple verse opens other meaning: (a) the speaker addresses the eyes, since eyes see all and know all (b) life may be too short if lived in pleasure but too long if lived in pain (c) the pains of life are more than the tears in eyes which implies that they need to be preserved for more pains waiting along the way (d) the eyes can best defend themselves by looking at their profit to live through a long life (e) after all, life is not for shedding tears alone, but for negotiating with life about profit as well (f) the speaker possibly knows that there is no chance of receiving love's favour which implies that he will have to shed tears all his life.

The idea of losing tears is contained in the first line—*na khovo ashk aa.nkho.n tum* (don't lose tears, eyes). This foreshadows another idea that they must be preserved for longer years ahead, which is qualified by—*ik 'umr* (a whole life). The second line turns the tide of thought by adding an alternative meaning to the verse. This implies that rather than shedding tears, thinking rationally and preparing to negotiate with the world should be far more reasonable. With this, a sense of wholeness is imparted to the verse as the speaker shows neither bitterness nor self-pity, not even disappointment. His voice is one of understanding and reconciliation. It should be worthwhile to recall how Mir reiterates this sentiment in a metaphoric frame in another verse: *ve din gae ke aa.nkhei.n dariyaa sii bahtiyaa.n thii.n / suukhaa paRaa hai ab to muddat se ye do-aabaa.*

Ghazal 523 | Verse 8

84

یعنی مانند صبح دنیا میں
ہم جو پیدا ہوئے سو پیر ہوئے

या'नी मानिंद-ए सुब्ह दुनिया में
हम जो पैदा हुए सौ पीर हुए

yaanii maanind-e sub'ha duniyaa mei.n
ham jo paida hue so piir hue

(*maanind*—like, as)

Like the arrival of morning
in this world;
I became old as I took my birth
in this world

The speaker articulates his musings that like the morning's arrival, he also took birth one day, but like the morning too, he turned old in the same moment of arrival/birth.

The paradoxical stance of this verse may be worked out with these interpretations in our mind: (a) man's birth on this planet and the dawn's appearance on the horizon bring out the beginnings of two cycles of life bearing upon one another (b) man's life ends in death as dawn settles down as dusk (c) both have limited spans of life, but both represent two parallel units in the larger scheme of life and death (d) one man's birth, therefore, merges into another man's birth, as one dawn joins another dawn which implies that even in birth both man and dawn are old; carrying a cycle of life and death infinitely (e) this accounts for the unity of life and time and the manifestations symbolized by nature and man.

The paradox involved in the second line imparts the verse its artistic and thematic value. In a simple confession, a man appears to unveil a truth in a state of self-indulgence but without any regrets about becoming old. The verbal order of the verse is based on a play of a tripartite relationship between words—*sub'ha* (morning in terms of time), *paidaa* (birth in the sense of beginning) and *piir* (old in the sense of an end). In this relationship also lies the scheme of meaning as spelt out above. Mir reminds here of one of his equally engaging verses, which also bears on this verse obliquely but meaningfully: *piirii mei.n kyaa javaanii ke mausam ko royiye / ab sub'ha hone aaii hai ik dam to soiiye.*

Ghazal 543 | Verse 1

85

پیری میں کیا جوانی کے موسم کو روئیے
اب صبح ہونے آئی ہے اک دم تو سوئیے

पीरी में क्या जवानी के मौसम को रोइए
अब सुब्ह होने आई है इक दम तो सोइए

piirii mei.n kyaa javaanii ke mausam ko roiiye
ab sub'ha hone aaii hai ik dam to soiiye

(*piirii*—old age)

Why cry over the lost season of youth
now that you have grown old;
Dawn beckons on the horizon,
better sleep a while, all is already told

Age withers a man. It makes him sad and drives him to tears as he can no longer enjoy the bliss of his youth. So, the speaker advises the aged man here to appreciate what cannot be undone. He urges him to stop shedding tears and go to sleep even if dusk is about to appear.

The implied meanings of the speaker's advice to the aged man are quite diverse: (a) youth is stereotypically represented as an age of enjoyment and old age as one of remorse, but it is not necessarily so in every case (b) weeping over the season of youth gone by implies grieving over the passing of youth which is only futile as it cannot be recalled (c) while night, in this case, may be appreciated as a metaphor of revelry and seeking fun, the dawn may be appreciated as that of old age and death (d) death may thus be taken as nothing but a moment of longer sleep (e) as such, one is left wondering if death is the morning of life and sleep is a passage to wake up again, and the two ages of man are lived in two phases of light and darkness (f) in this discourse on the two phases, lies a discourse on life itself with all its splendid gifts.

This verse develops on the contrasting conditions of *piirii* (old age) and *javaanii* (youth). It also persuades the listener to go and sleep even if dawn has shown up, which is precisely the time to wake up. The word—*mausam* (weather)—has a broader implication and stands for the different seasons of life, like the seasons in nature, which teach man to acclimatize with all seasons of life pleasantly. Even while the verse begins on a lighter note, it is overturned with the projection of night as a metaphor for youth and life and morning as a metaphor for decay and death. Recalling a contiguous verse by Mir in this context should be befitting: *'ahd-e javaanii ro ro kaataa, piirii mei.n lii.n aa.nkhei.n muu.nd / yaanii raat bahut the jaage sub'ha huii aaraam kiyaa.*

Ghazal 543 | Verse 6

86

اب جان جسم حاکی سے تنگ آ گئی بہت
کب تک اس ایک ٹوکری مٹی کو ڈھوئیے

अब जान जिस्म-ए ख़ाकी से तंग आ गई बहुत
कब तक इस एक टोकरी मिट्टी को ढोईए

ab jaan jism-e KHaakii se tang aa gaii bahut
kab tak is ek tokrii mitti ko Dhoiiye

(*jism-e KHaakii*—body composed of soil/clay)

My being is so bothered, trapped in this clay body,
and for so long;
How far shall I carry this basketful of soil
and for how long

Here is a verse that reflects the poet's attitude towards life. In a moment of exasperation, the speaker expresses his impatience with life's longevity and wonders how long he will have to carry his body, which is, after all, composed of a basketful of soil.

The speaker addresses some of the more profound questions about life and living: (a) the body is composed of soil, but it contains a thriving spirit that has turned incompatible with the fleshly abode of a body in which it is made to reside (b) the tired spirit is a failed spirit indeed that is unable to attain its lofty status (c) the inability to guess the longevity of suffering leads to frustration and makes the suffering longer than life itself (d) this state of the suffering spirit leads to a realization of failure in life while life, ironically enough, is the best gift man obtains from the divine power (e) in spiritualist terms, body is a prison, and spirit is the prisoner (f) the physical human body, distinct from the etheric (energy), astral (emotional), mental (thought), and spiritual (higher self) bodies is at best a vehicle of vices which underlines a disdain for the body (g) this further brings to mind that carrying the burden of the body calls for putting in hard labour but without earning any profit.

This verse is instantly remarkable for the striking metaphor of *tokrii* (basket), as the body is ultimately destined to be buried, burnt and/or disposed of in different ways till the arrival of doomsday. Thinking of the body in terms of soil reminds us of the Quranic and Biblical dictum that man is born of soil and to soil he returns. Furthermore, the idea of carrying the body's soil in a mere basket of the so-called human body underscores the concept of life and the body as essentially insignificant. The first line marks the speaker's weariness, and the second line marks his exasperation. Khwaja Haider Ali Atish comes to mind with yet another reminder: *is mushaqqat se use KHaak na hogaa haasil / jaa.n 'abas jism kii begaar liye phirtaa hai.*

Ghazal 544 | Verse 6

87

پیار کرنے کا جو خوباں ہم پہ رکھتے ہیں گناہ
ان سے بھی تو پوچھتے تم اتنے کیوں پیارے ہوئے

प्यार करने का जो ख़ूबाँ हम पे रखते हैं गुनाह
उन से भी तो पूछते तुम इतने क्यों प्यारे हुए

pyar karne kaa jo KHubaa.n ham pe rakhte hai.n gunaah
un se bhii to puuchhte tum itne kyu.n pyaare hue

(*KHuubaa.n*—revered; loved one)

Why does my love blame me
for the sin of loving her;
Why don't you ask her why
she's so enticing as it were

Playfulness in love adds a pinch of salt and pepper to love affairs. This is a pleasantly excitable situation in which the lover tells someone why the lady love blames him for the sin of loving her. To defend himself, he asks a counter question and wants her to be asked in turn why she is so charming after all.

This light-hearted and naughty verse has amusing suggestions: (a) the beloved blames the lover for committing the sin of loving her, but the lover knows well that loving is no sin and he has committed none (b) the speaker present behind the verse finds a unique way to praise the beloved by blaming her in turn for being so lovely and amenable to his love (c) the fun is all about the beloved being absent yet remaining at the centre of the fun-filled play of love (d) the speaker, the lover and the beloved constitute a delightful dramatis personae to present a play on and off the stage.

This endearing verse gains its impact with its light tone, jovial mood, and colloquial diction. Remember Dagh Dehlvi in this context: *aa hii jaatii hai tabi'at laut hii jaataa hai dil / kyu.n banaa dii hai KHuda ne teri suurat pyaar kii.*

Ghazal 546 | Verse 3

88

عریاں پھریں کب تک اے کاش کہیں آ کر
تا گرد بیاباں کی بالائے بدن بیٹھے

उर्यान फिरें कब तक ऐ काश कहीं आ कर
ता गर्द बयाबाँ की बाला-ए बदन बैठे

'uryaan phirei.n kab tak ai kaash kahii.n aa kar
taa gard bayaabaa.n kii baalaa-i badan baiThe

(*'uryaan*—naked, nude;
baalaa-i badan—over the body)

How long to walk naked—
I wish the dust of the wilderness
would blow and sit on my body
in this wilderness

Here is one person who has risen above the worldly ways and seeks his earthly deliverance now. He has been walking naked for a long time, but has grown tired of that now. So, he wishes to make friends with the dust of the wilderness, where the wind stirs and sits over his body to offer him a protective costume.

There is a mystical aura the speaker seems to represent in this verse: (a) the idea of covering the body with clothing is only a fantasy rather than a reality (b) the speaker wishes to cover his nakedness not with clothes but with dust (c) indeed, the human body is made of dust and yearns to be with dust, which is the ultimate reality testified by all religious faiths across the board (d) without the covering of dust, the body remains naked, which the speaker realizes with a quiet intensity (e) keeping to his nature, he is already in the wilderness where he seeks the meaning of his existence (f) the verse unveils the yearning of the seeker who discovers that life and the physical world are mere shadows of a desire that are essentially spiritualist.

A tone of exhaustion characterizes the first line of the verse, especially the first clause—*'uryaan phirei.n kab tak* (how long to walk naked) followed by the subsequent clause *ai kaash kahii.n aa kar* (wish it came over). The second line expresses the speaker's desire in two well-measured clauses—*taa KHaak bayaabaa.n kii* (so that the dust of the wilderness) followed by—*baalaae badan baiThe* (sat over the body). It is also important to note that *gard* (dust) and *bayaabaa.n* (wilderness) go together to create an atmospheric condition of barrenness corresponding to nakedness. A brilliant configuration of this nakedness can be seen in Rasikh Azimabadi: *vahshat mei.n kahaa.n mujh ko hosh apne badan kaa thaa / tah gard-e bayabaa.n kii jaama mire tan kaa thaa.*

Ghazal 558 | Verse 2

89

کھول کر آنکھ اڑا دید جہاں کا غافل
خواب ہو جائے گا پھر جاگنا سوتے سوتے

खोल कर आँख उड़ा दीद जहाँ का ग़ाफ़िल
ख़्वाब हो जाएगा फिर जागना सोते सोते

khol kar aa.nkh uRa diid jahaa.n kaa Ghaafil
KHvaab ho jaaigaa phir jaagnaa sote sote

(*Ghaafil*—heedless, careless, negligent)

Open your eyes, blow up the spectacle
of this world, you careless one!
Lest your waking up should become
a dream, you careless one!

The speaker in this verse refers to this world of manifestations in multiple terms. He addresses the careless man of this world and asks him to open his eyes first and then scan the spectacle that spreads all around. He warns in time lest it's too late before sleep or ignorance overtake completely, and it becomes a far-off dream to stay awake and alert.

We can draw a deeper analysis of the verse with these ideas: (a) man is expected to cultivate a higher consciousness to appreciate the manifestations of this world properly (b) the world's manifestations open up only to the probing eyes that attempt to access them in all their richness (c) if one fails to do so, their consciousness will seal, and one would be unable to visualize what the supremely abled man can, even in the state of sleep (d) there is an intimate relationship between the seer and the seen, and sleep and awakening, which are not too distant from each other, and indeed are precariously balanced in their mutual relationship.

This verse is complex in terms of ideas and their treatment. It works on the principle of inversion, which may be found in the second line with a play on *KHvaab* (dream), *jaagnaa* (state of awakening) and *sote sote* (state of sleeping). Mir resorts to this idea further in another verse: *daaGh-e firaaq-o hasrat-e vasl aarzuu-e dost / kyaa kyaa liye gae tere 'aashiq jahaan se.* A modernist poet, Ahmad Mushtaq, adds another perspective: *tamaasha-gaah-e jahaa.n mei.n majaal-e diid kise / yehi bahut hai agar sarsarii guzar jaaei.n.*

Ghazal 558 | Verse 5

90

جم گیا خوں کفِ قاتل پہ طرح میرؔ زبس
ان نے رو رو دیا کل ہاتھ کو دھوتے دھوتے

जम गया ख़ूँ कफ़-ए क़ातिल पे तरह 'मीर' ज़ि-बस
उन ने रो रो दिया कल हाथ को धोते धोते

jam gayaa Khuu.n kaf-e qaatil pe tarah Mir zi-bas
un ne ro ro diyaa kal haath ko dhote dhote

(*kafe-e qaatil*—killer's palm/sleeve/hand)

Blood congealed on the assassin's hand,
Mir, yet again;
He wept and wept, washing his hands,
again and again

Here is a dramatic representation of a strange human action that man indulges in and ultimately suffers for doing so. The scene of the killer's hand bearing the marks of blood is terrifying. All the more pathetic is his attempt to wash his hands and shed tears with a sense of guilt and repentance while doing so.

We may approach the verse along some of the possible lines of interpretation as these: (a) man's motivations may be enigmatic sometimes, and they may impel him to do that which he would not have done otherwise (b) such motivations brings suffering to those who indulge in them (c) there is an existential dilemma between cause and action that characterizes the broader human predicament (d) the realization of the consequence after the deed is done, and the suffering it entails, characterizes the essential nobility of the person in question, which is to say that it is this recognition of his culpability and penitence that makes him worthy of himself.

The phrase *kaf-e qaatil* (assassin's hand) is a traditional symbol and proof of the oppression caused by the perpetrators of crime. The impossibility of undoing his heinous act is best represented by the idea of congealed blood stains on the hand and their stubbornness to go away, which is well represented in the repetitive act of *dhote dhote* (washing again, yet again). This verse is clearly reminiscent of Macbeth's impassioned words of doubt and apprehension after murdering Duncan in *Macbeth*, Act 2, Scene 2: 'Will all great Neptune's ocean wash this blood clean from my hand?'

Ghazal 584 | Verse 7

91

ہے گی تو دو سالہ پر ہے دختر رز آفت
کیا پیر مغاں نے بھی اک چھوکری پالی ہے

हैगी तो दो साला पर है दुख़्तर-ए रज़ आफ़त
क्या पीर-ए मुग़ाँ ने भी इक छोकरी पाली है

hai gii to do-saala per hai duKHtar-e raz aafat
kya piir-e muGhaa.n ne bhii ik chhokrii paalii hai

(*do-saala*—two-year-old, too young;
duKHtar-e raz—wine made of fermented grape juice;
piir-e muGhaa.n—tavern keeper, spiritual guide)

She's too young, yet that daughter of the grape
is a calamity
Has the preacher, too, taken a fancy to her
this calamity?

Wine is a recurring motif in Urdu ghazal, used in two ways. Literally, it leads drinkers to a state of self-enjoyment and loss of senses, clouding their wits. Metaphorically, it signifies a state of divine reverie and complete submission to the Almighty. This verse offers new insights into the types of wine and their consumers.

The different perspectives of this verse are worth noting: (a) there are three subjects here that emerge as characters—old wine configured as the daughter of grape, the tavern keeper as the master of his space, and his alter ego—the spiritual guide—as the witness and moving force behind all that happens around (b) all three interact with each other in a dramatic manner and weave a playful plot together (c) even if it is only two years old, this wine is considered superior to freshly produced wine, and it appears to influence both the tavern keeper and the spiritual guide (d) the element of wonder and questioning in the second line regarding the spiritual guide gives him a unique feature, as he is enamoured by that wine and has taken her as his flirtatious mistress (e) even if there is an ironic tone in the second line, it also highlights the value of both—the spiritual guide and the wine-mistress—who complement each other.

Three phrases—*do-saala* (two-year-old), *duKHtar-e raz* (literally, daughter of grape), and *piir-e muGhaa.n* (tavern-keeper or spiritual guide)—provide the essential props for the structure of this verse. At the root of the verse is the word *chhokrii* (young lass), which qualifies the wine as a playful thing that plays upon the senses.

Ghazal 585 | Verse 8

92

عالم میں آب و گل کا ٹھہراؤ کس طرح ہو
گر خاک ہے اڑے ہے ور آب ہے رواں ہے

आलम में आब-ओ-गिल का ठहराव किस तरह हो
गर ख़ाक है अड़े है वर आब है रवाँ है

'Aalam mei.n aab-o gil kaa Thahraao kis tarah ho
Gar KHaak hai uRe hai var aab hai ravaa.n hai

(*aab-o gil*—water and clay;
var—if)

In this world of water and clay,
how can things ever go slow;
If it is dust, it will fly
if it is water, it will flow

Constancy in nature goes against the very principle of nature itself. Therefore, the speaker in this verse asserts that constancy in nature negates nature. Two examples of dust and water suggest this. They keep to the roles assigned to them by providence; that is, dust being dust, will fly, and water being water, will flow.

The verse speaks to the philosophy of existence in broad terms: (a) there is an equilibrium in nature, and all the elements reciprocate mutually to maintain harmony (b) constancy is death, and movement is life, which is reflected best in the life of nature itself (c) water and dust/clay, represent both the life of nature and the life of human beings, and the two together represent nature in its complete balance (d) human life and the life of nature reinforce each other, and in doing so, they compose and constitute God's kingdom in all its grandeur.

The first line of the verse makes a proposition with a question, and the second line offers a resolution with an answer. This mutual relationship also underlines the mutuality between human life and the elements of nature. A paradigm of meaning is constructed with the contrast projected with the idea of constancy negated by the acts of dust flying and water flowing. The ever-changing face of nature becomes a subject of broader concern in a strong modernist voice in Majeed Amjad: *pihnaa-i zamaa.n ke sine per ik mauj angRaaii letii hai / is aab-o gil kii daldal mei.n ik chaap sunaaii deti hai.*

Ghazal 588 | Verse 3

93

رونا تو ابر کا سا نہیں یار جانتے
اتنا تو روئیے کہ جہاں کو ڈبو سکے

रोना तो अब्र का सा नहीं यार जानते
इतना तो रोइए कि जहाँ को डुबो सके

ronaa to abr kaa saa nahii.n yaar jaante
itnaa to roiiye ke jahaa.n ko dubo sake

(*abr*—cloud;
jahaa.n—world)

Friends know their crying is
not like the crying of clouds
Cry enough to drown the world,
wail aloud

Shedding of tears has many meanings and implications. Although no one wants to weep, the speaker makes an unusual plea to shed more tears, even more than the clouds shedding their tears in the form of rain. The plea to shed such tears so the world may be drowned in them is far more meaningful than it appears in the verse.

The speaker's appeal takes a different turn from Aristotelian poetics, in the sense that Aristotle theorizes in terms of pity, fear and catharsis, while Mir puts it in a context in poetic terms and turns a theory per se into poetry. Alternatively, the verse suggests: (a) considering tears as an expression of grief is formulaic and the staid idea does not hold value beyond a point (b) clouds bring rain only intermittently and scantily; they soak the earth only partially and bring vegetation only insufficiently (c) but a deluge like the one brought by the rains that caused Noah to save each species in his boat, announced the coming of a new world order replacing the one marked by utter degeneration (d) from this perspective, shedding of tears that could drown the world might also be a way of initiating a new order.

The visual of *abr* (cloud) and the emotional condition of *ronaa* (weeping) work together to create a complex meaning. This also brings to mind the simile of a cloud representing rain and the eyes shedding tears. Both work towards building the core intent of the verse. The second line introduces the actual message, where creation is revealed through a churn as induced by a deluge. This sentiment is expressed distinctly in Sheikh Ibrahim Zauq's verse: *ham rone pe aa jaaei.n to dariyaa hii dubo dei.n / shabnam kii tarah se hamei.n ronaa nahii.n aataa.*

Ghazal 591 | Verse 3

94

شب خواب کا لباس ہے عریاں تنی میں یہ
جب سویئے تو چادر مہتاب تانیے

शब ख़्वाब का लिबास है उर्यां-तनी में ये
जब सोइए तो चादर-ए महताब तानिए

shab-KHvaab kaa libaas hai 'uryaa.n tanii mei.n ye
jab soiiye to chaadar-e mehtaab taaniye

(*shab-KHvaab*—night-sleeper, night-sleeping;
'uryaan.tanii—naked state of body,
mehtaab—moon)

This is the garb of the night
for a state of nakedness;
When you go to sleep, draw the moon's drapes
on your nakedness

Here is a playful speaker who proposes to a willing addressee, whose gender is not revealed, that when the addressee goes to sleep, they go in a state of nakedness, and they may draw the veil of moonlight over their body.

This naughty idea tickles the imagination but it proposes deeper meanings too: (a) the speaker makes a seemingly fabulous suggestion to an addressee who has no qualms about how or how not to observe the ways of sleeping (b) the idea of sleeping naked under the shade of a moonlit night is unique, but it verges more on fancy (c) sleeping naked under the sky may be an outrageous idea morally, but it is a fascinating one romantically, as the moon's rays are imagined as a diaphanous veil on the naked body.

The verse sounds like a piece of advice to a listener, but it is a teasing idea poeticized like a queerly romantic thought. It is a fine example of imaginative exuberance. The creative touch in this verse lies in the idea of spreading the sheet or veil of moonlight, which is too thin to conceal the body, yet it can still act as a veil for the body. The expression—*shab-KHvaab*—contains two meanings: it qualifies the sleeper at one time and the state of sleeping at another. In totality, the verse reads like a pleasant idea rendered romantically. While this verse seems to turn the abstract into the real, another verse in Mir turns the real into the abstract: *'uuryaa.n tanii kii shoKHii se diivaangii mei.n Mir / Majnuu.n ke dasht-e KHaar kaa daamaa.n bhii chal gayaa.*

Ghazal 594 | Verse 5

95

روز آنے پہ نہیں نسبت عشقی موقوف
عمر بھر ایک ملاقات چلی جاتی ہے

रोज़ आने पे नहीं निस्बत-ए इश्क़ी मौक़ूफ़
उम्र भर एक मुलाक़ात चली जाती है

roze aane pe nahii.n nisbat-e 'ishqii mauquuf
'umr bhar ek mulaaqaat chalii jaatii hai

(*mauqoof—dependent*)

The bond of love does not rely
on meeting one's love on all the days;
A lone meeting may stretch over
all of the lover's days

This verse has a romantic-cum-mystical aura. The speaker, who may also be the lover himself, asserts that meeting the beloved daily is not a necessary condition or sign of his love for her. Instead, even one meeting may carry on its magic for his lifetime.

It's interesting to note how there are various related expositions that could be drawn from this verse: (a) emotional proximity with the beloved in her absence may also be an experience far more gratifying than the physical proximity with her every day (b) constant vicinity dissipates the romantic heft of a relationship while distance makes it more deeply rewarding (c) this idea reaches its peak in the verse when a single meeting is conceived as good enough to last a lifetime than meeting every day because the access of physical closeness loses its charm when it is constant (d) this is how the fundamental nature of love may be redefined in a broader context (e) meeting daily may be a sign of one's overwhelming desire for physical closeness with the beloved, or even an expression of lust, whereas meeting sparingly may bring blissful contentment, anchored in yearning.

The gestural aspect in the second line is remarkable; it is achieved by a long articulation of *ek* (one). It also adds a specific tone to the verse and creates a dramatic condition. The overstretching of one meeting over *'umr bhar* (all life) enhances the dramatic impact further. The expression—*nisbat-e 'ishqii* (relationship in love)—is critical to the verse as it gathers its value through the simplicity of expression. A verse by Hasrat Mohani may be read as a reconstruction of this experience where the lover pined for love all his life, but the courage to express that love eluded him forever: *kaT gaii ihtiyaat-e 'ishq mei.n 'umr / ham se izhaar-e mudd'aa na huaa.*

Ghazal 601 | Verse 8

96

ٹک گریباں میں سر کو ڈال کے دیکھ
دل بھی کیا لق و دق جنگل ہے

टुक गरेबाँ में सर को डाल के देख
दिल भी क्या लक़-ओ-दक़ जंगल है

tuk garebaa.n mei.n sar ko daal ke dekh
dil bhii kyaa laqq-o daqq jungle hai

(*garebaa.n*—collar, neck of a dress;
laqq-o daqq—bleak and barren)

Look into your collar,
into your heart, to see
What a massive jungle is this
for a sight to see

The heart has been a much-adored and much-maligned subject in the Urdu ghazal. This verse is a tribute to the heart, especially its overpowering massiveness and untameable wilderness. The speaker invites the listener to peep into his own heart and discover what a colossal jungle this heart is.

The inferences of this verse help us realize the following: (a) in turning the heart from an abode of desires to a bleak and barren jungle, Mir's speaker tells lots about what has happened to it, as there is an untold story of suffering hinted between the two lines (b) although he knows that the phrase 'peeping into one's *garebaa.n*' amounts to being ashamed of one's actions, yet he asks the listener to do so and realize that the bleak heart could also have an awesome grandeur about it (c) this makes the heart immensely beautiful in its grandeur and the verse philosophically loaded (d) the sense of awe on the part of the speaker is expressed in the way he addresses his listener and shares his sense of utter surprise with him.

This verse is a fine example of Mir's mastery over precise expression. The first line is an endearing invitation to a willing listener, but even before he peeps into his *garebaa.n*, the speaker cannot control himself; instead, he tells the listener what lies inside the *garebaa.n*. The immensity of the heart's jungle is most admirably expressed with the word—*laqq-o daq* (massively spacious)—which carries a sense of awe and admiration. The auditory impact of the heavily accented word *laqq* in the phrase *laqq-o daq* dramatizes the immensity of space. This experience is represented in a different metaphor of great value in another of Mir's verses: *dil ko jo KHuub dekha to huu kaa makaan hai / hai is makaa.n mei.n saarii vahii laa-makaa.n kii tarh.* It is also tempting to quote a verse from Qaim Chandpuri in this very context: *ghabraae hai jii vus'at-e dil dekh ke har dam / Allah re ye dasht bhii kitnaa laq-o daq hai.*

Ghazal 605 | Verse 1

97

فقیرانہ آئے صدا کر چلے
کہ میاں خوش رہو ہم دعا کر چلے

फ़क़ीराना आए सदा कर चले
कि म्याँ ख़ुश रहो हम दुआ कर चले

faqiiraana aae sadaa kar chale
ke miyaa.n KHush raho ham du'aa kar chale

Like a *faqiir* I came,
said what I had to say;
May you live happy
and happy stay

A *faqiir* expects nothing; he only prays for others. Mir's speaker identifies himself with the *faqiir* here. He aspires to reach out to those who would pay heed to his blessing. And having done that, he moves along ...

We can read the verse in the following ways: (a) a *faqiir* is an institutionalized figure of spiritualist Islamic culture who can be a completely selfless and a metaphysically empowered and overpowering being (b) he bears out his qualities by giving a call which is a call of blessing for his listeners (c) this is a call that has echoed through generations and has given him his unquestioned place in the cycle of existence (d) in performing his acts of blessing, he acquires the status of a giver and turns his listener into a receiver of his blessings.

Mir has developed the figure of the *faqiir* by adjectivizing the noun *faqiir* as *faqiiraana* which qualifies his action. He is, thus, not the one who begs and seeks alms, as one assumes by listening to this word, but gives his listener the most precious gift of his blessing. The second line bears out his objective detachment from the listener, yet it shows a passionate association with him. This adds immensely to the image of the *faqiir* and helps us appreciate Mir's mastery over constructing him as a figure of reverence. We have a configuration of such a *faqiir* in a verse by Qalandar Bakhsh Jurat: *sadaa tum salaamat raho merii jaa.n / ham aa kar yehii bas duaa kar chale.* Ghalib also defines him more straightforwardly and emphatically: *haa.n bhalaa ka tira bhalaa hogaa / aur darvesh kii sadaa kyaa hai.*

Ghazal 611 | Verse 1

98

ظالم کہیں تو مل کبھو دارو پیے ہوئے
پھرتے ہیں ہم بھی ہاتھ میں سر کو لیے ہوئے

ज़ालिम कहीं तो मिल कभू दारू पिए हुए
फिरते हैं हम भी हाथ में सर को लिए हुए

zaalim kahii.n to mil kabhuu daaru piye hue
phirte hai.n ham bhii haath mein sar ko liye hue

Meet me, my oppressor, all drunk,
here or there;
I, too, wander—keen to be slain,
here and there

This verse might appear frivolous and light-hearted, but it represents man's natural response to the curious conditions and bizarre moments of human life. The speaker in this verse assumes the role of the one seeking a drinker's company as he, too, is ready to sacrifice himself before him and join the fun of life. Mir is known to have exposed man to the serious and the sacrosanct, but here, his speaker exposes man to the plebeian and the popular, which is only a happy-go-lucky way of living one's life.

This verse embodies a queer condition of life in different ways: (a) it portrays a character who is seemingly an errant lover, but he unveils his atypical concern for life (b) the aura of the verse rests in its levity with which the poetic persona offers to be beheaded by an inebriated drinker (c) the two together express their desire to live life according to their whims without negating each other (d) the thin line of distinction between levity and sobriety is what distinguishes one attitude towards life from another (e) the invitation to get drunk is because the beloved will not kill him if she is in her senses, but only when she is drunk (f) the killing is indeed metaphorical than real which establishes a high level of intimacy between the two.

The word *zaalim* (oppressor) does not embody the speaker's hatred for his addressee; instead, it sounds like an address of endearment. The expression—*phirte hai.n* (I too roam around)—suggests his desire to seek an ally of his kind to celebrate life in their carefree manner. Carrying the head in his hands is an idiomatic expression of the day-to-day kind, but it is turned to creative usage in the verse. The word—*daaruu* (wine)—as opposed to the elitist *baada* and *sharaab*—has a ring of the *desi* about it and adds to the frolicsome nature of the lover and the verse. Mir uses this expression in another verse in a highly suggestive manner for his addressee: *suna jaataa hai ai ghaTiye tire majlis nashiino.n se / ke tuu daaruu piye hai raat ko mil kar kamiino.n se.*

DIIVAAN 2

Ghazal 664 | Verse 7

99

اس کے فروغ حسن سے جھمکے ہے سب میں نور
شمع حرم ہو یا کہ دیا سومنات کا

उस के फ़रोग़-ए हुस्न से झमके है सब में नूर
शम-ए हरम हो या कि दिया सोमनात का

us ke faroGh-e husn se jhamke hai sab mei.n nuur
sham-'e harem ho yaa ke diyaa somnat kaa

(*faroGh-e husn*—effulgence of beauty;
nuur—light, divine light)

It's the effulgence of His beauty
that fills all with glow;
Be they the lamps of Harem;
or Somnath's—all aglow

This verse celebrates divine beauty that fills all spaces with radiance. The speaker liberally states that God's beauty is seen in all its glory at both the centres of worship, be that the Islamic space of the Harem or the Hindu space of Somnath.

The secular approach towards the divine presence in two seemingly dissimilar spaces opens avenues of further inferences: (a) divine power is one, and divinity is indivisible (b) all faiths have an essential unity, although they prescribe different ways to reach the divine (c) this strengthens the idea that light cannot be divided as it fills both the spaces and enlightens the hearts of all believers (d) the integrative power of faith is far greater than the divisive power created by people in different times and places.

The diction of this verse deserves our critical attention. Two contiguous words—*sham'a* (lamp), and *diyaa* (wick- lamp)—lead us to another word—*nuur* (divine light)—which emanates from these two sources. It is worth noting that *nuur* is different from *raushnii* (light) as one fills the heart with divine light, and the other dispels only the darkness of physical space. Furthermore, both *sham'a* and *diyaa*, hailing from two different linguistic registers, fill the hearts of the worshippers with the glorious light of faith, even though *sham'a* typically represents the harem and *diyaa* represents the temple. In this context, the clause—*jhamke hai sab mei.n nuur* (an effulgence shows up in all spaces)—enlivens the connotational and auditory fields and contributes to the aesthetic appeal of the verse. Two verses by Insha Allah Khan and Ghulam Hamadani Mushafi, respectively, hold great relevance in the context of Mir's verse: *haasil kiyaa jo ham ne qadam bos-e piir-e dair / aaii sadaa-e 'ishq dar-e Somnat se* and *Allah re kaafiiri tire tarz-e KHaraam kii / naqsh-e qadam se kar diyaa K'abe ko Somnat.*

Ghazal 667 | Verse 1

100

لذت سے نہیں خالی جانوں کا کھپا جانا
کب خضر و مسیحا نے مرنے کا مزہ جانا

लज़्ज़त से नहीं ख़ाली जानों का खपा जाना
कब ख़िज़्र ओ मसीहा ने मरने का मज़ा जाना

lazzat se nahii.n KHaalii jaano.n kaa khapaa jaanaa
kab KHizr-o masiihaa ne marne kaa maza jaanaa

(*lazzat*—relish. delight;
Khizr—prophet of immortality;
masiihaa—messiah, healer)

The sacrifice of life
is never without a delight;
Did *Khizr* or a messiah ever
discover this delight?

Mir's speaker makes a point here concerning the pleasure of dying that neither *Khizr* nor any redeemer could ever realize, which implies that they remained only partially enlightened about life.

Mir is expressly philosophical here and helps us draw distinct inferences: (a) investing life in the pursuit of realizing the value of pain is not without relish (b) man struggles to deny death, but that is an exercise in vain (c) life and death are not incompatible; they are rather complementary (d) both *KHizr* and messiah are mocked at as they symbolize life and do not know what it means to relish death (e) in the suggestion that these two who keep death away are sadly ignorant, there is a submission that pain is better than pleasure and death is greater than life (f) here is a reversal of a popular notion about life and death which reminds us that this verse should not be read as a nihilistic take on death but as a treatise on the deeper awareness of its reality.

The first word of the verse—*lazzat* (relish)—which has a positive meaning, incorporates the central idea of the verse, which capitalizes upon the importance of death. The two figures of *Khizr* and *Masiihaa* play a seminal role in concretizing the idea of life and death that lies behind this verse. *Khizr*, known as the eternal path-finder, is celebrated for living eternally, and as *Masiihaa,* for curing men of their diseases to avoid death. They are mocked in the second line of the verse, where the essential import of the verse lies. The first line appeals as a helpful statement, and the second line holds the key to a broader domain of meaning. Shah Hatim has a verse that glosses over Mir's verse: *faqiiro.n se sunaa hai ham ne Hatim / maza jine kaa mar jaane mei.n dekhaa.* Asadullah Khan Ghalib develops a different but relevant perspective on such a verse: *havas ko hai nishaat-e kaar kyaa kyaa / na ho marnaa to jiine kaa maza kyaa.*

Ghazal 667 | Verse 11

101

اے شور قیامت ہم سوتے ہی نہ رہ جاویں
اس راہ سے نکلے تو ہم کو بھی جگا جانا

ऐ शोर-ए क़यामत हम सोते ही न रह जावें
इस राह से निकले तो हम को भी जगा जाना

ai shor-e qayaamat ham sote hii na rah jaavei.n
is raah se nikle to ham ko bhii jagaa jaanaa

(*qayaamat*—doomsday)

O, the din of the doomsday!
May I not languish in my sleep
When you walk this way,
wake me up too out of my sleep

This is a unique verse, charged with the speaker's desire to be awakened on the day of judgement. As a stock figure, he suggests that men have been indifferent to the life hereafter, which is worrisome. Therefore, the need to be woken up is urgent, to avoid becoming a loser in this world and the hereafter.

There are several questions and assertions that we come across here: (a) the speaker has lived this life recklessly and has been in a state of deep sleep, remaining apathetic to this world and oblivious of everything around (b) that he cannot be shaken off his deep sleep except by the din and clamour of the doomsday, shows his deep-rooted indifference towards this world (c) as he would like to present himself on the doomsday in the world hereafter, he seems to nourish some hope for his redemption even while he utterly disregarded this world and did not meet his obligations here (d) he considers the call of the day of judgement much more consequential than the affairs of this world which is why he cannot miss to present himself on the doomsday in the world hereafter (e) he is far more worried about the day of judgement because his actions will be weighed there, and he would be rewarded or punished accordingly.

A contrasting situation is represented here with the phrase—*shor-e qayaamat* (din of the doomsday)—and the apprehension of *sote hii na rah jaavei.n* (lest I am left sleeping). These phrases create a mixed sense of apprehension and fear as well as a sense of impending deprivation, which imparts a mood and a condition to the verse. It should be relevant to recall this verse by Khwaja Mir Dard in this respect: *ai shor-e qayaamat rah uudhar hii mai.n kahtaa huu.n / chaunke na abhii yaa.n se koii sar-e shoriida*

Ghazal 689 | Verse 3

102

بلبل کو موا پایا کل پھولوں کی دوکاں پر
اس مرغ کے بھی جی میں کیا شوق چمن کا تھا

बुलबुल को मुआ पाया कल फूलों की दूकाँ पर
उस मुर्ग़ के भी जी में क्या शौक़ चमन का था

bulbul ko muaa paayaa kal phulo.n kii duukaa.n per
us murGh ke bhii jii mei.n kyaa shauq chaman kaa thaa

I found the bulbul lying dead
at the flower shop yesterday
What love this poor bird cherished
in her heart for the garden gay

This is a verse story in which Mir's speaker draws upon the mythic love of the bulbul for the blossom. The bulbul lived in the garden, loved the flowers and sang ceaselessly for them. When the flower-picker picked the blossoms from the garden, the bulbul followed them to the shop, where they were brought and sold to buyers. Unable to bear its separation from flowers, the bulbul reached its life's end at the flower shop. This makes the speaker wonder why the bulbul chose to shed its life for the flowers after all.

Different layers of meaning may be marked here in a sequence: (a) love demands sacrifice, which the bulbul made for its love for flowers (b) the bird sang for them in the garden, but could no longer sing when they were plucked from their branches and taken to the shop for sale (c) being away from the garden spelt death for flowers which the bulbul could not bear (d) the bulbul left the garden and followed them to their new destination which was like leaving a cherished home (e) thus it chose to shed its own life and be together with the blossoms even in death (f) it seems pretty probable that the bird had seen the flower-picker who had mercilessly plucked the flowers from the branches and taken them to the shop for selling for his gain (g) following the flower-picker from the garden and being unable to bear the pain of parting with the flowers, the bulbul chose to sacrifice her life at the flower shop, which was no less than a grave for flowers as well as the bulbul.

Phrases like—*muaa paayaa* (found her dead) and *kyaa shauq chaman kaa thaa* (what love for the garden she nursed)—bear out the speaker's deep sympathy for the bulbul. A blend of irony and pathos may also be marked in *kal phulo.n kii dukaa.n per* (at the flower shop yesterday) and *us murgh ke bhi jii mei.n* (in the heart of that bird). The dramatic narration and the sense of melancholy that permeates the verse also reflect upon the possible human predicament, which is essentially marked by pathos. Ghalib echoes the plaintive echoes of the bulbul, which also bear closely upon Mir's verse: *kahtaa hai kaun naala-i bulbul ko be-asar / parde mein gul ke laakh jigar chaak ho gaye.*

Ghazal 711 | Verse 6

103

آئینے کو بھی دیکھو پر ٹک ادھر بھی دیکھو
حیران چشم عاشق دمکے ہے جیسے ہیرا

आईने को भी देखो पर टुक इधर भी देखो
हैरान चश्म-ए आशिक़ दमके है जैसे हीरा

aaiine ko bhii dekho per tuk idhar bhii dekho
hairaan chashm-e 'aashiq damke hai jaise hiiraa

Look at the mirror,
but look here, too;
Lover's wondering eyes
shine like diamonds, too

A lover's message to the beloved finds a thousand ways to reach her. Here, the lover seeks the beloved's attention but finds it missing. So, he asks her to set the mirror aside and look at him since his wondering eyes reflect her image, just like the mirror does. This is the finest and the most pleasing praise for the beloved from the lover.

The implications of this verse are exquisite: (a) the lover is as appreciative of the beloved's beauty as she is of her love for the mirror (b) he considers his own eyes as her mirror, which implies he wishes for her to look into his eyes (c) if she looked into her lover's eyes, she would see the shades of pleasure reflected prominently in them(d) she would also see his eyes glittering like diamonds there (e) these diamonds reflect nothing else but her resplendent face.

Mir constructs a scene in the two lines of this verse with a mirror and diamond as the predominant images. As for the mirror, there are two mirrors here—one on the wall and the other in the lover's eyes. Similarly, as for the diamonds, there are two here—one is the face of the beloved, and the other is the glittering eyes of the lover. Mir's ingenious craftsmanship is well borne out in this verse's two simple yet too-pungent lines. Here is a variation on this verse by Mir himself: *jo dekho to nahii.n ye haal apnaa husn se KHaalii / damak almaas kii sii hai hamaarii chashm-e hairaa.n mei.n.*

Ghazal 716 | Verse 2

104

اڑتی ہے خاک یارب شام وسحر جہاں میں
کس کے غبار دل سے یہ خاکداں بنایا

उड़ती है ख़ाक या-रब शाम-ओ-सहर जहाँ में
किस के गुबार-ए दिल से ये ख़ाक-दाँ बनाया

uRtii hai KHaak yaa Rab shaam-o sahar jahaa.n mei.n
kis ke Ghubaar-e dil se ye KHaakdaa.n banaayaa

(*KHaak*—dust, ashes, earth;
Ghubaar—cloud of dust, haze;
Khaakdaa.n—receptacle/box of dust, earthen pot)

Dust flies all day, all night
through this world, O God;
With whose heart's haze did you
Make this box of dust, O God

This highly philosophical and self-reflexive verse addresses God, the creator and sustainer of this universe. Here is an impatient and highly inquisitive speaker who wishes to understand the source of the world's creation. Was it the haze of someone's heart, he wonders, that configured the world, which is at best like a receptacle or pot of dust.

The verse opens up several avenues of meaning that may be identified as follows: (a) this vast world is a configuration of haze that resembles an earthen pot or receptacle made of soil (b) this pot is made of the haze of someone's heart that is hollow from within (c) born of dust, the haze flies day and night all over the space and gathers ultimately into the physical form of this world (d) the world is a massive earthen pot, but the human body and the heart also are the receptacles or the pots of dust (e) they emerged out of the haze as they were born out of the whirling wind blowing all around (e) all three—the human heart, the human body and the physical world—are thus abstract and wandering images that are essentially hollow and ephemeral (f) all these three, especially the world, are the homes of desires laid waste and are turned ultimately into dust and haze.

The most striking word—*KHaakdaa.n* (receptacle/earthen pot)—in this verse serves as a metaphor for the hollowness of the world, the heart and the body. The address to God—*kis ke Ghubaar-e dil se ye KHaakdaa.n banaayaa* (with whose heart's haze did you make this earthen pot)—sounds like a question and also a helpless thought, which determines the tone and drift of the verse. This idea occupies Mir once again in another verse with a fresh metaphoric construction: *thii jumla-tan lataafat 'aalam mei.n jaa.n ke ham to / mittii mei.n at gae hai.n is KHaakdaa.n mein aa kar.*

Ghazal 717 | Verse 5

105

صبر و حواس و دانش سب عشق کے زبوں ہیں
میں کاوش مژہ سے عالم کو چھان مارا

सब्र-ओ-हवास-ओ-दानिश सब इश्क़ के ज़ुबूँ हैं
मैं काविश-ए मिज़ा से आलम को छान मारा

sabr-o havaas-o daanish sab 'ishq ke zubuu.n hai.n
mai.n kaavish-e mizha se 'aalam ko chhaan maaraa

(*sabr-o havaas- o daanish*—patience, senses, wisdom;
zubuu.n—aim, target;
kaavish-e mizha—effort of eyebrows)

Patience, senses, wisdom—
are the targets of love;
With my eyebrows scanning
I explored the world I love

Love tries, tests, and tears the hearts apart. This verse asserts that love is too demanding; it tries our forbearance, challenges sanities and tests sensitivities. It's difficult to achieve success in love. A true lover may, however, stand all tests and tribulations but only with the efforts of his all-seeing eyes. It implies thus that the lover can ultimately win, but only after enduring all the challenges.

The expectations associated with love open up other aspects of the pursuit of love and loving: (a) love is a natural human urge, and its conditions are daunting both in the case of divine as well as romantic love (b) love presupposes two participants and it calls for exploiting the potential of complete communion between the two (c) only those with extra sensorial powers, especially the power to see the concealed aspects of nature, may succeed in love (d) this amounts to exploring the manifestations of creation in their complete variety and developing a perspective to ascertain love as a moving force behind the functions of nature.

The first line of the verse is essentially axiomatic, but the second line underlines the value of experiential wealth. As spelled in the first line, the three targets of love are often insurmountable. The second line, however, minimizes their power that could ravage love. This establishes the supremacy of love, which enables a man to look beyond the obvious and realize the eternal truth of nature.

Ghazal 724 | Verse 2

106

بے خودی لے گئی کہاں ہم کو
دیر سے انتظار ہے اپنا

बे-ख़ुदी ले गई कहाँ हम को
देर से इंतिज़ार है अपना

be-KHudii le gaii kahaa.n ham ko
der se intizaar hai apnaa

(*be-KHudii*—selflessness)

Where has my selflessness driven me now
I've waited to meet myself for long now

Selflessness is a prized quality. This verse praises this state because it transports man to greater heights of his earthly existence. In such a state, man is not aware of himself and cannot keep in touch with himself; that is, he cannot even have the opportunity to meet himself, even briefly.

Closer reading of this verse reveals other meanings too: (a) man possessed by his selfhood is not the one who can fulfil his social duties as God's supreme creation (b) this implies that one who negates the self transcends to a higher state of existence (c) being in a state of selflessness is being in the state of a quest that is essentially mystical (d) negating the self is a purificatory exercise of the ascendence of the self (e) in such a state, finding no time to meet one's 'self' is only a result of accessing the higher states of existence where self is annihilated in the quest for selflessness.

There is a tension of ideas built into the two lines of this verse. While the first line is a statement of one condition of selflessness, the second line eases that tension. This dramatic situation is woven into two clauses—*be-KHudii le gaii kahaa.n ham ko* (where has my selflessness taken me to) and *der se intizaar hai apnaa* (I have been waiting all the while to meet myself). Mir frequently engages with this idea. One example is worth consideration: *Khudaa jaane hamei.n is be-KHudii ne kis taraf phai.nkaa / ke muddat ho gaii ham khainchte hai.n intizaar apnaa.* Ghalib has also drawn upon this experience: *ham vahaa.n hain jahaa.n se hum ko bhii / kuchh hamaarii KHabar nahii.n aatii.*

Ghazal 735 | Verse 4

107

ایک تھے ہم وے نہ ہوتے ہست اگر
اپنا ہونا بیچ میں حائل ہوا

एक थे हम वे न होते हस्त अगर
अपना होना बीच में हाइल हुआ

ek the ham ve na hote hast agar
apnaa honaa biich mei.n haail huaa

(*hast*—being, existence, desire;
haail—barrier)

I was but one,
if only he had not been there;
But my being stood in-between
to be a barrier here

Only poets and those with extra intellectual grit can propose a discourse between themselves and God. This verse moves boldly in that direction and asserts that man alone could be the one to survey all and move all, but God's overpowering presence did not allow that to happen. In other words, it is proclaimed that man's presence on the scene and his oneness ultimately served as a barrier that prevented the two from crossing each other's paths and perhaps also man's true union with God.

This daring posture of the speaker takes us to other thoughts as well: (a) the speaker does not speak here as an individual in singular number but in the plural, representing man as a larger entity (b) one wonders if this stock figure of the man is too proud, too self-possessed, too challenging, or is he mislaid in his understanding of himself (c) one also wonders if he is subjected to wishful thinking, or is it his hidden desire to be God which he neither is, nor can ever be (d) the verse interrogates whether man considers the world as the be all and end all of everything, and is completely shorn of the capacity to look to other spheres beyond the earth, which he aspires to rule (e) he is aware of the presence of God in His absence and seems to acknowledge Him but only demurely (f) significantly enough, God in His absence and silence appears strong and man in his presence appears too fickle to stand God.

The key word in the verse—*hast* (existence)—must be read in the larger ideational context of *hastii* (being), which brings us to the idea of *niistii* (nothingness). Between these two states lie the states of existence and non-existence that regulate man's life and the life of the phenomenon or nature. Munir Niyazi writes on the dichotomy of being and nothingness in style that echoes Mir's: *ye bahr-e hast-o buud hai be-gauhar-e muraad / gahrayio.n mei.n us kii agar jaae aadmii.*

Ghazal 741 | Verse 1

108

کل میں کہا وہ طور کا شعلہ کہاں گرا
دل نے جگر کی اور اشارت کی یاں گرا

कल मैं कहा वो तूर का शो'ला कहाँ गिरा
दिल ने जिगर की ओर इशारत की याँ गिरा

kal mai.n kahaa vo tuur ka sh'ola kahaa.n giraa
dil ne jigar kii ore ishaarat kii yaa.n giraa

(*ishaarat*—indicate, mention)

I asked where the *Tuur*'s lightning
fell yesterday;
My heart gestured to itself,
here, o here, it fell yesterday

This verse draws upon the Qur'anic and Biblical episode of the fall of lightning as a token of God's existence and a sign of multiple manifestations, including Moses losing his consciousness. Mir appropriates this episode in the context of love. When asked where the lightning fell, the heart said it fell on itself and nowhere else.

The intended meaning in this verse may be deduced as follows: (a) falling in love is like experiencing the fall of lightning on the heart (b) as Moses fell unconscious at Mount Sinai in getting God's vision, the lover too became its victim and lost control over himself (c) as the fall of lightning annihilates, love too destroys the lover (d) in the case of this lightning falling on the lover's heart, there is a sense of pride and fulfilment (e) when vanquished in love, lovers attain their highest status and find themselves deserving of their due.

The element of drama is the most remarkable aspect of this verse. The first line poses a question, and the second line offers an answer, but the drama lies in the gestural response to the question—*sh'ola kahaa.n giraa* (where did the lightning fall) in the first line and its answer—*ishaarat kii yaa.n giraa* (made a gesture that it fell here). It must also be noted that *dil* and *jigar* in Urdu ghazal are used complementarily and interchangeably for heart only. In this context, the heart seems to ask the heart itself and gets an answer from the heart. In his verse, Imam Bakhsh Nasikh draws close to Mir: *hai dil-e sozaa.n mei.n tuur us kii tajalli-gaah kaa / ruu-e aatish naak per sh'ola hai merii aah kaa.*

Ghazal 770 | Verse 8

109

نالاں ہوئی کہ یاد ہمیں سب کو دے گئی
گلشن میں عندلیب ہماری زباں ہے اب

नालाँ हुई कि याद हमें सब को दे गई
गुलशन में अंदलीब हमारी ज़बाँ है अब

naalaa.n hui ke yaad hamei.n sab ko de gaii
gulshan mei.n 'andaliib hamaarii zabaa.n hai ab

(*naalaa.n*—lamenting, moaning, being put off;
'andaliib—nightingale, bird)

She sang her sad songs; she left us
with memories of the garden;
Now, the nightingale alone
is our tongue in the garden

Nightingale has been a frequent reference for longing in love poetry. This verse draws upon the fabled value of this bird to say that as she was in a blue state, she sang her sad songs in the garden. Now that she is no more, she has left memories behind, but more importantly, her song is everyone's song of love and longing now.

The inferences in this verse are worth noting: (a) nightingale is a stock symbol of love, longing and loss and has acquired a mythic status in the popular imaginary (b) songs of longing reflect the longings of lovers, which implies that lovers share their fate with the nightingale (c) even if the nightingale has lived and died in sorrow, she has left behind a language of love to sing in (d) her songs are the songs inherited by lovers and have kept the lovers' hearts alive with their plaintiff tones, as well as with songs of suffering and music of melancholia.

The crux of the verse lies in the second line—*gulshan mei.n 'andaliib hamaarii zabaa.n hai ab* (nightingale is our tongue in the garden now). This underlines that the nightingale is more than a bird now after her passing away; she is a word, a tongue, a tone of musical expression, and a metaphor of one with a sing-song voice. Mir appropriates the metaphor of a nightingale in another verse: *'ishq kaa shor koii chhuptaa hai / naala-i 'andaliib hai gulbaa.ng.*

Ghazal 771 | Verse 1

110

شبنم سے کچھ نہیں ہے گل و یاسمن میں آب
دیکھ اس کو بھر بھر آوے ہے سب کے دہن میں آب

शबनम से कुछ नहीं है गुल-ओ-यासमन में आब
देख उस को भर भर आवे है सब के दहन में आब

shabnam se kuchh nahii.n hai gul-o yaasman mei.n aab
dekh us ko bhar bhar aave hai sab ke dahan mei.n aab

(*gul-o yaasman*—flowers and jasmine
aab—water)

It is not from the dewdrops,
that the blossoms get their glow;
It's their own exuberance—
so tempting—to see them aglow

Here is an unusual idea put in an unusual style. It is rightly supposed that dewdrops bring a sheen to blossoms, but it is suggested here that they do not get this glow from the dewdrops because blossoms are beauteous on their own. They are so beautiful, as such, that their very glow becomes enticing and, in other words, mouth-watering, as the speaker says.

The verse celebrates the beauty of blossoms, which does not reflect nature's glow but only its own: (a) nature is a manifestation of God's grandeur, and it reflects God's glory (b) the dewdrops, too, are nature's creation, but the blossoms obtain their beauty due to the cycles of days and nights—the order of the universe itself (c) man envies nature's beauty represented here with the stock image of blossoms, but this envy is not harmful as it symbolizes the positivity of the man–nature relationship (d) both, nature and men, share the spirit of kinship as one is incomplete without the other.

The two key words—*shabnam* (dewdrops) and *aab* (water/glow)—that appear as central images in this verse are distinctly identifiable because of the quality of their liquidity, which will evaporate with the appearance of the sun. This implies that blossom is beautiful despite the temporal dewdrops. It must also be noted with profit that the word—*aab*—acquires a third meaning apart from water and glow and embodies the temptation that metaphorically fills the viewer's mouth with water.

Ghazal 815 | Verse 7

111

رنگین گور کرنی شہیدوں کی رسم ہے
تو بھی ہماری خاک پہ خوں کے نشان کر

रंगीन गोर करनी शहीदों की रस्म है
तू भी हमारी ख़ाक पे ख़ूँ के निशान कर

rangeen gor karni shahiido.n ki rasm hai
tu bhi hamari KHaakh pe khoon ke nishaan kar

(*gor*—grave, tomb;
KHaak—soil, dust, ashes)

Martyrs turn their graves colourful,
as is their custom;
You, too, should mark my soil with blood
as per the custom

It is an established custom to decorate the tombs of martyrs with flowers and emblems and to pay homage to them; however, this is not the case with lovers. They shed their lives in love but remain unknown and less cared for after their passing. This verse pleads for recognition of the lovers, too, but with bloodstains.

The parallel between a martyr and a lover makes way for exciting interpretations: (a) martyrs sacrifice their lives by shedding their blood for noble causes and are respected widely, but lovers remain neglected even though they also shed their lives for love which is another noble cause (b) the tombs of martyrs are decorated differently with wreaths and insignias, but those of lovers may best be marked with blood (c) martyrs achieve their status both in life and death, but lovers do not achieve any, either in life or in death (d) martyrs achieve their recognition ritualistically, but the martyrs of love lack it and call for their own (e) the speaker in this verse is the lover himself who extends the idea of martyrdom to include himself in that same tradition.

There is an ironic play on *gor* (tomb) and *KHaak* (soil) in the verse concerning martyrs and lovers respectively. Another level of irony may be marked in *rangiin* (colourful) for the martyrs and *nishaan* (mark) for the lovers. Sheikh Ibrahim Zauq thinks about the lover's lot in ironic terms and it comes closer to Mir's verse as well: *nahii.n paaegaa nishaa.n koii hamaaraa hargiz / ham jahaa.n se ravish-e tiir guzar jaaenge.*

Ghazal 826 | Verse 1

112

کیا کہیے کیا رکھیں ہیں ہم تجھ سے یار خواہش
یک جان و صد تمنا یک دل ہزار خواہش

क्या कहिए क्या रखें हैं हम तुझ से यार ख़्वाहिश
यक-जान-ओ-सद-तमन्ना यक-दिल हज़ार ख़्वाहिश

kyaa kahiye kyaa rakhei.n hai.n hum tujh se yaar KHvaahish
yak jaan o sad tamanna yak dil hazaar KHvaahish

(*tamanna*—yearning, desire;
sad—hundred)

How do I say how many yearnings I nurture,
how many desires
One life and a hundred longings, one heart
and a thousand desires

Man is a creature driven by desire, which is a perennial subject of countless literary texts. In this verse, the speaker directly shares his desires with the beloved and wonders if he might be able to put them into words himself. In precise terms, he suggests that his one heart is a vehicle of a thousand desires.

The lover's discourse on expressed and unexpressed desires may be appreciated thus: (a) instead of thinking wishfully or suffering individually, the lover chooses to address the beloved face-to-face (b) his address to her is an expression of his qualified inexpressiveness marked by a mixed sense of wonder and interrogation (c) his unexpressed desire remains ambiguous as he cannot say expressly what he desires (c) the sense of wonder comes out in the dichotomous placement of one heart against a thousand desires.

The beloved, addressed as *yaar* (friend), shows the lover's closeness to her, which adds an intimate tone to the verse. The phrase—*kyaa kahiye* (what/how to say)—underscores his inability to express his yearning. With the repetition of *yak* (one) against *sad tamanna* (hundred yearnings) as also *hazaar KHvaahish* (thousand desires), he underlines the infinite amount of love and longing he nourishes for the beloved, but this is only indirectly suggested. While Mir's verse is personalized, Ghalib's verse on the same idea, as follows, is generalized and compares rather weakly with Mir: *hazaao.n KHvaahishei.n aisii ke KHvaahish pe dam nikle / bahut nikle mire armaan lekin phir bhii kam nikle.*

Ghazal 837 | Verse 2

113

عشق ہی عشق ہے جہاں دیکھو
سارے عالم میں بھر رہا ہے عشق

इश्क़ ही इश्क़ है जहाँ देखो
सारे आलम में भर रहा है इश्क़

'ishq hii 'ishq hai jahaa.n dekho
ssare 'aalam mei.n bhar rahaa hai 'ishq

(*'aalam*—world)

Love is everywhere, only love,
wherever you see;
Brimming in this world, all over,
wherever you see

Love is a pervasive force. As a central motif in Mir's poetry, it appears in many ways in many of his verses. This verse capitalizes upon this idea and incorporates a larger ambit of meaning. It is quite possible to appreciate the value of this verse in greater detail parallel to the suggestions Mir has provided in his memoirs, *Zikr-e Mir*, on the value of love.

The following inferences enhance our understanding of this verse: (a) love is a condition of being that a lover alone may experience for all the magic and warmth it carries (b) love is also the essence of existence and the mover of the world at large (c) it appears as an illusion at times but also manifests itself as the ultimate reality (d) its pleasure may be realized through mystical cognisance, as also through the physical body (e) being an unambiguous expression of his perception of love, this verse bears upon Mir's aspirations that are so well reflected in his ghazals.

The first line highlights the omnipresence of love, which is further expanded upon in the subsequent line alongside the manifestations of the world. Furthermore, while the first line reads like an assertion, the following line substantiates that assertion through a gestural mode—*saare 'aalam mei.n bhar rahaa hai 'ishq* (love fills the world all over)—where the first word may be read with an extended breath. A verse quite close in meaning to this one comes from Mir only: *'ishq se jaa nahīn.'n koii KHaalii / dil se le 'arsh tak bharaa hai 'ishq.*

Ghazal 837 | Verse 3

114

عشق ہے طرز و طور عشق کے تئیں
کہیں بندہ کہیں خدا ہے عشق

इश्क़ है तर्ज़-ओ-तौर इश्क़ के तईं
कहीं बंदा कहीं ख़ुदा है इश्क़

'ishq hai tarz-o taur 'ishq ke taii.n
kahii.n banda kahii.n KHuda hai 'ishq

(*tarz-o-taur*—way, method, manner;
taii.n—towards)

Love is a means, a method; it's love alone
That fills the world all over, to the bone

This verse considers love as a means and a mode of living. In living love in these ways, love becomes both—a god and an individual—imparting the verse a definite metaphysical aura.

The associated ideas are even more remarkable to note: (a) love is a way unto itself, and it cannot be restricted to the set norms of life (b) it finds the most exalted space for itself in the world of lovers where it is personified as a being at one place and as a god at another (c) significantly, it is love that distinguishes both of them because both of them are the paragons of beauty unto themselves (d) we are left finally with yet another meaning that love is so magnificent that it becomes god at one time, and the same love is also so deprived at another that it gets reduced to an inconsequential human being.

The distinction between man and god as physical entities portrays love in concrete terms. This is why it is a way of living and experiencing life with love. The two analogous words—*tarz* (manner) and *taur* (way)—help define love as a concrete object that man relates with rather naturally. Mir testifies this again, as can be seen here: *arz-o samaa mei.n 'ishq hai saarii charo.n ore bharaa hai 'ishq / ham hai.n janaab-e 'ishq ke bande nazdiik apne KHudaa hai 'ishq.*

Ghazal 837 | Verse 4

115

عشق معشوق عشق عاشق ہے
یعنی اپنا ہی مبتلا ہے عشق

इश्क़ मा'शूक़ इश्क़ आशिक़ है
या'नी अपना ही मुब्तला है इश्क़

'ishq maashuuq 'ishq 'aashiq hai
y'anii apna hii mubtala hai 'ishq

(*mubtala*—entangled, involved, afflicted)

Love is the beloved, love the lover
Love is indeed afflicted by love

There comes a stage in love where all distinctions are erased forever. At such a level of a higher consciousness, love becomes both a cause and an effect. At this stage, the lover becomes the beloved and the beloved becomes the lover, as they embody the spirit of love in its purest form.

This verse allows us to draw some other important meanings: (a) love raises itself beyond the mundane when love becomes the beloved and also the lover (b) the act of switching these roles also involves the act of ungendering, which again is a mystical phenomenon(c) as the lover and the beloved fall for one another, they create a world unto themselves where they answer their natural instincts to attain, at times, even a metaphysical level of awareness.

The word—*mubtala* (involved, afflicted)—generally carries a negative connotation. In the context of this verse, however, it acquires a favourable implication in the sense of belonging. The interchangeability of lover and beloved is a uniquely striking way of establishing their necessity for each other. It should be pertinent to recall another Mir verse in this context: *log bahut puuchhaa karte hai.n kyaa kahiye mia.n kyaa hai 'ishq / kuchh kahte hai.n sirr-e Ilaahii kuchh kahte hain KHudaa hai 'ishq.*

Ghazal 843 | Verse 6

116

سبز ہے رونے سے میرے گوشہ گوشہ دشت کا
باعث آبادیٔ صحرا ہے چشم گریہ ناک

सब्ज़ है रोने से मेरे गोशा गोशा दश्त का
बा'इस-ए आबादी-ए सहरा है चश्म-ए गिर्या-नाक

sabz hai rone se mere gosha gosha dasht kaa
baa'is-e aabaadi-i sahraa hai chashm-e girya-naak

(*gosha*—corner, side;
dasht—wild lands or forest;
baa'is—cause, reason;
sahraa—desert;
girya-naak—tearful)

Each corner of the wilderness is green
because of my tears;
The cause of the wild's habitation is only
the shedding of my tears

Lovers go wild when disappointed in love. They shed tears endlessly and seek their consolation in that act. We have a disappointed lover here who has shed so many tears that the wildernesses have grown green and have turned into places suitable for inhabitation.

This verse has its meaning reposed in the images that constitute its structure: (a) wilderness and habitation, as also wild lovers and tears, complement each other and create a scheme of meaning here (b) the lover's tears are not wasted as they have turned the wilderness into greenery (c) in bringing pain to himself, the lover has brought life even to the wilderness which establishes his exalted status as a lover.

The scheme of meaning in this verse is owed to the placement of the conflicting images. *Sabz* (greenery) is placed here against *dasht* (wilderness), *aabaadii* (inhabitation) against *sahraa* (desert) and *chashm* (eyes) against *chashme-e girya-naak* (tearful eyes). All these, cumulatively, suggest two conditions of being that reflect upon the space and the inhabitant as they are characterized here. A pertinent reference may be made to Mir only for a corresponding representation of this experience: *aaj kal se kuchh na tuufaa.n zaa hai chashm-e girya-naak / m'ojaza barso.n se hai dariyaa hai chashm-e girya-naak.*

Ghazal 859 | Verse 5

117

کیا لطف تن چھپا ہے مرے تنگ پوش کا
اگلا پڑے ہے جامے سے اس کا بدن تمام

क्या लुत्फ़-ए तन छुपा है मिरे तंग-पोश का
उगला पड़े है जामे से उस का बदन तमाम

kyaa lutf-e tan chhupaa hai mire tang-posh kaa
uglaa pade hai jaame se us kaa badan tamaam

(*lutf-e tan*—pleasures of the body;
tang-posh—slim-fit wearer)

How well is the body's effulgence contained
in her slim-fit robe;
My love's whole body is boiling in and out
of her slim-fit robe

Along with the abstract concepts of love and passion, the beloved's body has also been adored in ghazal verses often. This verse eulogizes her body, which is clothed in a slim-fit robe that can hardly contain her opulent physical form. The beloved thus acquires a different kind of beauty when her body parts boil in and out in the robes she has put on.

This verse makes other suggestions as well: (a) the fullness of the beloved's body arouses passion when dressed in a certain kind of robe (b) both the body and sartorial elegance add to the eroticism of the body (c) she has made no special efforts to show or hide the curves of her body, but her body makes a natural statement on its own (d) one wonders if she shows up in her chosen dress for enticing or teasing the onlookers (e) the celebration of the female form and beauty does not necessarily have to be profane, it can also be aesthetically gratifying as in this verse.

This is a visually charged verse, clearly marked by the keen portrayal of the female body that evokes sensuality. The two lines of the verse represent a tension of ideas with two phrases—*chhupaa hai* (is hidden) and *uglaa pade hai* (is boiling out). These phrases spell out the pleasures of the female body contained in the phrase—*lutf-e tan*. The element of inherent sexuality is further intensified with the totality of her physical form represented by the phrase—*us kaa badan tamaam* (her whole body). Mir recreates this experience in two other verses as well: *ve kapRe to badle hue Mir us ko kaii din / tan per hai shikan tangii-i poshaak se ab tak* and *jii phat gayaa hai rashk se chaspaa.n libaas ke / kyaa tang-jaama liptaa hai us ke badan ke saath.*

Ghazal 863 | Verse 1

118

کب تک رہیں گے پہلو لگائے زمیں سے ہم
یہ درد اب کہیں گے کسو شانہ بیں سے ہم

कब तक रहेंगे पहलू लगाए ज़मीं से हम
ये दर्द अब कहेंगे किसू शाना-बीं से हम

kab tak rahenge pehluu lagaae zamii.n se ham
ye *dard ab kahenge kisuu shaana-bii.n se ham*

(*shaana-bii.n*—one who discovers hidden matters by studying omens)

For how long should I root myself
to the earth's side;
I shall share my agony with
a keen seer—in them confide

Miseries are a part of life and living, but it is only natural for man to seek his release and find his resolution. The speaker here is in a state of agony and seeks a keen sympathizer who may bring him release.

This common human predicament has other aspects to it as well: (a) pain and redemption from pain make their appearance in the cyclical movement of man's fate (b) one who suffers is a man, but one who brings relief is a man, too (c) seeking release from suffering is a human act, just as bringing release to the sufferer is a human act (d) earth is the home for the living and the dead, and it is the earth that causes suffering as it also brings release from suffering (e) it is suggested that an omen-reader, who discovers hidden matters, may treat the speaker (f) in Greek-Islamic medicine, the treatment of pain on the sides and shoulders is prescribed as such: lying straight on a firm bed or the ground (g) the pain on the shoulders is indicative of heart's ailment which makes it more relevant as one tends to associate it with the pain a lover's heart has suffered.

The implication of—*pehluu lagaae zamiin se* (to be stuck with the earth)—is one of being almost buried under the pressure of Earth and suffering immeasurably due *to* the pain caused. The intertextuality of *shaana* and *shaana-bii.n* is worth noting. The word *shaana* means both a comb and a shoulder, and *bii.n* qualifies a person who can see through the pins of the comb on the one hand and diagnose the cause of pain on the shoulder blades and the sides on the other. Such a person may be an actual seer and redeemer. Momin Khan Momin and Ghulam Hamadani Mushafi respectively appropriate this imagery to their advantage in their verses: *ham kisii shaana-bii.n se puchhenge / sabab ashuftagii-i kaakul kaa* and *uljhaa hai kis kii zulf-e pareshaa.n mei.n dil mira / ai shaana-bii.n samajh ke zaraa shaana dekhnaa.*

Ghazal 874 | Verse 7

119

آتش عشق نے راون کو جلا کر مارا
گرچہ لنکا سا تھا اس دیو کا گھر پانی میں

आतिश-ए 'इश्क़ ने रावन को जला कर मारा
गरचे लंका सा था उस देव का घर पानी में

aatish-e 'ishq ne Raavan ko jalaa kar maaraa
garche Lanka sa thaa us deo ka ghar paanii mei.n

The fire of love consumed Raavan,
the gigantic one;
Whose home, like Lanka,
was isled in the water for one

The ways of destiny are inscrutable. Time tells us that the mighty may prove fickle, and the fickle mighty. This verse testifies to this with the example of Raavan, who was calamitous and mighty, but ironically enough, he was burnt to ashes by the fire of love and desire, even though he lived in a country surrounded by deep waters.

The historical allusion employed in this verse opens more avenues of interpretation: (a) love is all fire; it engulfs man from all sides and vanquishes him irrespective of his power and position (b) this fire cannot be quenched with water, not even by a sea full of mighty waves of water (c) this is true of real-life situations and figures, as also of the mythical situations and figures (d) the beloved for whom one is burnt to ashes remains untouched by and uninformed of the lover's fate (e) the representation of Raavan as a martyr of love derives its strength from a reference to his fire of passion and alludes also to the custom of burning Raavan's effigy on Dussehra.

The figure of Raavan is well picturized with the word—*deo* (gigantic one)—and his raging love is compared with *aatish* (fire). The ironical layer in this verse lies in the second line—*garche Lanka saa thaa us deo kaa ghar paanii mei.n* (although, like Lanka, this huge one too had his home in the waters)—which implies that he lived in a p(a)lace surrounded by water, but could not escape the fire. Qaim Chandpuri's verse employs similar images to eulogise romantic love: *dil miraa tum ko to Lanka hai dashahre kii butaa.n / fat'h hai saal bhar us kii jo use luutegaa.*

Ghazal 877 | Verse 1

120

کس کنے جاؤں الٰہی کیا دوا پیدا کروں
دل تو کچھ دھنسکا ہی جاتا ہے کروں سو کیا کروں

किस कने जाऊँ इलाही क्या दवा पैदा करूँ
दिल तो कुछ धँसका ही जाता है करूँ सो क्या करूँ

kis kane jaauu.n Ilaahii kyaa davaa paidaa karuu.n
dil to kuchh dha.nskaa hii jaataa hai karuu.n so kyaa karuu.n

To whom shall I go, O God,
what remedy will make do;
My heart keeps on sinking now,
what shall I do, if I do

Helplessness is one of the myriad conditions of human destiny. The speaker here is helpless and seeks help from God, the eternal redeemer. His heart sinks every moment, and he desperately pleads with the maker of all destinies to save him from his suffering.

This condition of the sufferer makes way for further readings: (a) in pain lies the realization of the condition of pleasure, but man does not realize this until pain overpowers him (b) pain and pleasure alone represent the totality of life, as no life is either all pain or all pleasure (c) It is God alone who is remembered in times of misery, and forgotten soon after God redeems the misery of the sufferer (d) the most affected subject of human suffering is the human heart itself which holds a premium position in the human frame and sits high but is too delicate and too sensitive to pain.

The condition of helplessness is expressed in this verse. It becomes evident in all the clauses of the verse, which can be broken into four parts—*kis kane jaau.nn Ilaahii* (where shall I go, O God), *kyaa davaa paidaa karuu.n* (what remedy shall I produce) in the first line and *dil to kuchh dha.nskaa hi jaataa hai* (my heart keeps on sinking) and *karuu.n so kyaa karuu.n* (what shall I do, if I can do anything at all). The well-orchestrated movement of the two lines turns it into an impassioned appeal to God. The element of helplessness can be read comparatively in this verse by Ahmad Mushtaq: *vahii un kii satiizakaarii hai / vahii be-chaargii hamaarii hai.*

Ghazal 885 | Verse 4

121

اب کے جنوں میں فاصلہ شاید نہ کچھ رہے
دامن کے چاک اور گریباں کے چاک میں

अब के जुनूँ में फ़ासला शायद न कुछ रहे
दामन के चाक और गरेबाँ के चाक में

ab ke junuu.n mei.n faasla shayed na kuchh rahe
daaman ke chaak aur garebaa.n ke chaak me.in

(*faasla*—distance, space;
daaman—hem of a garment;
chaak—torn, slitted)

This time, perhaps no gaps
in my madness there will be
Nor gaps between the torn hems of my
collars and clothes as you see

The image of a lover with a torn collar is a stock image in the Urdu ghazal. The speaker presents the picture of a wild lover and surmises that his wildness will cross all limits this time. As such, he will appear as a picture of complete dishevelment symbolizing a true lover.

The visual representation of the wild lover has more to it: (a) the wildness of the lover is presented in terms of a season which is, arguably, the spring season when the lovers go wild (b) when they go wild, they tear their collar and hem apart and appear like *Majnuu.n*, the archetypal lover (c) the speaker is aware of the lover going wild and he can visualize how this will turn him into a wreck in the spring season knocking at the door (d) it appears that in the previous spring season, he had not reached complete dishevelment, but this season he will cross all limits and look completely torn apart.

This verse is a fine example of image-making. *Daaman* (hem) and *garebaa.n* (neck of the shirt) together personify the lover as *Majnuu.n*. This lover thrives best in his prime during spring, but he is not destined to bask in its pleasures and merriments. We have another verse from Mir on this theme: *ab ke junnu.n ke biich garebaa.n kaa zikr kyaa / kahiye bhii jo rahaa so koii taar darmiyaa.n.*

Ghazal 887 | Verse 1

122

آج ہمارے گھر آیا تو کیا ہے یاں جو نثار کریں
الا کھینچ بغل میں تجھ کو دیر تلک ہم پیار کریں

आज हमारे घर आया तो क्या है याँ जो निसार करें
इल्ला खींच बग़ल में तुझ को देर तलक हम प्यार करें

aaj hamaare ghar aayaa to kyaa hai yaa.n jo nisaar karei.n
illa khe.nch baGhal mei.n tujh ko der talak ham pyaar karei.n

(*nisaar*—sacrifice, offer;
Illa—except, if not)

Now that she has come to my abode,
what do I have to offer for too long,
But only to pull her close, love her closely,
and for a while to her belong

Waiting for the beloved and her coming to the lover are two experiences worth adoring for the lover. His desire is fulfilled here as the beloved has come to his abode. An overwhelmed lover wonders if he has anything worthy to offer her. The only offer, and the most appropriate one, he thinks of, is to pull her close to himself and love her for a long while.

Some more observations come to mind: (a) it is only a natural and innocent urge for every lover to seek physical proximity with the beloved (b) it is also natural to admit this with tenderness, frankness and without any inhibition (c) while the lover expresses his delight at her arrival to his abode, the beloved remains mute which points towards her desire to be loved (d) also, her coming to the beloved is in itself an act of her willingness to join her lover with all pleasure and be in her embrace for a while longer than usual (e) there could be a hidden erotic suggestion in the lover's desire that may not missed.

The clause—*kyaa hai yaa.n jo nisaar karei.n* (what do I have here to offer her)—portrays the lover as one in a state of wonder. This wonder turns into a rare pleasure for her with his offer of *der talak ham pyaar karei.n* (I may love her for long hours). Consider two verses by Abdul Hai Taabaan: *aaj aayaa hai yaar ghar mere / ye KHushii kis se mai.n kahuu.n Taabaa.n* and *b'ad muddat ke maah-ruu aayaa / kyu.n na us ke gale laguu.n Taabaa.n*.

Ghazal 897 | Verse 4

123

تھا سب کو دعویٰ عشق کا لیکن نہ ٹھہرا کوئی بھی
دانستہ اپنی جان سے دل کو اٹھایا ایک میں

था सब को दावा इश्क़ का लेकिन न ठहरा कोई भी
दानिस्ता अपनी जान से दिल को उठाया एक मैं

thaa sab ko d'ava 'ishq kaa lekin na Thahraa koii bhii
daanista apnii jaan se dil ko uThaayaa ek mai.n

(*d'avaa*—claim;
daanista—knowingly, deliberately)

Everyone had a claim to love,
but none could stand the test;
That was me alone who didn't care
for life and stood the test

There is an adage that love claims life, and lovers are destined to sacrifice their own lives for the beloved. The lover in this verse stands out as one who loved and paid with his own life for the sake of loving.

The lover in this verse has more suggestions to make: (a) more than a simple lover, he emerges here as the prime protagonist of love, a chivalrous lover so to say, as he willingly chose to sacrifice his life (b) he is unique because no one could stand the trials of love, but he alone was ready to sacrifice all for love (c) in sacrificing his life, he emerges victorious and asserts this with a sense of pride (d) in making the claim of shedding his life, he is easily distinguished as a genuine seeker and symbol of love.

The word *d'avaa* is used here more in the sense of claim than right, which underlines the primary intent of the verse. Another word—*Thahraa* (stood)—is an idiomatic corollary that accompanies the claim, which falls flat, as it asserts that making a claim is self-defeating. Mir's idiomatic and most expressive use of language, however, is best reflected in the clause—*jaan se dil ko uThaayaa ek mai.n* (I left the temptation of life behind only heartily). The phrase—*ek mai.n* (me, alone)—asserts his superiority over all other lovers. Mir reiterates this assertion of the lover's self in another verse as well: *bazaar-e vafaa mei.n sar-e saudaa tha sabho.n ko / per bech ke jii ek KHariidaar huaa mai.n.*

Ghazal 916 | Verse 9

124

دیر رہنے کی جا نہیں یہ چمن
بوئے گل ہو صفیر بلبل ہو

देर रहने की जा नहीं ये चमन
बू-ए गुल हो सफ़ीर-ए बुलबुल हो

der rahne kii jaa nahii.n ye chaman
buu-e gul ho safiir-e bulbul ho

(*jaa*—*place;*
buu-e gul—fragrance of flowers;
safiir-e bulbul—whistling/hissing of bulbul)

This garden is not the place
to stay for long,
Neither for the flowers' fragrance
nor for the bulbul's song

Transitoriness has been a subject of discourses throughout history. However beautiful, neither the world nor its manifestations have a perennial presence. This includes even terrestrial and aquatic spaces. This verse strikes a voice of caution that this garden is not the place to be in for too long.

This sobering and prophetic voice has specific inherent messages: (a) the world is yet another image of a garden with its own manifestation in the form of human beings and the elements of nature (b) this garden is not only transitory but unwelcoming for the seekers of permanence (c) not men and women alone, but even the most prized gifts of nature like fragrances and birdsongs cannot stay here for too long as this world is a place of vile passions and ephemeral attachments (d) while blossoms and songs appear to be ephemeral, they represent permanence, while the gardens of this world represent temporality.

In a philosophical context, *chaman* (garden) stands out in this verse as a metaphor for the world, which is ephemeral at best. A triangle of *chaman* (garden), *buu-e gul* (flower's fragrance), and *safiir-e bulbul* (bulbul's whistling) composes a macrocosm within a microcosm. The irony lies in the poetic construction of the idea that the garden is not the place to be, even for the fragrance of flowers and the whistling of the bulbul. Khwaja Mir Dard strikes a similar sentiment in his verse: *ne gul ko hai sabaat na ham ko hai 'etebaar / kis baat per chaman havas-e rang-o buu karei.n.*

Ghazal 936 | Verse 8

125

لذت دنیا سے کیا بہرہ ہمیں
پاس ہے رنڈی ولے ہے ضعف باہ

लज़्ज़त-ए दुनिया से क्या बहरा हमें
पास है रंडी वले है ज़ो'फ़-ए बाह

lazzat-e duniyaa se kyaa bahra hamei.n
pass hai randii vale zof-e baah

(*bahra*—concern;
zof-e baah—sexual incapacitation)

For the delights of this world,
I have no love lost;
I have a whore by my side, but
all my drive, I have lost

The world is often considered a place for getting embroiled in and pursuing desires, which may be awful at times. Some men are too attached to the pleasures of this world; others abhor it for what it is and what it brings to them. The speaker here has no love lost for the pleasures of this world and denies them because he has no drive to like or love them.

The rich ambiguity in this verse makes it worthy of deeper attention: (a) the world is not faithful to anyone, and like a prostitute it can be bought for a price (b) it affords temporal and false pleasures, but it corrupts both physically and spiritually (c) the speaker cannot make love with this prostitute because he is sexually incapacitated now; too old or weak (d) this implies, although paradoxically, that if he had the sexual power and drive, he would have bought her services (e) the sense of resignation concerning the world is, however, conveyed poignantly in the two lines.

This verse may be read as a corrosive attack on the falsity of the world. This comes out in the words—*lazzat* (pleasure) and *randii* (slut)—that go together and keep the speaker away from both. Akbar Allahabadi's discourse on the world echoes Mir: *duniyaa mei.n huu.n duniyaa kaa talabgaar nahii.n huu.n / baazaar se guzraa huu.n KHariidaar nahii.n huu.n.*

Ghazal 953 | Verse 2

126

کیا رنگ و بو و باد سحر سب ہیں گرم راہ
کیا ہے جو اس چمن میں ہے ایسی چلا چلی

क्या रंग-ओ-बू-ओ-बाद-ए सहर सब हैं गर्म-ए राह
क्या है जो इस चमन में है ऐसी चला-चली

kyaa rang-o buu-o baad-e sahar sab hai.n garm-e raah
kyaa hai jo is chaman mei.n hai aisii chalaa chalii

(*baad-e sahar*—morning breeze;
garm-e raah—on the move)

Are the colours, the fragrance, the morning breeze
on the move now;
What's this buzz in the garden, why this hurry
to leave just now

Permanence is an illusion; change is a reality. This verse underscores this idea and asserts that everything is in a state of flux, constantly transitioning from one state or stage to another. It does not say why there is such a hurry to leave or for which destination, yet it underlines the mutability of the world that characterizes it anyway.

The verse is essentially philosophical in its intent and brings us to appreciate the very nature of the world in such terms: (a) the world is in a constant state of mutability (b) composed of colours, fragrance and breeze, the world represents an imagined paradigm of physical existence (c) this garden represents the world itself which is at best a phenomenon of vanishing beauty (d) since nothing is tangible here and everything represents a picture of deception, there is a hurry to leave (e) the destination is not known to anyone since that too is illusory.

The spirit of the verse rests in the phrase—*chalaa-chalii* (the hurry for leaving). It creates a sense of urgency and some unknown kind of impending danger that might cause loss with any delay in departure. A corollary to this phrase—*garm-e raah* (busy leaving/travelling)—is pre-posted in the first line. Together, these phrases add to the urgency of departing without delay because there is some prompting from behind to set out immediately. The phrases—*kyaa rang-o buu* (what colour and fragrance?) and *kyaa hai* (what's there?)—are not questions; they affirm some doubt and apprehension of something unwelcome. Although with a variation on this theme, Sheikh Ibrahim Zauq reiterates his perspective on this world: *duniyaa ne kis kaa raah-e fanaa mei.n diyaa hai saath / tum bhii chale chalo yuu.n hii jab tak chalii chale.*

Ghazal 954 | Verse 2

127

خانہ آباد کعبے میں تھا میرؔ
کیا خدائی خراب ہے وہ بھی

ख़ाना-आबाद का'बे में था 'मीर'
क्या ख़ुदाई-ख़राब है वो भी

KHaana aabaad K'abe mei.n thaa Mir
kyaa KHudaaii-KHaraab hai vo bhii

So well placed was Mir in the *K'aba*, for one
Is he, too, a God-damned one, a God-soiled one

The dichotomy between reverence for God and impatience with Him often becomes a matter of serious deliberation among poets and philosophers. Mir, too, has engaged with this in many of his verses. Placing himself in the *K'aba*, he asserts that he was well stationed there, but soon he is also dogged by a strange doubt: whether he, too, is one, like many others, a God-damned one.

Mir's reflections on himself reveal more about him: (a) the difference between a believer and a non-believer is too thin but too consequential (b) every believer or non-believer reflects upon his duality or doubt that he embodies (c) one's belief and non-believing may be relative and may be both rational or irrational (d) the spirit of quest characterizes a man who remains incessantly in quest concerning God whom he has never seen.

The real magic of the verse lies in the second line—*kyaa KHudaaii-KHaraab hai vo bhii*—(Is he too, a God-damned one, a God-soiled one), which portrays Mir as a stock figure in a state of doubt or quest. *KHuddaii-KHaraab* is a highly creative phrase that eloquently speaks for many in this category. Mir draws upon this expression in another verse, emphasizing love and maintaining equal freshness: *'ishq Khudaaii Kharaab hai aisaa jis se gae hai.n ghar ke ghar / K'aba-o dair ke aivaano.'n ke gire pade hai.n dar ke dar.*

Ghazal 957 | Verse 7

128

پیدا کہاں ہیں ایسے پراگندہ طبع لوگ
افسوس تم کو میرؔ سے صحبت نہیں رہی

पैदा कहाँ हैं ऐसे परागंदा-तब्अ' लोग
अफ़सोस तुम को 'मीर' से सोहबत नहीं रही

paida kahaa.n hai.n aise paraaganda-tab'a log
afsos tum ko Mir se sohbat nahii.n rahii

(*paraaganda-tab'a*—a man of distracted nature;
*sohba*t—company)

Whence such men riddled by distractions
are ever born, Mir;
Alas! They could never enjoy
the hallowed company of Mir

Verses that reflect upon the poet's self are often difficult to decipher. They lead to the poet's persona opening up differently for different readings. Mir defines himself in this verse as a person of a distracted nature. He adds further that such men are not born so often.

This verse leaves us with some questions but also provides some answers: (a) one wonders whether Mir implies that being distracted holds value for him or his readers (b) also whether he means he was one of them, sadly or happily (c) both these doubts lead to affirmative answers, but he leaves us with a couple of innuendos: (i) sadly, you did not have his company, and (ii) you could not enjoy his company because he is no more (d) in sum, Mir characterizes the man as a complex being and compliments himself for being so, and more importantly, for being a poet who must have such a nature.

A note of self-praise, for entirely justifiable reasons, is borne out by two phrases—*paraaganda-tab'a* (distracted one) and *afsos* (sad). Interestingly, both words have negative connotations, but Mir turns them into positive phrases to portray himself as a person and a poet of unique worth. This portrayal is further strengthened with the clause *paidaa kahaa.n hai.n aise* (such men are hardly ever born). Mir carries his sense of superiority in several other verses as well. Here is one such: *muft yuu.n haath se na kho ham ko / kahii.n paidaa bhii hote hai.n ham se.*

Ghazal 968 | Verse 2

129

رنگین ہم تو تجھ کو ایسا نہ جانتے تھے
تو نے تو عاشقوں کا لوہو پیا پیارے

रंगीन हम तो तुझ को ऐसा न जानते थे
तू ने तो आशिक़ों का लोहू पिया पियारे

rangiin ham to tujh ko aisaa na jaante the
tuu ne to 'aashiqo.n kaa lohuu piyaa piyaare

(*lohuu*—blood)

That you were so colourful,
I didn't know;
That you are drunk on the blood of lovers
I didn't know

Moments of fun and frolic enliven the plot of love, presenting lovers as whimsical. An observer addresses a lover here and considers him too colourful. He surmises that his colourful countenance is a result of having drunk his beloved's blood.

As with all of Mir's verses, there is much more to this one than appears on the surface: (a) the observer who addresses the lover may himself be a lover like him, but he hides that (b) he may be envious of him because he has not had such a rosy appearance like him (c) he may be genuinely praising him and his countenance that is uniquely remarkable (d) love brings brightness on the face of the lovers, and it bears out the feeling of fulfilment in love.

The words—*rangiin* (colourful) and *lohuu* (blood)—which complement each other, should be read together as the lover has grown red because he has, metaphorically speaking, been brought up on the beloved's flaming blood. Conversely, drinking blood is a beastly act that the lover cannot ever do with his beloved. This is certainly not the speaker's intent, unless he is envious of the person and wishes to downgrade them. There is a sense of surprise on the part of the rival lover when he says—*rangiin ham to tujh ko aisaa na jaante the* (I didn't ever know you were that colourful). One should not also miss his endearing address to him as—*piyaare* (my dear)—which carries a sense of both praise and envy. Mir has capitalized on the proverb of *lohuu piinaa* (drinking blood) in several verses. Here is one as a variation on this theme: *lohuu piina jaan khaanaa dekhiye / kyaa mizaaj-e 'ishq mei.n marGhuub ho.*

Ghazal 1001 | Verse 9

130

رنگ گل و بوئے گل ہوتے ہیں ہوا دونوں
کیا قافلہ جاتا ہے جو تو بھی چلا چاہے

रंग-ए गुल ओ बू-ए गुल होते हैं हवा दोनों
क्या क़ाफ़िला जाता है जो तू भी चला चाहे

rang-e gul o buu-e gul hote hai.n havaa dono.n
kyaa qaafilaa jaataa hai jo tuu bhii chalaa chahe

The colours of blossoms, their fragrance too,
dissolve in the air;
Is the convoy set to depart that you too
should leave unaware

The world has a distinguished appearance, with its lovely objects scattered throughout the space. These objects appear and disappear with time. This verse presents a scenario where objects are about to disappear, along with those who nurtured and cared for them. It tells, in brief, how creation manifests and how it ultimately dissipates and disappears.

Some points for further inquiry into the verse are also notable: (a) wind is both empowered and empowering, and it allows for the movement of all the composites of nature from the colour and fragrance of flowers to the groups of humans that wander this earth (b) the speaker also wonders that if all are prone to be blown, what good is a man after all (c) hinting at a philosophical suggestion in the second line, the speaker reflects on the transience of man, as he does on that of the world.

The first line has two implications: (i) the colour of the rose and the scent of the rose are only that of the breeze blowing and passing by, and (ii) both the colour of the rose and the scent of the rose are departing from the garden. The second line has a dramatic appeal and is a poignant expression of the loss of the garden, which would be bereft of all its gifts, as well as of all those who testified in praise of them once. Wind is the central point of reference in this verse, and it is used in three different ways: as a noun, a verb and a metaphor. The verse is rich in nature imagery—*rang-e gul* (the colour of flowers), *buu-e gul* (the fragrance of flowers), and *havaa* (the wind). While the first two represent nature's beauty, the third is their unkind carrier that blows to unknown destinations. Mir develops this idea in another verse with distinction: *'aalam mei.n aab-o gil ke Thahraao kis tarah ho / gar KHaak hai uRe hai var aab hai ravaa.n hai.* A verse from Insha Allah Khan may be quoted in this context too: *juu.n mauj-e havaa apnaa thaa hosh bhii uRne per / ai nikhat-e gul tuu ne kyu.n itnii shataabii kii.*

Ghazal 1024 | Verse 4

131

کیا جانیے کہ چھاتی جلے ہے کہ داغ دل
اک آگ سی لگی ہے کہیں کچھ دھواں سا ہے

क्या जानिए कि छाती जले है कि दाग़-ए दिल
इक आग सी लगी है कहीं कुछ धुआँ सा है

kyaa jaaniye ke chhaatii jale hai ke daaGh-e dil
ik aag sii lagii hai kahii.n kuchh dhuaa.n saa hai

I don’t know if it’s my chest that burns
or my heart that is blotted;
There is fire to be sure,
some smoke in the air, clotted

Certainties and uncertainties punctuate human life. One knows this well enough, yet does not understand what is happening around them. The speaker knows for sure that there is some fire and smoke around him, but he does not know if it is his chest that burns or the marks of woe on his chest that are on fire. In both cases, suffering is his share or destiny.

Let us read between the two lines to find out what happens in this representation of a pathetic condition: (a) the speaker makes a distinction between his chest and scars on his heart, but he is tragically unaware which of the two burns indeed (b) he is, on the other hand, tragically aware, that some fire has erupted somewhere, causing smoke to billow (c) despite the uncertainty, he suggests that his very being is on fire for reasons certain and yet uncertain to him (d) the mixed senses of wonder, pathos and helplessness mark the verse and make it worthy of attention.

This verse is typically picturesque. The images of *siina* (breast), *daaGh* (blot), *aag* (fire) and *dhuaa.n* (smoke) create a macabre scenario together, where the speaker appears as the tragic protagonist without ever realizing the fuller proportions of what has happened to him. Pathos and irony are evident in the verse in no uncertain terms. This condition is visible in another of Mir's verses: *mohabbat ne shaaed ke dii dil ko aag / dhuaa.n saa hai kuchh us nagar kii taraf.*

Ghazal 1025 | Verse 2

132

حنا سے یار کا پنجہ نہیں ہے گل کے رنگ
ہمارے ان نے کلیجوں میں ہاتھ ڈالا ہے

हिना से यार का पंजा नहीं है गुल के रंग
हमारे उन ने कलेजों में हाथ डाला है

hinaa se yaar kaa panja nahii.n hai gul ke rang
hamaare un ne kalejo.n mei.n haath daalaa hai

(*kaleja*—heart, lung or courage, spirit)

It's not henna that has turned
my beloved's hand red like a flower;
She has clawed at my heart
her palms now red like a flower

The beloved in Urdu ghazals appears in many forms, symbolizing both kindness and cruelty. Here, the beloved is depicted as unkind, nearly killing the lover, and her hands are stained with his blood. The narrator, who is the lover himself, openly shares his fate, leaving us to wonder if the beloved could be so cruel, bringing such misery to the lover.

There are fascinating suggestions in the lover's narrative that deserve attention: (a) the beloved is cruel, and the lover can narrate his situation but only in a meek manner without any hope or chance of redress (b) there is a note of complaint in the lover's narrative that makes him appear as a helpless sufferer; which lovers often are (c) with marks of blood on her hand, she is no less than a killer (d) the narrative is as much a remonstration as it is a reflection on the narrator's lot (e) the lover's verse is aimed at anyone who might sympathize with lovers, as they are destined to suffer and remain in suffering ceaselessly.

The ironic tone of the verse is emphasized by henna's redness, which resembles the heart's blood—contrasting the celebratory application of henna with the violent redness of blood obtained by clawing at the lover's heart. Another aspect of the verse's irony involves *kaleja*, which means both heart and lung, as well as courage and spirit, but they fall prey to the beloved's machinations in both senses. The expression—*haath daalaa hai* (has slid a hand into my chest)—invokes the idea of robbing and ransacking, which intensifies the verse's impact.

Ghazal 1039 | Verse 5

133

لطف اس کے بدن کا کچھ نہ پوچھو
کیا جانیے جان ہے کہ تن ہے

लुत्फ़ उस के बदन का कुछ न पूछो
क्या जानिए जान है कि तन है

lutf us ke badan kaa kuchh na puuchho
kyaa jaaniye jaan hai ke tan hai

(*lutf*—pleasure)

Of the pleasures of her body,
oh, don't ask me;
Don't know if it's spirit or body
that charms me

The female body, as a paragon of beauty, is referenced frequently in the poetry of love and romance. But we have one of the more distinguished representations here where the young lady's admirer struggles to portray her beautiful form. He cannot distinguish whether her arresting charm is due to her winsome body or is it some spiritual miracle within a physical form.

There are some interrelated ideas we can take a note of: (a) the female body is imagined in two different ways for its physicality and also for the spirit it harbours (b) even if the admirer is unable to configure it as of one kind or the other, he looks at it in a state of wonderment (c) in one way, it so appears that he is the part-taker of the pleasures of this female body himself and attempts to define that body (d) in another, it appears that this is someone else who observes that body from a distance and enjoys its magical spell (e) the verse also reads as a monologue and expresses the inability of the admirer to describe the indescribable since he stands completely mesmerized (f) the body is represented here as spirit or phantom or fantasy or magic which is the highest poetic praise for the body.

Lutf (pleasures) is a condition of enjoyment in this verse, but it also represents the female body in all its glory. *Kuchh na puuchho* (don't ask me at all) conveys his inability to describe the speaker's state of being spellbound. The body, distinguished as *jaan* (pulsating life) and *tan* (physical form), ultimately proves to be an exercise in creating a fantasy. In another verse, Mir demonstrates this condition in comparable terms: *lutf-e badan ko us ke hargiz pahunch sake na / jaa paRtii thi hamesha apnii nigaah jaa.n par.*

Ghazal 1040 | Verse 1

134

ہم مست ہو بھی دیکھا آخر مزہ نہیں ہے
ہشیاری کے برابر کوئی نشہ نہیں ہے

हम मस्त हो भी देखा आख़िर मज़ा नहीं है
हुश्यारी के बराबर कोई नशा नहीं है

ham mast ho bhii dekhaa aaKHir maza nahii.n hai
hushyaarii ke baraabar koii nasha nahii.n hai

I found no pleasure in drunken revelry,
There's no intoxication equal to wisdom merry

The speaker distinguishes here between the two states of blinding drunkenness and actual consciousness and concludes that the state of consciousness is far more enabling than that of hollow intoxication.

We can trace wider meanings in this verse: (a) in putting premium on consciousness against drunkenness, the traditional idea of being drunk on the divine wine, associated with Sufis, is squarely contradicted (b) as such, those who are 'mystified' as per the Sufi belief are not really mystified, and those who are not mystified are indeed mystified (c) absolute ecstasy lies in a state of consciousness than in a condition of transitory intoxication (d) one need not take pride in temporal pleasures induced by intoxicants because they do not enrich man in any possible way (e) the states of consciousness and drunkenness relate with the philosophy of truth and untruth (f) awareness too is an intoxication in which wisdom is duly valourized.

This verse is constructed on the logic of antithesis. The basic idea of being in a state of consciousness akin to the state of drunkenness is driven home through the antithetical placing of *hushyaarii* (consciousness) and *nasha* (drunkenness). Instead of using the personal pronoun *mai.n* (I), Mir uses the collective pronoun *ham* (we) to convey the greater strength of more than one subscribing to the philosophy of meaningful drinking and drunkenness. He also represents this dichotomy between consciousness and drunkenness in another verse that may be read comparatively: *aa.nkh mastii mei.n kisuu per nahii.n paRti us kii / ye bhii us saada-o pur-kaar kii hushyaarii hai.*

Ghazal 1040 | Verse 4

135

زیر فلک رکا ہے اب جی بہت ہمارا
اس بے فضا قفس میں مطلق ہوا نہیں ہے

ज़ेर-ए फ़लक रुका है अब जी बहुत हमारा
इस बे-फ़ज़ा क़फ़स में मुतलक़ हवा नहीं है

zer-e falak rukaa hai ab jii bahut hamaaraa
is be-fazaa qafas mei.n mutlaq havaa nahii.n hai

(*zer-e falak*—under the sky;
be-fazaa—lacking in openness, unpleasant condition;
mutlaq—unrestricted, absolute, not in the least)

Often enough, I suffocate
under the sky
To realize that there's no air at all
in this cage dry

In existentialist philosophy, living on this earth has often been presented as a despairing experience. In line with that idea, this verse identifies the earth as a place without the requisite air that helps man breathe. Thus, the speaker finds it too difficult to survive in such a place.

The speaker seems to imply that: (a) the earth is indeed a cage despite being limitless (b) living here, thus, is living in a state of unbearable suffocation (c) the keeper of the earth and the sky does not bless man with kindness (d) his predicament gives him no space to live and breathe easily (e) the verse creates a condition of sadness and utter lack of enthusiasm on the part of the speaker.

Mir's existential angst is distinctly conveyed in this verse. The phrase—*zer-e falak* (under the sky) refers here to the earth spatially. It is compared with *be-fazaa qafas* (bare cage), which has no wind passing through, making it difficult to breathe and survive. The definiteness of no wind passing through the constricting cage is best conveyed through *mutalaq havaa nahii.n hai* (there is no air here at all). The double adjectives—*be-fazaa* (lacking in openness) and *mutlaq* (not in the least)—portray a condition of double deprivation. Qaim Chanduri's verse may be quoted here for its reciprocity with Mir's verse: *kyu.n na jii ghabraae zer-e aasmaa.n / ghar to hai matb'u par bas muKHtasar.*

Ghazal 1047 | Verse 4

136

دیدنی ہے شکستگی دل کی
کیا عمارت غموں نے ڈھائی ہے

दीदनी है शिकस्तगी दिल की
क्या इमारत ग़मों ने ढाई है

diidnii hai shikastagii dil kii
kyaa ‘imaarat Ghamo.n ne Dhaaii hai

(*diidnii*—worth seeing;
shikastagii—defeat;
‘imaarat—building, edifice)

The fall of this heart is indeed
a fall to witness;
What an edifice have the pains
pulled down to nothingness

The heart holds a prime position in the hierarchy of the body but more importantly, in the domains of living, loving and surviving with passion. It can, however, be hurt easily and even left in despair. The speaker compares it to an edifice that has fallen due to the onslaught of pain, which left the speaker bereaved at its fall.

The following inferences of this verse should also be noted: (a) for the speaker, heart's palpitation announces life; its seizure announces death (b) the poetic persona has kept it well with care and saved it from all onslaughts in the multiple affairs of love and life (c) despite its susceptibility to breaking easily, it has been a house of energy and virility for him (d) as such, the heart for him is a grand edifice that needs protection, failing which it would present a pathetic site of a devastating fall (e) the fall of heart which is too small is the fall of a world that is too big to bear for him, which also brings pain to the onlookers and deprives them of their inner vitality.

The two lines of this verse work in a close logical sequence. The first line pre-empts the second line in presenting the scene of a grand edifice's fall, and the second line, which strikes a note of mixed wonder and sorrow with—*kyaa 'imaarat Ghamo.n ne Dhaaii hai* (what an edifice have the pains pulled down)—provides the reason for the fall. Mir maintains this pain of loss in another verse as well: *nahii.n taaza dil kii shikastagii yehii dard thaa yehii KHastagii / ise jab se zauq-e shikaar thaa ise zaKHm se sarokaar thaa.*

Ghazal 1047 | Verse 11

137

مرگ مجنوں سے عقل گم ہے میرؔ
کیا دوانے نے موت پائی ہے

मर्ग-ए मजनूँ से अक़्ल गुम है 'मीर'
क्या दिवाने ने मौत पाई है

marg-e Majnuu.n se 'aql gum hai Mir
kyaa divaane ne maut paaii hai

(*marg-e Majnuu.n*—*Majnuu.n*'s death)

Senses are at a loss to make sense of
the loss of *Majnuu.n*;
What a death has the wild one got,
known as *Majnuu.n*

Death has to kiss every mortal being, but every death does not leave us with shock or surprise. *Majnuu.n* serves here as an institution, a figure of loss and an epitome of the grand tradition of sacrifice. In remembering him, the speaker reiterates the value of a mythic figure of love who only experienced longing in life and loss in death.

We might deliberate further: (a) the speaker does not reveal any reasons, but he suggests that *Majnuu.n*'s death has left his wisdom challenged and his wits at its end (b) as *Majnuu.n* epitomized his name, the speaker implies that his death is the death of the institution of love (c) further, in calling *Majnuu.n* a *divaana* who had long lost his identity as Qais and got mythicized as *Majnuu.n*, the speaker clearly expresses his admiration for him with his gesture of wonder mixed with a sense of shock (d) the speaker also sounds overawed even as he cannot stop from admiring him for pursuing his life's passion and losing his life in that pursuit (e) it is also a prized death for him although he is utterly surprised which takes one to wonder how both of them command respect.

There are three key words—*'aql* (wisdom), *Majnuu.n* (wild lover incarnate) and *divaana* (wild person literally)—which constitute the verse's thematic kernel. These three create a condition for the verse and develop an aura of wonder that is hard to believe otherwise. There are frequent references to *Majnuu.n* in Mir. Two verses that come close to this verse may be read with pleasure: *barso.n se Mir maatam Majnuu.n hai dasht mei.n / rota hai aa ke abr-e siyah is taraf hanuuz* and *Majnuu.n na dasht mei.n hai na Farhaad koh mei.n / thaa jis se lutf-e zindagii ve yaar mar gae.*

Ghazal 1050 | Verse 5

138

ہم طور عشق سے تو واقف نہیں ہیں لیکن
سینے میں جیسے کوئی دل کو ملا کرے ہے

हम तौर-ए इश्क़ से तो वाक़िफ़ नहीं हैं लेकिन
सीने में जैसे कोई दिल को मला करे है

ham taur-e 'ishq se to vaaqif nahii.n hai.n lekin
siine mei.n jaise koii dil ko malaa kare hai

(*taur-e 'ishq*—manners of love)

I know not the ways of love,
but this I do know;
Someone rubs my heart from within
my chest as though

One of the greatest philosophers of love among the canonical Urdu poets across ages, Mir makes his speaker reveal an open secret about love. He pretends that he does not know the ways of love; he only knows that someone seemingly scours his heart, which is a painful experience for him, and he can only suffer it intensely—which is the way he feels love, perhaps.

The verse draws our attention for its experiential richness and artistic representation: (a) the speaker makes an assertion in the first line that he knows nothing about the ways of love and loving, but curiously enough, he inverts this idea in the second line (b) he identifies an entirely new perspective on love and defines it as a silent way of sustaining a constant rubbing of his heart within his chest (c) love to him thus becomes a condition which is deeply internalized (d) it is a condition of being, an amorphous state of existence, in which he realizes the mysterious presence of someone who acquaints him with a sensation of love as a constant source of suffering without relief.

The art of this verse can best be appreciated in terms of how Mir turns it into a felt thought. He imparts concrescence to an experience of suffering as each word is put together like a bead in the garland in the second line—*siine mei.n jaise koii dil ko malaa kare hai* (someone rubs my heart within my chest, as though). This is one of the finest examples of portraying the abstract feeling of pain as a reality. A similar reonstruction of this idea may be seen again in another verse of Mir: *kis Gham mei.n mujh ko yaa rab ye mubtala kiyaa hai / dil saarii raat jaise koii malaa kiyaa hai.*

Ghazal 1052 | Verse 7

139

شعر میرے ہیں سب خواص پسند
پر مجھے گفتگو عوام سے ہے

शेर मेरे हैं सब ख़वास-पसंद
पर मुझे गुफ़्तुगू अवाम से है

sh'er mere hai.n sab KHavaas pasand
per mujhe guftuguu 'avaam se hai

(*KHavaas pasand*—something liked by the elite)

The elites love all my verses,
my verses all
But I converse most freely with the
common folks all

Poets write what lies within them, but they also know what their readers like to read. Here is Mir's plain statement on his poetics and his admirers. In this verse, he identifies his intended readership and establishes a rewarding relationship with them.

Further readings of this verse afford us more significant insights into it: (a) the poet's awareness of two kinds of readerships speaks of his discriminating taste (b) in prioritizing the common reader over the elite one, he defines poetry as secular speech (c) as he projects his stance as a critically informed poet, he leaves us wondering if poetry can ever be written to cater to a particular class of readers and if the ordinary readers are valued more than the elite readers (d) genuine poetry discovers its readership, and it stands on its own (e) he assigns the role of a people's poet to himself which implies that the common man may appreciate him better those in the elite class.

The class of readership in this verse is marked with the phrases—*KHavaas* (elite) and *'avaam* (commoner). A simple monosyllabic word—*per* (but) is crucially important. It is well-placed in the second line to distinguish the elite from the ordinary and expresses his personal choice of readership. Mir finds an ironic way to express his sentiments towards the elite in the following verse: *jaisi 'izzat mire diivaa.n mei.n amiiro.n kii huii / vaisii hii un kii bhii hogii mire divaan ke biich.*

Ghazal 1052 | Verse 8

140

شیطنت سے نہیں ہے خالی شیخ
اس کی پیدائش احتلام سے ہے

शैतनत से नहीं है ख़ाली शैख़
उस की पैदाइश एहतेलाम से है

shaiṭanat se nahii.n hai KHaalii sheiKH
us kii paidaaish ihtilaam se hai

(*shaitanat*—evil-doing;
ihtilaam—male nocturnal emmision)

The *sheiKH* is not wholly without satanic acts
He is born of wet dreams, nocturnal acts

Poets alone have had the privilege of being irreverent. They can be corrosive with their words and derisive with their comments like no other. Here is a fine example of a poet aiming once again at the much-maligned *sheiKH*, the guard of faith, with all his strength.

The institution of *sheiKH*, known for its dualities and falsities, is explored here afresh: (a) he is painted as one embodying Satan whose prime concern is to waylay men and bring them to disaster (b) being born of a nocturnal emission, he is only a preposterous being (c) born of the sperm ejaculated in a dream without actual copulation with a female partner, he is only a false entity (d) this rejection of the *sheiKH* is the rejection of the institution of sheikhdom, assiduously iconized and religiously followed by the common folk.

This verse exemplifies personification that adds value to its artistic merit. More than a person, the *sheiKH* is presented as an embodiment of vices. The spirit of hatred against him and his rejection is strongly represented in the second line—*us kii paidaaish ihtilaam se hai* (he is born of wet dreams, nocturnal acts)—even while he is portrayed in the first line as one, not empty of evil acts—*shaitanat se nahii.n hai KHaalii sheiKH* (the *sheiKH* is not wholly without satanic acts).

Ghazal 1052 | Verse 10

141

سہل ہے میرؔ کا سمجھنا کیا
ہر سخن اس کا اک مقام سے ہے

सहल है 'मीर' का समझना क्या
हर सुख़न इस का इक मक़ाम से है

sahl hai Mir kaa samajnaa kyaa
har suKHan us kaa ik maqaam se hai

(*suKHan*—word, saying;
maqaam—state, status, station)

Is it easy to comprehend Mir; is it easy?
Each verse hails from a high station; it isn't easy

Creative artists, in general, and poets, in particular, have always had a desire to be appreciated favourably. These desires are sometimes expressed openly but are often held secretly in the heart. Mir speaks directly to us here and places himself on the highest pedestal regarding his poetic output.

By assigning a high status to himself as a poet, Mir makes multiple points about himself: (a) mentioning his extraordinary status, he draws our attention to artistic aspects and defines his rank in the hierarchy of poets (b) he does not run down other poets; instead he underlines with confident humility the significance of his own poetry in critical terms (c) in asking if it is easy to understand him, he underlines the rich complexity of his poetry (d) he does not eulogize his work in parts, but as a whole, being an aesthete who refined language, developed a poetic diction and configured poetry as a heightened speech for representing everyday experiences.

The verse can be read simultaneously in both the poet's voice and the reader's voice. The first line projects a question—*sahl hai Mir kaa samajhnaa kyaa* (is it easy to comprehend Mir?), and the second line suggests an answer—*har suKHan us kaa ik maqaam se hai* (each verse hails from a high station). It should be easy to note that the word *sahl*, meaning 'easy', also conveys an implied meaning of 'complex'. Furthermore, the importance of his poetry is distinctly qualified by the adjective *maqaam,* which carries multiple meanings, including place, status, rank, station and hierarchy. Interestingly, this word is also used to define the status of Sufis, which qualifies Mir as one of them in this verse. Mir plays on this idea differently in another verse: *dil aur 'arsh dono.n pe goyaa hai un kii sair / karte hai.n baatei.n Mir ji kis kis maqaam se.*

Ghazal 1054 | Verse 1

142

عبرت سے دیکھ جس جا یاں کوئی گھر بنے ہے
پردے میں چشم ڈھکنے دیوار و در بنے ہے

'इबरत से देख जिस जा याँ कोई घर बने है
पर्दे में चश्म ढकने दीवार-ओ-दर बने है

'ibrat se dekh jis jaa yaa.n koii ghar bane hai
parde mei.n chashm Dhakne diivaar-o dar bane hai

(*'ibrat*—lesson;
chashm—eye)

When a house is made here,
look at the house and learn;
Walls and doors are made
to veil the eyes so you learn

Perspectives make all the difference in how we look at an object. This verse reflects on this idea and suggests, through the example of a house, that it is not made for habitation but to keep the eyes in the veil with the help of doors and walls.

This verse presents an entirely fresh perspective on the philosophy of human habitation. It makes unique suggestions: (a) the idea of making a house is mundane because it only reflects one's worldly desire (b) houses are temporal, illusory and false reflections of man's desire and status (c) living within the walls of a house, one is separated from the world outside even though the windows offer a view, but only partially (d) a house is therefore only a veil to save the sanctity of eyes that hold a far greater status in the hierarchy of human body and have the capacity to see the immediate and visualize the remote.

Two words—*'ibrat* (lesson) and *chashm* (eye)—are the key words in this verse. The first line invites the viewer to look at a house and seek a lesson. Still, the second line elevates the act of seeing to a greater height, where the eyes that see must be duly protected with a veil because the all-seeing eyes are more precious than a house made of dead material, such as brick and mortar. Muneer Niazi has revisited this idea of seeking a lesson from the worldly habitat in a different but meaningful frame: *aa.nkho.n mei.n uR rahii hai lutii mehfilo.n kii dhuul / 'ibrat-saraae dahr hai aur ham hai.n dosto.*

DIIVAAN 3

Ghazal 1058 | Verse 7

143

بشرے کی اپنے رونق اے میرؔ عارضی ہے
جب دل کو خوں کیا تو چہرے پہ رنگ آیا

बुशरे की अपने रौनक़ ऐ 'मीर' आरज़ी है
जब दिल को ख़ूँ किया तो चेहरे पे रंग आया

bushre kii apne raunaq ai Mir 'aarzii hai
jab dil ko Khuu.n kiyaa to chehre pe rang aayaa

(*bushra*—countenance, face;
'*aarzii*—ephemeral, temporary)

This glow on my face, Mir,
is only a passing one;
It was when I bloodied my heart,
that this red was won

Human countenance does not always remain the same; it varies with the internal season a person carries within him and the surrounding environment of his physical existence. Mir unassumingly states that his face's glow is only transitory. The more critical idea he shares is that his face got its natural hue and spark only when he shed his heart's blood.

What Mir intends to say has deeper insinuations: (a) a face is a face only if it has a distinguishing glow (b) there is a distinction between the acquired glow that is fake and natural glow that is genuine (c) the fake glow is transient not only for the viewer but also for those who bear that face (d) the natural glow is deep-rooted; it shows its distinct hue only when the heart's blood is shed, which implies that the heart too pays for getting that colourful countenance (e) the speaker may be sharing this with his alter ego or with an attentive addressee (f) the verse also seems to address the question of aesthetics regarding genuine and fake art.

Mir employs two corresponding words—*raunaq* (glow) and *rang* (colour)—for two different impacts and puts a premium on *raunaq* over *rang* for the depth of meaning it embodies. This choice of words acquires a more significant layer of meaning in—*Khuu.n* (blood)—which refers to the heart's blood. Therefore, the redness of the heart's blood shows up brightly on the face, which excels *raunaq*. Sarwat Hussain, a modernist poet, configures the genuineness of a face in inimitable terms in a verse that reflects obliquely upon Mir: *paao.n saakit ho gae Sarwat kisii ko dekh kar / ik kashish mehtaab jaisii chehra-i dilbar mei.n thii.*

Ghazal 1086 | Verse 2

144

تحقیق کروں کس سے حقیقت کے نشے کو
خضر آب اسے کہتا ہے آتش کہے موسیٰ

तहक़ीक़ करूँ किस से हक़ीक़त के नशे को
ख़िज़्र आब उसे कहता है आतिश कहे मूसा

tehqiiq karuu.n kis se haqiiqat ke nashe ko
Khizr aab usey kahtaa hai aatish kahe Musa

(*tehqiiq*—confirm, ascertain, research;
haqiiqat—reality)

With whom do I confirm
the intoxication of the real;
Khizr says it is water, Musa says
the fire alone is real

The phenomenon called the cosmos is a riddle. Its realities manifest themselves through the elements. Khizr and Musa, known for their prowess, have experienced the intoxication of reality through water and fire, respectively, and visualized the reality only through those elements.

The answer to this riddle brings the religious and the philosophical angles to the fore: (a) the tug between illusion and reality and discourses around those underline the multiplicities of the visible phenomenon (b) the search for reality can be as intoxicating as is the vision of the reality which rarely unveils itself (c) reality lies hidden in the elements of the earth and the air which are terrestrial, as well as water and fire which are antithetical to each other, but storehouses of energy anyway (d) despite all his extraordinary reach at different levels, man's inability to decode and decipher any of these to discover the reality only underlines his limited potential (e) the quest remains ongoing and endless which makes the speaker ask if Khizr could unveil reality as he had drunk the water of life and could show the path to the seekers of destination or Musa who could visualize the real in the flashes of lightening on mount Sinai.

The spirit of this quest is reflected in the phrase—*tahqiiq* (ascertain)—which qualifies the seeker of the answer. Thematically, the intoxication to explore reality is evident in the first line, for which a paradigmatic answer is proposed in the second line. Qayam Chandpuri reflects upon this dichotomy of the real and the unreal, which may be appreciated as a gloss over Mir: *us ko na raast kah tuu na us ko bataa Ghalat / kyaa jaane kyaa sahih hai vaaqa'e mei.n kyaa Ghalat.*

Ghazal 1088 | Verse 9

145

کیا تم کو پیار سے وہ اے میرؔ منہ لگاوے
پہلے ہی چومے تم تو کاٹو ہو گال اس کا

क्या तुम को प्यार से वो ऐ 'मीर' मुँह लगावे
पहले ही चूमे तुम तो काटो हो गाल उस का

kyaa tum ko pyar se vo ai Mir mu.nh lagaave
pehle hii chume tum to kaato ho gaal us kaa

How can she share her love with you, O Mir
In the very first kiss, you bite her cheek, O Mir

Love and lust are common themes in the ghazal tradition. In a lighter vein, the lover in this verse is frankly told that his beloved will not yield to him since he has shown his overpowering lust in his very first kiss by biting her cheek.

Even if the verse is light-hearted, it makes exciting suggestions: (a) there is a thin line between love and lust, but all lovers cannot control themselves and often cross the line and express their lust when they mean to express the former emotion (b) lust is a subliminal act on the part of the lover, but it is so overpowering that it may deter the beloved from getting close to the lover (c) biting the cheek is an expression of his brimming lust that is usually associated with male lovers (d) loving can be as playful and pleasurable as lusting, and together they write the story of the lover and the beloved.

The verse is conversational in tone and idiomatic in expression, just as its mood demands. The first line is a kind advice mixed with a reprimand from a keen observer to the lover. The second line's idiomatic turn in the phrase *pehle hii chuume* (in the very first kiss) adds an edge to his words and imparts a biting touch to the verse. *Gaal kaatnaa* (biting the cheek) is a proverb for loving mischievously, even if it hurts the beloved. Yagana Changezi puts this experience lightly in his verse: *pahle hii chuume gaal kaat liyaa / ibtidaa ye to intihaa kyaa hai.*

Ghazal 1091 | Verse 1

146

بوسہ اس بت کا لے کے منہ موڑا
بھاری پتھر تھا چوم کر چھوڑا

बोसा उस बुत का ले के मुँह मोड़ा
भारी पत्थर था चूम कर छोड़ा

bosa us but ka le ke mun.h moRaa
bhaarii patthar thaa chuum kar chhoRaa

(*bosa*—kiss)

I kissed that idol
and turned my face away;
She was a heavy stone I kissed
before I walked away

When determined lovers succeed in their tactics, they take pride in their success. The lover here is one who intended to kiss an unyielding beloved but could not for long. Finally, when he succeeded and kissed her, he felt proud and chose to share his success story.

Other than being a naughty declaration of the lover's success, the verse has some other interesting aspects to it: (a) in the determination to kiss an unyielding beloved, there is also a will on the lover's part to take revenge for her coldness, which is happily realized (b) supposedly, the beloved is hard as a stone, which makes her look literally like a statute or an idol (c) the beloved seems to have been defeated and suffered a loss in the game of love, when the lover kisses her (e) this is indeed a unique moment in the story of the proud lover and makes the verse both animated and expressive.

The beloved is often likened to a statue in the ghazal tradition. It turns acutely meaningful in this verse as it portrays her as stubbornly rigid. The metaphor of a stone, as expressed in—*bhaarii patthar thaa chuum kar chhoRaa* (she was a heavy stone, I didn't spare her, I kissed her)—also configures her status further, even as it reflects the lover's sense of determination.

Ghazal 1093 | Verse 1

147

دل عجب چرچے کی جا گا تھی سو ویرانہ ہوا
جوشِ غم سے جی جو بولایا سو دیوانہ ہوا

दिल अजब चर्चे की जागा थी सो वीराना हुआ
जोश-ए ग़म से जी जो बौलाया सो दीवाना हुआ

dil 'ajab charche kii jaagaa thii so viiraana huaa
josh-e Gham se jii jo baulayaa so divaana huaa

(*jaagaa*—place;
josh-e Gham—abundance of sorrow/pain/grief)

This heart was once a favoured site for chatter,
but it turned into a wilderness,
When it turned crazy with plentiful pain,
it became a home of madness

In the ghazal tradition, a lover's heart is a highly revered and also a deeply mourned subject. In this verse, the speaker celebrates it as a prized repository of desires but submits that it turned into a wilderness when subjected to excessive pain and suffering. The two states of the heart drive the speaker to reflect on it ruefully.

The underpinnings of this verse are worth noticing further: (a) a lover's heart in a state of joy reflects him in his happiest state, but that is not a permanent state of being for him (b) suffering, being an inevitable part of the lover's saga, has made him crazy (c) the alternating rhythms of lovers' lives define the nature of love and heart that are unstable (d) love life is marked necessarily by both pleasure and pain just like human destiny that is characterized by the two phases of gain and loss.

The sense of praise blended with pleasant wonder for the heart is conveyed in the clause—*dil 'ajab charche kii jaagaa thii* (heart was once a favoured site for chatter)—but the following clause—*so virrana huaa* (it turned into wilderness)—brings it to an anticlimax. The second line serves as a sequel where the first clause—*josh-e Gham se jii jo baulaayaa* (when it turned crazy with plentiful pain) prepares for the resultant sequence—*so divaana huaa* (it became a home of madness). Reading this verse with two clauses in both lines should be rewarding. The wilderness of the heart, as represented in a verse by Ahmad Faraz, is worth referring to in the context of Mir's verse: *ai mire abr-e karam dekh ye viiraana-i jaa.n / kyaa kisii dasht pe tuu ne kabhii baarish nahii.n kii.*

Ghazal 1094 | Verse 8

148

اس گل تر کی قبا کے کہیں کھولے تھے بند
رنگوں گلبرگ کے ناخن ہے معطر اپنا

उस गुल-ए तर की क़बा के कहीं खोले थे बंद
रंगों गुल-बर्ग के नाख़ुन है मोअ'त्तर अपना

us gul-e tar kii qaba ke kahii.n khole the band
rango.n gulbarg ke naaKHun hai mu'attar apnaa

(*gul-e tar*—precious beauty;
qabaa—apparel;
gulbarg—garden;
mu'attar—fragrant)

I had untied the knots of that precious
beauty's apparel, then,
Like the garden's myriad hues
my nails are fragrant till now, as then

The ways of praising the beloved and her apparel are rich and varied in the ghazal tradition. This lover appears close enough to his beloved and has the liberty of untying the knots of her apparel. This brings him to the realization of a different pleasure as his nails retain the fragrance of her apparel and please him.

This verse of enduring beauty may be read more deeply by mining its extended meanings: (a) the beloved is a paragon of beauty and this brings him to experience an entirely different kind of pleasure when he realizes that his nails carry the fragrance of her apparel (b) as the beloved wore her apparel, the apparel reflected the radiance of her body (c) being in love with such a beauteous being is akin to experiencing an aesthetic pleasure for this lover (d) he finds himself doubly fulfilled; once for the chance of untying the knots with his nails and then for seeking the pleasure of carrying her fragrance with him embedded in them.

The verse is remarkable for its acute, sensual quality and vividness. The transference of one quality into another, known as a synaesthetic process, enriches it further. While the beloved is defined as *gul-e tar* (precious beauty), she is further qualified as *gulbarg* (garden), a complete garden unto herself. The following verse by the modernist poet Rajendra Manchanda Bani can be read to appreciate how the resourceful lover approaches the precious beauty for his own gain: *ik gul-e tar bhii sharar se niklaa / bas-ke har kaam hunar se niklaa.*

Ghazal 1109 | Verse 2

149

پھرتی ہے اڑی خاک بھی مشتاق کسو کی
سر مار کے کرتا ہے پہاڑوں میں بسر آب

फिरती है उड़ी ख़ाक भी मुश्ताक़ किसू की
सर मार के करता है पहाड़ों में बसर आब

phirtii hai uRi KHaak bhii mushtaaq kisuu kii
sar maar ke kartaa hai pahaRo.n mei.n basar aab

(*KHaak*—dust, soil;
mushtaaq—curious, inquisitive;
basar—accomplish, execute;
aab—water)

Eager to see someone,
the dust keeps flying all around;
Water beats its head against the foothills,
and flows all around

The speaker in this verse visualizes the wind blowing all around as a curious seeker for someone or some object. This is just like the water that beats against the unmoving rocks, and seeing no passage further for itself, it ultimately settles down with them for good.

The verse is decidedly philosophical in its intent and conveys multiple meanings: (a) nature is in a constant state of meeting a mission where its different incarnations like dust, mountains and water keep exploring their respective paths (b) while dust represents the earth below, the mountain represents the astounding heights divinely incarnated over the earth, and water the seeker of a passage through the mountains (c) that which was materially present once has turned to dust and the clouds of dust move around tracing those lost or left behind (d) this dust could be a personification of the man himself who lived once in a physical form but is turned into dust now (e) the dust, perennially associated with wilderness, keeps flying and water crashing against the foothills—the seeker of love or truth is generally associated with both (f) being essentially a verse representing the cycles of nature, it unfolds the essential meaning of existence and perishing.

Constructed around the words and images of *KHaak* (dust), *pahaaR* (mountains), and *aab* (water), this verse unravels the philosophy of existence in states of mutation. The sense of continuous quest by these elements of nature that results in futility is richly picturized in two clauses—*phirtii hai uRii KHaak* (the dust keeps flying all around) and *sar maar ke kartaa hai basar* (beating its head, it keeps surviving). The play of *sar* (head) against *basar* (survive) is equally remarkable, as it portrays life as an act of beating one's head against rigid objects.

Ghazal 1112 | Verse 2

150

مت ان نمازیوں کو خانہ ساز دیں جانو
کہ ایک اینٹ کی خاطر یہ ڈھاتے ہیں گے مسیت

मत इन नमाज़ियों को ख़ाना-साज़-ए दीं जानो
कि एक ईंट की ख़ातिर ये ढाते हैंगे मसीत

mat in namaaziyo.n ko KHaana saaz-e dii.n jaano
ke ek iint kii KHaatir ye Dhate hai.nge masiit

(*KHana-saaz-e dii.n*—makers of the house of faith;
masiit—mosque)

Don't think of these men as praying
for faith's sake;
They demolish whole mosques
for a single brick's sake

Appearances can be deceptive sometimes. This verse meditates on the dichotomous relationship between the idea of appearance and reality. It illustrates the example of such individuals who appear to be praying to God but are fake and preposterous in real life. They, indeed, are the ones who can sacrifice more incredible things to gain a petty advantage.

This rejection of fake persons and their fake postures conveys that: (a) despite being empowered and enabled, human beings fail to perform their duties (b) this is truer of the hypocritical people who appear virtuous but indeed defy virtuosity (c) paradoxically, people of religious leanings and practices are sometimes far more susceptible to irrationality and sinful indulgences (d) the roles we assign to people in a social structure can be ill-informed (e) a liberal view of life helps make critical distinctions and act proportionately.

There is an element of irony in the first line. It also warns those who judge things at face value and are pitiably misled. The second line emerges as a corrosive attack on those who lose far more than they gain because they are too constricted in their approach. The phrase—*KHaana-saaz-e dii.n* (makers of the house of faith)—is sarcastic at its core and contributes immensely to the richness of the verse. Mir executes this idea yet again in another verse: *KHaana-saaz-e dii.n jo hai vaa'iz so ye KHaana-KHaraab / iint kii KHaatir jise masjid ko Dhaayaa chaahiye.*

Ghazal 1125 | Verse 11

151

دھوتے ہیں اشکِ خونی سے دست و دہن کو میرؔ
طور نماز کیا ہے جو یہ ہے وضو کی طرح

धोते हैं अश्क-ए ख़ूनी से दस्त-ओ-दहन को 'मीर'
तौर-ए नमाज़ क्या है जो ये है वुज़ू की तरह

dhote hai.n ashk-e KHuunii se dast-o dahan ko Mir
taur-e namaaz kyaa hai jo hai ye vuzuu ki tar'ha

(*ashk-e KHuunii*—tears of blood;
dast-o dahan—hand and mouth;
vuzuu—ablution performed before saying prayers)

Mir washes his hands and mouth
with the tears of blood for resolution;
What's the method of honest prayer,
if this be the way of ablution

The idea of washing oneself with blood has had relative implications in different texts and contexts. This verse, however, reflects upon the speaker, who has taken pains to live an uneasy life, but all his efforts have fallen short and failed to bring him to a point of resolution.

The verse is not essentially about religious prayers and the methods of its offering as it might appear on the surface; it takes us in a different direction to reflect upon the speaker's condition: (a) living life is akin to offering prayers as life is as holy as prayer itself (b) ablution needs water to prepare for praying to God, but life demands shedding tears of blood to live it (c) the speaker has made all efforts to meet his ends and metaphorically washed his hands and mouth with blood-like tears, but failed to live his life well (d) he wonders, therefore, that if the first stage of making an ablution is so challenging, then the subsequent stage of the actual offering of prayer would be unimaginably more arduous and well-nigh impossible to sustain (e) this implies that preparing to live a life is a blood-sucking experience and the travails of an actual living of life are simply unimaginable (f) this also implies that if ablution to prepare for prayers needs washing with blood, the actual prayer in religious terms would be much more demanding where sinners are destined to fail (g) it is to be kept in mind that with blood oozing from any part of the body, prayers cannot be offered, but here it is only a metaphoric way of portraying pain.

The acts of *namaaz* (prayer) and *vuzuu* (ablution) are essentially religious rituals. Still, they serve here as metaphors for the two stages of living—first, the act of preparing to live, and second, living it in actual terms. The speaker's exasperation is richly reflected in the second line—*taur-e namaaz kyaa hai jo hai ye vuzuu ki tar'ha* (what's the method of real prayer if that be the way of ablution?) Mir reminds us of another verse for an extended comparison of metaphors employed: *vo dil nahii.n rahaa hai ta 'ab jo uThaaegaa / yaa lohuu ashk-e KHuunii se mu.nh per bahaaega.*

Ghazal 1160 | Verse 2

152

کیا کوئی اس کے رنگوں گل باغ میں کھلا ہے
شور آج بلبلوں کا جاتا ہے آسماں تک

क्या कोई उस के रंगों गुल बाग़ में खिला है
शोर आज बुलबुलों का जाता है आसमाँ तक

kyaa koii us ke rango.n gul baaGh me.in khilaa hai
shor aaj bulbulo.n kaa jaataa hai aasmaa.n tak

Has a blossom unfurled in her colours
in the garden today;
The clamours of bulbuls reach up to
the high skies today

As we have encountered in many verses so far, the bulbul and the blossom are two of the stock symbols in Urdu poetry, especially in the ghazal tradition. The bulbul is known for loving the blossom and even shedding its life for the blossom. This verse is developed around this idea. The speaker asks if a new blossom has appeared in the garden that the bulbul's calls—inspired by joy—reach the heights of the sky.

What are the implications of the blossom showing up and the bulbul's call, one may wonder: (a) the blossom bears the same colour as that of the bulbul, so the bulbul's clamour reaches up the sky in celebration of its beauty (b) the ebullience of the colour and the clamour are akin to each other which makes the bulbul cheerful (c) while the garden represents the earthly beauty, the sky represents the divine beauty, and the two correspond with each other (d) the love of both the bulbul and the blossom is as pure as those of the earthly garden and the heavenly sky.

The verse seems to pose a question, but it strikes us more as a wonder and a surprise than a question. Similarly, the expression *shor* (clamour) does not imply a raucous noise but a welcoming, loud voice of appreciation and praise for the blossom. Mir configures this idea in another verse worthy of attention: *mastaana saath mere rotii phire hai bulbul / gul se jo dil lagaa hai abtar hai haal us kaa.*

Ghazal 1175 | Verse 4

153

وفا صد کارواں رکھتا ہوں لیکن شہر خوبی میں
خریداری نہیں مطلق کہاں جا کر بکاؤں میں

वफ़ा सद-कारवाँ रखता हूँ लेकिन शहर-ए ख़ूबी में
ख़रीदारी नहीं मुतलक़ कहाँ जा कर बिकाऊँ मैं

vafaa sad-kaarvaa.n rakhtaa huu.n lekin shahr-e KHuubii mei.n
KHariidaarii nahii.n mutlaq kahaa.n jaa kar bikauu.n mai.n

(*sad-kaarvaa.n*—a hundred caravans;
KHubii—merit, splendour;
mutlaq—at all)

In this town of splendours, I carry
a hundred caravan-loads of love within myself
But there is no buying here at all,
where shall I go and sell myself

Love is a common human experience but indeed rarely offered or achieved in its truest forms. Those who realize its value are rarer still. The speaker asserts that he carries a load of a hundred caravans of love with him, but there are no takers anywhere. He mourns and wonders if there is a place where he might find someone who would buy the treasure of love he carries with him.

Several ideas go together with this verse: (a) even precious emotions like love are wasted if not received and valued (b) a city of all splendours is no city if it does not have space for love in it (c) ironically, one who has loads of love to make himself rich is indeed impoverished as he has none who could value his treasure of love (d) this love is not merely romantic; it encompasses humane warmth and values that sustain human beings and their world (e) the bearer of love is the image of love himself, but he remains a non-entity in the town of all spectacle and splendour.

The speaker's pride over his possession of love is brought out in the first clause of the first line—*vafaa sad-kaarvaa.n rakhtaaa huu.n* (I carry a hundred caravan-loads of love within myself). This, however, is belied in the first clause of the second line—*KHariiidaarii nahi..n mutlaq* (but there is no buying here at all). His ironic helplessness comes out with greater force in the last clause of the verse, both as an exclamation and a question—*kahaa.n jaa kar bikaau.n mai.n* (where do I go to sell myself). A verse from Ibn-e-Insha is well recalled here: *vahshat-e dil ke KHariidaar bhii na-paid huve / kaun ab 'ishq ke bazaar mei.n kholegaa dukaa.n.*

Ghazal 1185 | Verse 1

154

رفتگاں میں جہاں کے ہم بھی ہیں
ساتھ اس کارواں کے ہم بھی ہیں

रफ़्तगाँ में जहाँ के हम भी हैं
साथ उस कारवाँ के हम भी हैं

raftagaa.n mei.n jahaa.n ke ham bhii hai.n
saath us kaarvaa.n ke ham bhii hai.n

(*raftagaa.n*—those gone by/departed)

Of those who left this world, I too am one
Of that very passing caravan, I too am one

Man's place in this world and the world hereafter are not entirely separated or disconnected from each other. This verse reiterates this idea with a difference, through one who has left this world and joined the caravan of those who have gone before him.

We can interpret this verse more with these ideas in place: (a) those in the caravans have left a habitat behind and are homeless now (b) their traces are left behind which reminds that they have left, but only symbolically (c) their reaching the other world remains un-visualized, and they are yet to reach the other world (d) there is an impending sense of loss in leaving this world which is still tempting, but a retreat to it is against the law of nature (e) it is worth pondering if the speaker is calling out from here or the other world and this ambiguity adds greater value to the verse.

The idiomatic and lexical meanings of *raftagaan* (those gone by) are worth noting, as they refer to those who are entranced, absorbed, or lost in the passages of time. Similarly, the caravan represents the journey motif, and those on the journey represent a visual condition in the first line. This caravan and the traveller are visualized as belonging to this space reflected in the second line—*saath us kaarvaa.n ke ham bhii hai.n* (among that passing caravan, I, too, am one). The sense of pride and pity are carried together in the speaker's admission of his belonging to both that caravan that has gone ahead and this caravan of the world that is left behind. Ahmad Faraz harks back to Mir and develops another perspective in his verse: *ab raftagaa.n kii baat nahii.n kaarvaa.n kii hai / jis simt bhii ho gard-e safar jaanaa chaahiye.*

Ghazal 1193 | Verse 6

155

جہاں سے دیکھیے اک شعر شور انگیز نکلے ہے
قیامت کا سا ہنگامہ ہے ہر جا میرے دیواں میں

जहाँ से देखिए इक शेर-ए शोर-अंगेज़ निकले है
क़यामत का सा हंगामा है हर जा मेरे दीवाँ में

jahaa.n se dekhiye ik sh'er shor-angez nikle hai
qayaamat kaa saa hangaama hai har jaa mere diivaa.n mei.n

(*shor-angez*—clamour-absorbing)

A clamour-absorbing verse rises
from wherever you see;
In my *diivaan* is the din of the doomsday
as you may see

Poets can also be their first critics. Here is a verse where Mir defines the nature of his poetry in precise terms. He postulates that his *diivaan* is a collection of clamour-raising verses. This clamour reminds him of the clamour likely to be heard on the day of doom.

This seemingly straightforward verse offers layered meanings: (a) poetry imitates life, and life is filled with noise (b) the poet bears this clamour in his life and echoes it in his poetry too (c) he has not seen the doomsday yet he can visualize it in terms of the din that is heard in his poetry (d) clamour is heard and experienced in both the worlds here and hereafter, and the poet stands as a witness at both the spheres (e) poetry absorbs sounds, even the clamorous ones, and echoes the sounds of life, as is abundantly found in Mir's poetry.

The verse may be read as a brilliant example of personification. In the first line itself, we come across something that raises a ruckus—*jahaa.n se dekhiye ik sh'er shor-angez nikle hai* (a clamour-absorbing verse rises, wherever you see). This appears as a concrete entity rather than an abstract concept. Three closely corresponding words in particular—*shor* (clamour), *hungaama* (din), and *qayaamat* (doomsday)—create a menacing situation. This verse naturally leads us to another verse of Mir: *agarche gosha-guzii.n huu.n mai.n shaairo.n mei.n Mir / pa mere shor ne ruu-e suKHan tamaam liyaa.*

Ghazal 1194 | Verse 1

156

تھا شوق مجھے طالب دیدار ہوا میں
سو آئنہ سا صورت دیوار ہوا میں

था शौक़ मुझे तालिब-ए दीदार हुआ मैं
सो आइना सा सूरत-ए दीवार हुआ मैं

thaa shauq mujhe taalib-e diidaar huaa mai.n
so aaiina saa suurat-e diivaar huaa mai.n

I passionately longed to see her,
to see her alone
So when she looked, I became still like a mirror,
like a wall, a stone

The world of the beloved can be amazingly inviolable. She remains ensconced there and keeps the lovers curious about her appearance. The lover in this verse has yearned for the beloved's gaze and presently takes a step to reach her. As he reaches out and looks at her, he finds himself in such a state that he cannot move and remains transfixed thereafter.

The two states of the lover's desire and fulfilment make curious suggestions: (a) a lover's desire may meet with success, but success always remains relative (b) the beloved, often configured as statuesque, turns the lover himself into a statue of amazement (c) the beloved's face shows up in the lover's eyes, and the lover gets transfixed at the sight of the beloved before him (d) despite all life and spirit in him, the lover becomes lifeless as a wall (e) the difference between his seeing the beloved, and yet not seeing her, characterizes all three—the lover, the beloved and the wall—as objects of fantasy than reality.

The first line is assertive, but the beauty of the verse lies in the second line. There is a deeper pun in two phrases—*so* (therefore) and *suurat-e diivaar* (like the wall). The second phrase is doubly suggestive, implying 'like the wall' on the one hand and 'the face of the wall itself' on the other. This fine distinction enriches the verse by representing the lover as a living person and an inanimate wall. Mir revisits this idea in another verse as well but with a different metaphoric reconstruction: *kaasa-i-chashm le ke juu.n nargis / ham ne diidaar kii gadaaii kii.*

Ghazal 1205 | Verse 5

157

اب لاغری سے دیں ہیں ساری رگیں دکھائی
پر عشق بھر رہا ہے ایک ایک میری نس میں

अब लाग़री से दें हैं सारी रगें दिखाई
पर इश्क़ भर रहा है एक एक मेरी नस में

ab laaGharii se de.n hai.n saarii ragei.n dikhaaii
per ‘ishq bhar rahaa hai ek ek merii nas mei.n

(*laaGharii*—feebleness, thinness)

I am feeble;
all my veins are visible now;
But this love courses through
all my veins now

Age is no impediment in love. In this verse, the lover acknowledges that even though he is too old now, he continues to long for the beloved. Rather, his situation is empowering him, as each vein in his body is filled with the pure and vibrant spirit of love. However, one wonders if he is thinking of romantic love alone or some other form of love.

The suggestions made in this verse alter our understanding of love in different ways: (a) love is not necessarily romantic, amorous or libidinal, and a lover is not necessarily driven by these impulses (b) love is enabling and ennobling, and it may transform a lover into a spiritualist to whom God is the beloved (c) the intensity of either kind of love varies from one age to another and takes the lover from a mundane stage to the mystical stage (d) tempered by time, a lover can realize the illuminating nature of love unlike others who are still to see the turn of time and age (e) the spirit of love filling each vein of the lover, turns the old lover into a young and zealous lover and helps the lover enjoy the bliss of love in its pure glory.

An irrational idea becomes a substantial poetic material in Mir's verse here. He defines love as an empowering passion in the second line—*per 'ishq bhar rahaa hai ek ek merii nas mei.n* (but love, love courses through my vein now)—where *per* (but) acts as a qualifying phrase to define the lover and his understanding of love. Mir engages with this inexhaustible idea in another verse using corresponding words: *tan-e zard-o laaGhar mei.n zaahir ragei.n hai.n / bharaa hai magar 'ishq ek ek nas mei.n.*

Ghazal 1219 | Verse 6

158

اب کے بہت ہے شور بہاراں ہم کو مت زنجیر کرو
دل کی ہوس ٹک ہم بھی نکالیں دھومیں ہم کو مچانے دو

अब के बहुत है शोर-ए बहाराँ हम को मत ज़ंजीर करो
दिल की हवस टुक हम भी निकालें धूमें हम को मचाने दो

ab ke bahut hai shor-e bahaaraa.n ham ko mat zanjiir karo
dil kii havas tuk ham bhii nikaalei.n dhuumei.n ham ko machaane do

(*bahaaraa.n*—spring;
havas—lust)

It is spring, all around,
do not enchain me now;
Let my heart be filled to the brim
let me go abuzz for now

Spring is the time to revel in the magic of nature. In the Urdu ghazal, lovers have been mythicized as going wild in such a season, but to keep them in control, they are traditionally kept in chains. This lover makes an impassioned plea that he should not be kept enchained and deprived of the spring's bliss this season. He expresses his desire to enjoy this season and shout and dance in ecstasy.

Drawing upon the traditional image of a lover who goes wild, Mir makes intriguing suggestions about this lover: (a) he is a lover of his kind because he can go wild, unlike others, and seek his blissful freedom (b) being wild is a boon for him, but it is a bane for others (c) his association with spring speaks of his lust for life's ecstasies and liberties (d) the lover and his beloved signify together the spirit of freedom and the ecstasy of spring in human terms (e) his impassioned plea is directed to the constraining agents of life who see life in mundane manners (f) this year's springtime is far more inviting, which is why he has been chained, but he negates that imprisonment with his plea.

This verse is a fine example of a wild lover's imagination. He speaks in a language marked by the tone of entreaty, using it to make his plea. The set of expressions—*bahaaraa.n* (spring), *zanjiir* (chain), *havas* (lust), and *dhuum* (buzz)—together develop the mood for the verse and portray a condition that projects a dramatic plot with the lover as a protagonist. The phrase—*shor-e bahaaraa.n* (buzz of springtime)—has two implications: buzz about the springtime and the springtime raising its voice of passion. Mir's verse comes very close to Mohammad Aman Nisar's verse: *hamaaraa haath mat pakRo bahaar aaii hai jaane do / garebaa.n kii hamei.n ab dhajjiyaa.n yaro uRaane do.*

Ghazal 1220 |Verse 7

159

خال سیاہ و خط سیاہ ایمان و دل کے رہزن تھے
اک مدت میں ہم نے بارے چوٹٹے یہ پہچانے دو

ख़ाल-ए सियाह ओ ख़त्त-ए सियाह ईमान-ओ-दिल के रहज़न थे
इक मुद्दत में हम ने बारे चोट्टे ये पहचाने दो

KHaal siyaah o KHatt-e siyaah iimaan-o dil ke rahzan the
ik muddat mei.n ham ne baare chotte ye pehchaane do

(*KHaal*—dimple;
KHatt—curve;
rahzan—looters;
chotte—mean, smalltime thief)

These dark dimples, these dark curves,
the looters of heart and faith—two together;
It took me ages to know them both,
that they were the thieves—two together

Sometimes, lovers describe and identify their beloveds playfully. The lover here does precisely this when he defines her with her dark dimple curves. He adores her for these distinguishing marks but naughtily calls them names as he has become a helpless prey to those enticing marks.

We can draw the following inferences too: (a) lovely ladies do not loot the heart alone; they impoverish the lovers of their faith too (b) lovers are also known, otherwise, for being farther away from the matters of faith (c) this lover is complaining, but he also seems to be paying a backhanded compliment to the beloved (d) the lover feels emotionally enriched even if he is robbed of his faith.

The two markers of the beloved's face—*KHaal* (dimple) and *KHatt* (curve)—are the typical markers of beauty for which the beloveds are profusely celebrated in subcontinental poetry. The lover's infatuation with his lady emerges with a seemingly abusive address—*chotte* (looters)—which turns into an address of endearment. This entirely new way of describing the beloved has a ring of both playfulness and mischievousness. Mir extends the idea of this verse in another verse as well: *dar-pae dil hii rahe us chehre ke KHaal-e siyaah / Dar hamein un chotto.n kaa roz-e raushan mei.n rahaa.*

Ghazal 1243 | Verse 5

160

ہیں مسلمان ان بتوں سے ہمیں
عشق ہے لا الہ الا اللہ

हैं मुसलमान उन बुतों से हमें
'इश्क़ है ला-इलाहा-इल्लल्लाह

hai.n musalmaan un buto.n se hame.in
'ishq hai laa ilaah illallaah

(*but*—statue, idol;
laa ilaah illallaah—there is no God except one God)

I'm a Musalmaan,
Yet an idol I love;
There is no God
except love

The proclaimer of love is also a proclaimer of a religious faith, but they do not contradict each other. The lover is the speaker here who proclaims that he is a lover because he has some idols before him to love and adore, although they are physical embodiments of flesh and blood, unlike the idols cast in stone that one worships as a matter of one's faith. He is then reminded that love is loving one idol only and making that idol the cynosure of one's life.

Marked by an apparent dichotomy, this verse opens up exciting avenues of meaning: (a) there is no dichotomy between being a Muslim and being a lover as both imagine and proclaim one God—one being of flesh and blood and the other being divine (b) a Muslim's proclamation of faith lies in the first *kalima* (proclamation of the Islamic faith) which says there is no God except one God, but for the lover this God has two forms (c) imaging the beloved—one of flesh and blood—as a God does not turn him into a heretic, but it only reiterates his faith in the earthly idol (beloved) created by the divine power known as God (d) even though the beloved in the ghazal tradition is treated as an idol and idol worship is prohibited in Islam, he sees the image of the divine in the earthly (e) an antithetical position does not necessarily deny either of these two gods but redefines them in a liberal perspective (f) the claim to be a lover of idols and to support that claim with the *kalima* verges on the lover's mischievousness and audacity.

The element of antithesis in this verse is built upon two key words—*Musalmaan* (follower of Islamic faith) and *but* (idol). The meaning of the verse lies in the resolution of the antithetical position. While both the lines of the verse are assertive, the second line is more emphatic and is heard more as a chant than a mute statement. Insha Allah Khan plays upon the key Islamic proclamation like Mir and comes up with this verse: *Kahuu.n ba-qaid-e qasam La Ilaah Illallaah / ke taab-e hijr bas ab mujh mei.n ai Ilaah nahii.n.*

Ghazal 1252 | Verse 4

161

گھر دل کا بہت چھوٹا پر جائے تعجب ہے
عالم کو تمام اس میں کس طرح ہے گنجائی

घर दिल का बहुत छोटा पर जा-ए तअ'ज्जुब है
आलम को तमाम इस में किस तरह है गुंजाई

ghar dil kaa bahut chhota per jaai ta'ajjub hai
'aalam ko tamaam is mei.n kis tar'ha hai gunjaaii

(*jaai ta'ajjub*—occasion for surprise/wonder;
gunjaaii—the ability to contain)

The heart's chamber is too small
but a place of wonder;
How is the whole world contained there,
that too is a wonder

The heart is a small entity but unimaginably rich in its ability to store the vast ideas of the world in its chambers. The speaker wonders how a small heart can encompass all that the world has, and indeed be a world unto its own. He questions this with wonder but finds no answer.

We can read the verse further with these ideas in place: (a) the heart is a small chamber in the human body, but it is an astonishing phenomenon of creation, on which the existence of man depends (b) the phenomenon that moves man is also the one that moves the world (c) this imparts a high spiritual intent to the potential of both man and the world (d) heart is thus an abode of all that the world harbours and all that human beings preserve for their spiritual sustenance (e) further, the heart is a marvel, a macrocosm unto itself, and incorporates many other worlds to create the balance of existence (f) a small heart may be a vast continent of love in the mystical order, and it is the creator's magic that bequeaths the small heart massive abilities (g) this also reminds one of William Blake who wrote about seeing the world in a grain of sand in 'Auguries of Innocence'.

An element of utter surprise qualifies the essential tone and intent of the verse. This is suggested by the last clause in the second line—*kis tar'ha hai gunjaaii* (how does it find a place). The element of surprise gathers its strength from the dichotomy posed by the smallness of the heart in terms of space and the magnitude of the world in terms of its vast appearance. Mir comes back to this theme once again: *hai farsh 'arsh tak bhii qalb-e hazii.n kaa apne / is tang ghar mei.n ham ne dekhii hai.n kyaa fizaaei.n.*

Ghazal 1286 | Verse 6

162

لوہو پانی ایک کر دیتا ہے عشق
پانی کر دے چشم دل لوہو کرے

लोहू पानी एक कर देता है इश्क़
पानी कर दे चश्म दिल लोहू करे

lohu paanii ek kar detaa hai 'ishq
paanii kar de chashm dil lohu kare

Love equals both—water and blood
Turns the eyes to water, heart to blood

Love does magical things and conveys profound messages. As the speaker suggests, it can transform its subject in the simplest of manners. He shares his observation, which could also be his experience of watching water and blood as one and turning the eyes to water and the heart to blood.

The change of one into the other has layers of meaning that mark the value of the verse: (a) turning the eyes to water implies the eyes losing their worth and becoming all tears (b) similarly, turning the heart to blood implies the heart losing its fire and shedding blood (c) both eyes and heart, thus, become one in losing their worth and becoming the images of loss (d) eyes and heart are the two objects that help the lover see and feel and the loss of both turns him into another picture of loss.

The essential mark of this verse is its intricate simplicity. Mir's unassuming posture of expression may be appreciated further in how he configures the four images of eyes, heart, water, and blood in this verse to make more profound suggestions about their transformation from one state to another, enriching the verse with an extra layer of meaning. With the same kind of diction, this idea is expressed in another verse of Mir: *lohuu paanii ek dono.n ne kiyaa meraa nidaan / y'anii dil lohu huaa sab chashm sab paanii huii.*

Ghazal 1310 | Verse 1

163

بات کیا آدمی کی بن آئی
آسماں سے زمین نپوائی

बात क्या आदमी की बन आई
आसमाँ से ज़मीन नपवाई

baat kyaa aadmii kii ban aaii
aasmaa.n se zamiin napvaaii

How well has man succeeded on this earth
He made the sky measure this earth

This verse reflects on the nature of the relationship between man and God, where man's potential is presented as surpassing even the divine design.

The kernel of the verse may be explored as follows: (a) man is the mover of and also sole surveyor of all that happens on this earth (b) he thus considers his potential akin to God's potential and seems to think as if God does what he wishes (c) sky is presented as God's sphere and earth as man's domain, and the implications of making God measure the earth reflects on man's prowess (d) measuring the earth implies creating the cartography of this earth as man wishes to be made for himself, to run its functions according to his wishes.

The verse weaves a plot with four key constituents: sky, earth, God and man. The dynamics of their mutual relationship are evident in how the verse constructs the plot in an unexpectedly daring manner. The sky measures the earth; that is, God, who rules the skies, stands subservient to man, who rules this earth. The mutual relationship between the earth and the sky is also a subject of poetic discourse in Mufti Sadruddin Azurda: *naalo.n se mere kab tah-o baalaa jahaa.n nahii.n / kab aasmaa.n zamiin-o zamii.n aasmaa.n nahi..n.*

DIIVAAN 4

Ghazal 1312 | Verse 6

164

ہم وحشیوں سے مدت مانوس جو رہے ہیں
مجنوں کو شوخ لڑکے کہنے لگے ہیں کاکا

हम वहशियों से मुद्दत मानूस जो रहे हैं
मजनूँ को शोख़ लड़के कहने लगे हैं काका

ham vahshiyo.n se muddat maanuus jo rahe hai.n
Majnuu.n ko shoKH laRke kahe lage hai.n kaakaa

(*vahshii*—uncouth, uncivilized, boorish;
muddat—a span of time;
maanuus—familiar, attached;
kaakaa—elder brother, paternal uncle)

I have been too familiar
with those boorish ones—far too long;
The naughty boys have been calling this *Majnuu.n*
a *kaakaa*—far too long

Memories of and responses to specific human figures are passed down through generations without modification. The speaker in this verse has been familiar with such beings for a long time. One of these idiosyncratic beings is no one else but *Majnuu.n* whom the naughty boys have now taken to calling *kaakaa,* as he looks like a wild lover of long years and is fit to be laughed at.

Apart from the element of fun that can be easily marked in this verse, there are other inferences we may draw: (a) *Majnuu.n* is a stock figure of an unkempt, wild lover who evokes excitement and amusement for the philandering boys (b) it is not surprising how *Majnuu.n* is treated and given a name that imparts him a status of superiority as a lover, but only mockingly (c) it would be surprising, contrarily, if he was not treated the way he is treated (d) the speaker calls such persons boorish, which evokes a sense of rejection for *Majnuu.n*, but the naughty boys address him with joviality and see in him as an archetypal figure tried by love, although sardonically (e) it is, however, ironic that this figure is not known by his name of Qais but by a representative word coined to configure such a figure.

Two words—*vahshii* (boorish) and *kaakaa* (an address for a respected one)—are not complementary to each other, but they represent the same person, albeit in different ways. While it defines the speaker as one who disparages a lover who has gone wild, it presents the naughty boys as more accepting of such a figure. It also implies two diametrically different ways of looking at a lover. Mir has constructed and reconstructed the figure of *Majnuu.n* in dozens of his verses. Here is one where he compares himself with him irrespective of how the naughty boys call him: *diivangii mei.n Majnuu.n mere huzuur kyaa thaa / laRkaa saa un dino.n thaa us ko sh'uur kyaa thaa.*

Ghazal 1336 | Verse 6

165

آستاں کی کسو کے خاک ہوا
آسماں کا بھی کیا ستارہ تھا

आस्ताँ की किसू के ख़ाक हुआ
आसमाँ का भी क्या सितारा था

aastaa.n kii kisuu ke KHaak huaa
aasmaa.n kaa bhii kyaa sitaara thaa

(*aastaa.n*—threshold)

I turned to dust at someone's threshold
What strange stars for the sky, so old!

The speaker in this verse reflects on the sky and the earth and comments on their supposed compatibility and astounding incompatibility.

In this seemingly paradoxical verse, we have philosophical intents imbued in good measure: (a) the earth and the sky face each other from a limitless distance, yet they develop a camaraderie (b) the sky represents divinity, but the earth suggests mundane realities, characteristically signified as sinful (c) the realities of the world here and hereafter are infinitely mutable as the sky may punish and the earth may preserve its manifestations (d) even the sky is run and regulated by luck which is also ironic, as much as it is tragic (e) the poet may also be hinting at the downfall of a lover; once exalted now fallen from the pedestal of love.

The pattern of meaning in this verse is woven into the contrariness of images that are also symbolic. This is further strengthened by the paradoxical nature of the speaker's assertion. The rhyming words—*aasmaa.n* (sky) and *aastaa.n* (threshold)—are brought closer to each other, and the magic of sound creates a condition of kinship between them. The use of the phrase—*KHhak honaa* (turning into ashes)—makes the verse even richer, both idiomatically and metaphorically. Mir views the sky as a keen sympathizer, and by doing so, he develops a different perspective for us to deliberate upon: *naala jab khe.nchtaa hai sar meraa / shor ik asmaa.n se uThtaa hai.*

Ghazal 1337 | Verse 2

166

روند کے جور سے ان نے ہم کو پاؤں حنائی اپنے کیے
خون ہمارا بسمل گہ میں کن رنگوں پامال کیا

रौंद के जौर से उन ने हम को पाँव हिनाई अपने किए
ख़ून हमारा बिस्मिल-गह में किन रंगों पामाल किया

raun.d ke jaur se un ne ham ko paao.n hinaaii apne kiye
KHuun hamaaraa bismil-gah mei.n kin rango.n paamaal kiyaa

(*jaur*—oppression, coercion;
bilmil-gah—slaughterhouse;
paamaal—destroy, ruin)

Her feet dyed red as if after henna,
when under them she crushed me;
She squandered my blood away
like in slaughterhouses plenty

The beloved as a tormentor is a figure of intrigue even for those not directly subjected to her tyranny. The lover presents her as one who has crushed him under her feet in a cruel manner. By indulging in such an act, she has turned her feet red as if after the application of henna. He complains further that his blood has met a terrible fate with its shedding in the slaughterhouse of love.

The verse makes these prominent points: (a) the images of both the lover and the beloved have been represented as the tormenter and the tormented ones but with a difference (b) instead of painting a horrendous picture, the verse mythicizes both the lover and the beloved in their stereotypical roles (c) the acts of crushing, arguably under one's feet, underline the brutal nature of the beloved and confirms her stereotypical identity as a tormentor (b) her severity is further suggested by her selfish act, which seems to have turned her soles red with the lover's blood, but the lover compares it with the colour that henna leaves behind (d) the sanctity of the lover's blood is squandered in the slaughterhouse where it was made to flow freely.

As many as five words—*rau.nd* (smash), *jaur* (oppression), *KHuun* (blood), *bismil-gah* (slaughterhouse), and *paamaal* (ruin)—create a gruesome scene with the beloved at its centre. The word—*rango.n* (colours)—does not mean the colour of blood here but a way or manner of crushing the lover under the beloved's feet. This is characteristically ironic as squashing him under her feet turns her feet red as if after the application of henna—which represents gaiety and celebration. Consider another verse by Mir that develops a befitting alternative perspective: *ham ve hai.n jin kii Khuu.n se tiri raah sab hai gul / mat kar KHaraab ham ko auro.n mei.n saan kar.*

Ghazal 1341 | Verse 1

167

دل کو کہیں لگنے دو میرے کیا کیا رنگ دکھاؤں گا
چہرے سے خوں ناب ملوں گا پھولوں سے گل کھاؤں گا

दिल को कहीं लगने दो मेरे क्या क्या रंग दिखाऊँगा
चेहरे से ख़ूँ-नाब मलूँगा फूलों से गुल खाऊँगा

dil ko kahii.n lagne do mere kyaa kyaa rang dikhaau.ngaa
chehre se KHuu.naab maluungaa phulo.n se gul khaau.ngaa

(*KHuu.naab*—tears of blood;
gul khaau.ngaa—I will wound myself)

Let my heart find a friend first,
I'll show you then my myriad desires;
With my face, I'll rub the tears of blood
from flowers, I'll devour the fires

In this verse, the lover-turned-speaker opens his heart and expresses his bizarre ambitions. He says that once he finds his beloved, he will express his pleasure in strikingly original ways. He will rub his face with the tears of blood and consume the fire from blossoms that will make his face glow.

This uniquely confessional verse from the lover has many meanings: (a) this lover is uniquely identified with his soaring passion, unlike other lovers (b) he exudes a sense of pride with the yearnings he nurses within his heart (c) his rubbing of blood-tears with his face rather than his face with the the blood-tears radiates his exceptional passion—one is the actor, the other one is acted upon (d) this is extended further with his desire to devour the fire embodied in flowers which implies that he will cauterize and burn himself with its heat (e) cumulatively, it is suggested that love demands smearing blood and bearing burns, which only the most committed of the lovers can do (f) his act will thus be a reiteration of what the lovers in the olden days used to do, that is, torture themselves by burning their hands and legs with hot iron to prove their love and loyalty to the beloved (g) burning is also an ancient way of treatment to cure a patient of his pain which this lover chooses for himself.

The most striking line in the verse is the second line, which reverses the order of the lover's action and distinguishes him from other lovers. The successive clause in particular—*phulo.n se gul khaaungaa* (I will devour fire from flowers)—is a distinctive use of an idiom that represents the act of cauterizing one's own body by heating the ring and placing it against the skin to prove one's love for the beloved. The uniqueness of this idea fascinates Mir, and he uses it in other verses as well: *gul khaae hai.n ifraat se mai.n 'ishq mei.n us ke / ab haath miraa dekho to phulo.n kii chhadii hai* (ghazal 883, *diivaan* 2); *bubul ko naaz kyu.n na KHayaabaan-e gul pe ho / kyaa jaane jii ne chaatii pe bhar kar na khaae gul* (ghazal 987, *diivaan* 3); and *bulbul ne kal kaha ke bahut ham ne khaae gul / lekin hazaar haif na thehrii havaa-i gul* (ghazal 1204, *diivaan* 4). Imam Bakhsh Nasikh has also used this idiom: *jaantii hai.n shaaKH-e gul mujh natavaa.n ko bulbulei.n / kyaa hii KHush-asluub mai.n ne apne tan per khaae gul.*

Ghazal 1342 | Verse 2

168

قیامت کو جرمانۂ شاعری پر
مرے سر سے میرا ہی دیوان مارا

क़यामत को जुर्माना-ए शायरी पर
मिरे सर से मेरा ही दीवान मारा

qayaamat ko jurmaana-i shaa'irii per
mire sar se meraa hii divaan maaraa

(*qayaamat*—doomsday;
jurmaana-i shaa'irii—punishment for writing poetry)

On the doomsday, as a fine
for composing verses,
My *diivaan* was thrust upon my head
for composing verses

Let this verse be read as the first voice of the poet about himself. He anticipates that on the doomsday, he will be punished for writing verses. Pitiably, this punishment comes to him in the form of his *diivaan* being hit on his head, which makes him into a pitiable being in the present.

This verse, which is essentially self-reflexive, raises some pertinent questions: (a) what is a poet's due after all that he may present to the world in the form of his craft, or how does he assuage himself if not by writing poetry? (b) why and how does poetry hold together his readers and the world spread all around? (c) does poetry not reveal the mysteries of the world for which the poet should be rewarded rather than punished? (d) how well does a poet write himself and his times to hold a mirror up to them? (e) is writing poetry a crime, and why is it prohibited in the divine domain and attracts punishment on the doomsday? (f) is this verse an expression of the poet's self-pity, or an elegy on his work, or does he suffer the sorrow of rejection? (g) finally, does it also reflect, more broadly, on the eternal question of the validity of art?

The verse is humble yet assertive, marked by a sombre tone. It should also be appropriate to distinguish between two clauses in the second line—*sar* **se** *diivaan maaraa* (hit the head with *diivaan*), which the poet appropriates, rather than *sar* **pe** *diivaan maaraa* (hit the *diivaan* on the head), which is commonly used in spoken and written forms to convey the idea of hitting or beating. It is notable that Mir's deft facility with language embedded greater meaning in the verse by making this choice. Look at this verse by Mir that compliments poets: *'ajab hote hai.n shaa'ir bhii mai.n is firqe kaa 'aashiq huu.n / ke be-dhaRke bharii majlis mei.n ye asraar kahte hain.*

Ghazal 1349 | Verse 1

169

چاہت کا اظہار کیا سو اپنا کام خراب ہوا
اس پردے کے اٹھ جانے سے اس کو ہم سے حجاب ہوا

चाहत का इज़हार किया सो अपना काम ख़राब हुआ
उस पर्दे के उठ जाने से उस को हम से हिजाब हुआ

chaahat kaa izhaar kiyaa so apna kaam KHaraab huaa
us parde ke uTh jaane se us ko ham se hijaab huaa

(*izhaar*—expression;
hijaab—veiling)

I expressed my love
and spoiled my chance with her;
With one veil lifted,
she wore for me, yet another

The difference between loving silently and expressing love before the beloved unveils the story of two kinds of love and lovers. Here, the lover laments that he unnecessarily expressed his love to her, and by doing so, he spoiled his prospects of being accepted respectably. Also, by lifting the veil of silence and expressing his intent, he only made the beloved conscious of and diffident towards him, which accounted for his loss.

This delicate relationship between the lover and the beloved is further marked as follows: (a) love calls for patience and waiting, and it loses its charm in impatience and making undue advances (b) words of love that remain unexpressed are more eloquent than the words expressed (c) with silence, love acquires sobriety but with expression it becomes ostentatious (d) the lover in this verse laments his act which, quite ironically, moves the beloved away from him than drawing her closer to him.

The verse features two key words—*izhaar* (expression) and *parda* (veil)—that stand in opposition to each other. The veil that separates the two is further qualified by *hijaab*. This reinforces the fundamental intent of the verse, which the lover comes to realize more fully after he has expressed himself to the beloved. A modernist poet, Saqi Farooqui creates a tension between veiling and unveiling in a comparably dichotomous manner: *tamaam jism kii 'uryaaniyaa.n thii.n aa.nkho.n mei.n / vo merii ruuh mei.n utraa hijaab pehne hue.*

Ghazal 1373 | Verse 4

170

ہم ہیں قلندر آ کر اگر دل سے دم بھریں
عالم کا آئینہ ہے سیہ ایک ہو کے بیچ

हम हैं क़लंदर आ कर अगर दिल से दम भरें
आलम का आईना है सियह एक हू के बीच

Ham hai.n qalandar aa kar agar dil se dam bharei.n
'aalam kaa aaiina hai siyah ek huu ke biich

(*qalandar*—wandering monk)

(*qalandar*—wandering spiritualist without the makings of one;
dam bharei.n—to speak up, recite heartily;
huu—a howling in the wilderness, sharp-toned magical chant)

I am a *qalandar*; if I take on
and hanker, heartily;
The world's mirror would turn black
with a *huu* of mine, heartily

The extraordinary power and prowess that the men of God are endowed with can do wonders and shock ordinary mortals. In this verse, we encounter a remarkable figure, not a ritualistically religious one but one spiritually charged, exercising his magical skill to effect consequential changes in the phenomenon known as the world.

The spiritual power of this holy man and the reality of the world may be appreciated thus: (a) being a profound spiritualist, lost in his hallowed world, and otherwise known as *qalandar*, he has the potential to unveil the universe with his robust magical chant of *huu* (b) he is possessed by his self-assured defiance and in raising his chant, he can dim out the world which is a mirror that reflects the phenomenon (c) in turning the mirror black, he can turn it blind to the world, which is essentially a web of fancies (d) while God is the creator of the universe, a *qalandar* is endowed with spiritual powers to do seemingly inconceivable things and make the world and its inhabitants realize that they are inconsequential (e) in this respect, the *qalandar*, the world, and its inhabitants are absolute realities, but they draw their light only from the divine—the absolute source of absolute power who has empowered the *qalandar* with the exceptional magic of transforming the world.

The fiery chant of *huu* has long been a part of the spiritualists' primal language by which they are known, recognized and respected. The power of this verse lies in the chant figured in the second line. It can turn the world's mirror blind and show the world to the seeker only through his chant. Khwaja Mir Dard unveils this reality: *mit jaaei.n ek aan mei.n kasrat-numaaiyaa.n / ham aaiine ke saamne jab ek huu karei.n.*

Ghazal 1374 | Verse 7

171

دل کو جو خوب دیکھا تو ہو کا مکان ہے
ہے اس مکاں میں ساری وہی لامکاں کی طرح

दिल को जो ख़ूब देखा तो हू का मकान है
है इस मकाँ में सारी वही ला-मकाँ की तरह

dil ko jo KHuub dekhaa to huu kaa makaan hai
hai is makaa.n mei.n saarii vahii laa-makaa.n kii tar'ha

(*huu*—a howling in the wilderness, sharp-toned magical chant; *laa-makaa.n*—of no abode or place, a house of no borders)

When I looked into my heart intently,
I found it a home of *huu;*
This, too, has the ways of a home
shorn of a home, echoing *huu*

A desolate heart is no heart; it lacks reverberations and is characterized by void and voicelessness. As a keen observer, the speaker configures a heart that echoes only its silence, akin to the voice of *huu*.

A verse devoted to defining the desolate heart offers various insights: (a) a heart-house being a derelict space which offers no abode for someone to live in; it could be the heart of one unable to reach out to the divine (b) it could as well be the heart of a lover lying in a state of ruin marked by the echoes of utter void (c) in both the ways, the heart without a kin—divine or earthy—is a place of bereavement (d) one who has such a heart is thus himself a house of echoes with no enlivening energy within (e) it is either music or noise that announces life and a house or a heart devoid of one or the other is the home of lifelessness.

This verse is built around two keywords—*makaa.n* (house) and *laa-makaa.n* (houselessness) placed in opposition to each other. Comparing a house to a derelict space representing a void reveals the pathos of one who owns such a house. It is also vital to note that *laa-makaa.n* also implies a divine world, adding another layer of meaning to the verse. The condition of void and voicelessness is constructed in a another verse by Mir: *dil kyaa makaa.n phir us kaa kyaa sehn Mir lekin / Ghalib hai sa'ii mei.n to maidaan la-makaa.n per.*

Ghazal 1437 | Verse 5

172

میر فقیر ہوئے تو اک دن کیا کہتے ہیں بیٹے سے
عمر رہی ہے تھوڑی اسے اب کیوں کر کاٹیں بابا ہم

'मीर' फ़क़ीर हुए तो इक दिन क्या कहते हैं बेटे से
उम्र रही है थोड़ी इसे अब क्यूँकर काटें बाबा हम

Mir faqiir hue to ik din kyaa kahte hai.n bete se
'umr rahii hai thoRii ise ab kyu.nkar kaatei.n baabaa ham

Mir became a *faqiir*, see what he told
his son one day:
Only a few days left, tell me
how to live for another day

In a moment of sharing one's vulnerabilities, one seeks both consolation and resolution. This verse, composed in the poet's own voice, narrates his poignant plot. In a monologic engagement with his son, he ruefully tells him that he has grown old and turned into a *faqiir* after a long life. At this stage, he seeks guidance from his son on how to live the days ahead.

There are many philosophical issues in this verse that call for attention: (a) life is configured as two ages of man—old and young—and they are put face-to-face in a kind dialogue (b) while the father has passed through the seasons of life, the son has yet to pass through his own (c) despite that, the father turns back to the son and proves the Wordsworthian adage that the Child is the father of the Man (d) the father returning to his son also underlines the cycle of life as a continuum (e) it is not the fear of decay and death that haunts the father but it represents his care for the son whom he has nursed all his life and who can now, in turn, nurse the father with his words (f) the answer-seeking father and the mutely-observant son present a drama of life marked by love and sympathy at one end and pathos and pain on the other (g) the old father, now turned into a *darvesh*, more than a *faqiir,* knows that he has brought up his son with care, so that the latter can offer wise counsel to his own father.

The verse renders a saga of living with three persons involved—the observant speaker, the aged father and the young son. The speaker maintains a distance and chooses to act only as a narrator of the father-son togetherness, which encompasses the entire saga of human life. The sympathetic tone of the narrator also unfolds the sympathetic chord the verse strikes in the readers. The conversational tone suits the nature of the verse perfectly. Mir's other verse may be quoted here as a gloss on this verse: *ho koii baadshaah koii yaa.n zaviir ho / apnii balaa se baiTh rahe jab faqiir ho.*

Ghazal 1457 | Verse 2

173

کچھ تفاوت نہیں ہستی و عدم میں ہم بھی
اٹھ کے اب قافلۂ رفتہ کو جا لیتے ہیں

कुछ तफ़ावुत नहीं हस्ती-ओ-अदम में हम भी
उठ के अब क़ाफ़िला-ए रफ़्ता को जा लेते हैं

kuchh tafaavut nahii.n hasti-'adam mei.n ham bhii
uthh ke ab qaafila-i rafta ko jaa lete hai.n

(*tafaavut*—dissimilarity, difference;
hastii-o 'adam—being and nothingness;
qaafila-i rafta—caravan gone by)

There is no difference between being
and nothingness now,
Let me get up and retrace the
caravans gone by now

The two states of being and nothingness hold the universe in a delicate balance. The speaker philosophically underscores that there is no dissimilarity or difference between them. Consequently, he proposes to retrace his steps and reach the caravans that have gone by.

A proposition that appears too simple in the verse turns out to be complex subsequently: (a) both the visible and the invisible constitute the complex paradigm of existence (b) in this respect, both of them obliterate the distinction between being and non-being, seen and unseen, as also life and death (c) together, they constitute the larger paradigm of human and terrestrial being and nothingness (d) a retreat to all that has preceded is therefore not an act of withdrawal, but one of more extensive belonging to a grander scheme of existential design (e) this philosophical stance also underscores the liberal expansiveness of divine design and man's place in that design (f) finally, it comes out that there is no distance between life and death as both complement each other.

The philosophical structure of the verse rests on the seeming dichotomy of being and nothingness or existence and non-existence. *Qaafila* (body of travellers) serves as a metaphor for generations, which keep multiplying with time and adding people into their fold. The clause—*jaa lete hai.n* (will get up and retrace) qualified by *ab* (now)—in the second line brings times past and present together. The speaker's easy and informal tone adds to the appeal of the verse, which cumulatively suggests that retracing is no big matter as it appears to be. Ghulam Hamadani Mushafi puts it with extraordinary precision: *kuchh is qadar nahii.n safar-e hastii-o 'adam / gar paao.n uThaaiye to ye 'arsa hai do qadam.*

Ghazal 1460 | Verse 3

174

گوندھ کے گویا پتی گل کی وہ ترکیب بنائی ہے
رنگ بدن کا تب دیکھو جب چولی بھیگے پسینے میں

गूँध के गोया पत्ती गुल की वो तरकीब बनाई है
रंग बदन का तब देखो जब चोली भीगे पसीने में

guu.ndh ke goyaa pattii gul kii vo tarkiib banaaii hai
ra.ng badan ka tab dekho jab cholii bhiige pasiine mei.n

Kneading the petals of flowers,
such magic is met;
Look at her body's colours when
her bodice is wet with sweat

The delicacy of the female body tests a poet's talent for an equally delicate poetic idiom. This is a fine example where the poet's imagination soars high and configures the female body as delicate and sensually charged, with her bodice soaked in sweat.

The verse is decidedly sensual, but it also embodies other qualities: (a) as flowers get their beauty from their colourful petals, the female body, too, gets its gracefulness from an artful configuration of natural elements (b) this body is a joy to both sight and senses (c) it is not the human hand or imagination that makes this body, but the divine power that forms it as a paragon of beauty (d) the female body emerges as an object unaware of how it appears, but the seer with his characteristic male gaze adds a definite touch of sensuality to it (e) this impression is strengthened with the representation of the body's contours as objects of male desire (f) both the verse and the body emerge as a fine blend of the sensual, the visual and the emotional.

An abundance of images—*pattii* (petals), *gul* (flower), *badan* (body), *cholii* (bodice) and *pasiina* (sweat)—constitute both a picture and a plot for the verse, which is markedly sensual as well as sexual in nature. Apart from this, *tarkiib* is the most consequential word, with multiple meanings that include construction, configuration, assemblage and style. It suggests that the said female body is a magical configuration that inspires visual and sensual pleasure. In addition, *rang* stands for the body's sheen and astounding appearance, besides holding its usual meaning of colour. *Rang* is a loaded expression, as can be seen in yet another verse by Mir: *ba-rang-e barg-e gul saath ek shaadaabii ke hotaa hai / 'araq-chii.n bhiigtaa hai dilbaro.n ke jab pasiino.n se.*

DIIVAAN 5

Ghazal 1545 | Verse 2

175

وصل میں رنگ اڑ گیا میرا
کیا جدائی کو منہ دکھاؤں گا

वस्ल में रंग उड़ गया मेरा
क्या जुदाई को मुँह दिखाऊँगा

vasl mei.n rang uR gayaa meraa
kyaa judaaii ko mu.nh dikhaaungaa

(*vasl*—union)

In union, I lost all my colour and sheen
In parting, how will I show my face so lean!

Union and parting tell the story of love lived at large. Between the two, there is a cycle of bliss and suffering. The lover here makes an innocent confession about his love life, punctuated by these forces. He finds himself at a loss when in a state of union with the beloved, and he wonders if he has a face at all to face separation since he has lost all his sheen in the state of union with the beloved.

This simple verse raises several questions: (a) what turned the lover pale, nervous, or ashamed? (b) was the union too demanding, or was it too disappointing? (c) did the fear of separation make him pale, or did overindulgence in love dull his senses? (d) did the pleasure of union fade in separation, or did the pain of separation disappear in union? (e) the poet puts a premium on separation, which is perennial, rather than on union, which is temporal, and wonders if he may dare to show his face to anyone in the moment of the former.

The speaker's tone is morose. The lover finds himself at a loss, which is carried well by the second line. This line may be read as one expressing helpless wonder and ambiguity. The phrase—*rang uRnaa*—does not carry the literal meaning of discolouration but of losing the gloss and gleam on the lover's face. More importantly, it embodies a sense of him being staggered and flabbergasted. Consider this verse by Momin Khan Momin in this perspective: *thii vasl mei.n bhii fikr-e judaaii tamaam shab / vo aae to bhi nii.nd na aaii tamaam shab.*

Ghazal 1577 | Verse 5

176

پاؤں پہ سر رکھنے کی مجھ کو رخصت دی تھی میرؔ ان نے
کیا پوچھو ہو سر پر میرے منت سی منت ہے اب

पाँव पे सर रखने की मुझ को रुख़्सत दी थी 'मीर' उन ने
क्या पूछो हो सर पर मेरे मिन्नत सी मिन्नत है अब

paao.n pe sar rakhne ki mujh ko ruKHsat dii thii Mir un ne
kyaa puuchho ho sar per mere minnat sii minnat hai ab

(*ruKHsat*—concession, leave;
minnat—bequeathing, request, kindness)

She had offered me the privilege of bowing
my head down at her feet;
What shall I tell you now; it's a blessing
to have bowed down at her feet

The lover recalls that his beloved had allowed him to bow down and put his head at her feet. He considered it a privilege, and indeed it has rendered countless blessings upon him ever since.

Other inferences can also be drawn: (a) bowing at someone's feet amounts to worshipping them as an idol—which in this context is the beloved (b) seeking the beloved's favour and receiving it is only a temporal pleasure (c) as such, the lover's devotion to the beloved has turned into a cause for his trepidation (d) what was a desire and a request once is a reversal of request that has gone awry.

While the two opposite words—*paa.on* (feet) and *sar* (head)—create, by implication, images of the lover and the beloved as the seeker and the sought, the word *minnat* (request) is doubly empowered by its repetitive use with two connotations put against one another. Ghalib brings us closer to this experience: *puuchhaa thaa garche yaar ne ahvaal-e dil magar / kis ko dimaagh-e minnat-e guft-o shunuud thaa.*

Ghazal 1617 | Verse 1

177

اک آدھ دن نکل مت اے ابر ادھر سے ہو کر
بیٹھا ہوں میں ابھی ٹک سارا جہاں ڈبو کر

इक आध दिन निकल मत ऐ अब्र इधर से हो कर
बैठा हूँ मैं अभी टुक सारा जहाँ डुबो कर

ek aadh din nikal mat ai abr idhar se ho kar
baiTha huu.n mai.n abhii tuk saaraa jahaa.n dubo kar

For a day or two now,
O Cloud, don't pass by this side;
I sit here aimlessly,
having drowned my whole world wide

Arid plains and rains look towards each other now with hope and now with apprehension. In this verse, the speaker addresses the clouds literally and asks them not to pass by the place where he is in. He makes this plea because he seems to think that he has drowned his whole world and is sitting there helplessly now.

In this unusual plea to the cloud, there are other intimate suggestions: (a) the speaker is in a state of disarray and speaks metaphorically of his drowning the world in despair (b) his condition is expressed in his plea to the cloud to bring no rains any more to the plains of his arid life (c) since he has drowned everything and sits ruefully now, it will take time for his sorrows to dissolve still (d) it is then that the cloud would be welcome with rains, to make his wasteland of a life green with the vegetations of promise (e) as in nature, life too is punctuated by seasons that represent different states of living which are metaphorically presented in this verse.

A tone of pleading and pathos marks this verse. This is reflected well in the first line of the verse itself, followed by a reason for the speaker's plea. The image of the cloud representing nature is a metaphor for hope; it sets aside the despair that hits the poet and leads him to drown his world into nothingness. One point that strikes further is that the speaker drowned his world, which means there was abundant water, but that was indeed the river of his despair. This prompts him to ask the cloud to withhold the rains of suffering for now. Mir constructs this state of despair differently in another verse: *sar talak aab-e teGh mei.n huu.n gharq / ab taii.n aab aab kartaa huu.n.*

Ghazal 1626 | Verse 3

178

راتوں پاس گلے لگ سوئے ننگے ہو کر ہے یہ عجب
دن کو بے پردہ نہیں ملتے ہم سے شرماتے ہیں ہنوز

रातों पास गले लग सोए नंगे हो कर है ये अजब
दिन को बे-पर्दा नहीं मिलते हम से शरमाते हैं हनूज़

raato.n paas gale lag soye na.nge ho kar hai ye 'ajab
din ko be-parda nahii.n milte ham se sharmaate hain hanuzz

(*hanuuz*—still)

For nights, she slept arm-in-arm
stark naked with me;
In daytime, she never meets
without a veil, shy of me

The speaker in this verse makes an unreserved comment on one he has slept with naked during the nights, but when the day appears, she puts on a veil in accordance with social rules. Is this hypocrisy or fear of censure on the part of the beloved, the lover wonders.

A bold verse that makes sense, irrespective of time and place, leaves us pondering further: (a) there is a moral code that regulates sexual behaviour, and its violation results in severe outcomes (b) all said and done, hypocrisy is a way with both men and women even in love, although there is no room for hypocrisy in love (c) typically proud as a male lover, he is eloquent and yet sarcastically comments on the beloved, who has brought him the pleasure of union in the darkness of the night (d) the beloved remains incognito as many remain in love that verges on lust (e) the thread of distinction between love and lust is too thin and its preservation makes vast differences in the lives of lovers (f) the verse is an exemplary representation of eroticism and an unpretentious statement of libidinal desire, both of which are natural in male–female relationships.

The verse is punctuated by irony and light wit, making for pleasant reading. It is a frank and uninhibited study of love and love-making. It is built around two characters and tells a story in which the lover is gratified by what he does to the beloved and wonders at the difference in her demeanour between daytime and night-time. Consider Mir again here: *suhbat hai ye vaisii hii ai jaan kii aasaaish / saath aan ke sonaa bhii phir mun.h ko chhupaanaa bhi.*

Ghazal 1719 | Verse 1

179

اب کچھ مزے پر آیا شاید وہ شوخ دیدہ
آب اس کے پوست میں ہے جوں میوۂ رسیدہ

अब कुछ मज़े पर आया शायद वो शोख़-दीदा
आब उस के पोस्त में है जूँ मेवा-ए रसीदा

ab kuchh mazey per aayaa shayed vo shoKH diida
aab us ke post mei.n hai juuu.n meva-i rasiida

(*shoKH-diida*—one with a naughty look;
post—skin,
rasiida—ripe, received)

That sharp-eyed one has come to terms now,
so it seems;
Like fruit has juice, her body has too,
so it seems

Unfulfilled desires constantly irk the lovers, and their fulfilment compensates for all the yearnings they have suffered. A chasing lover has ultimately found signs of favour from the one he has been pining for all along. He is secretly happy about the favour he will receive from the evading one now.

Finer shades of meaning distinguish this verse: (a) the desired one combines the qualities of a naughty, playful, and sprightly beloved, which is evident from her sharp looks (b) after testing the lover's patience all the while, she is now softer towards him, which makes the lover feel elated (c) as the lover looks at her shiny skin, erotic thoughts drive him crazy (d) the element of erotica is expressed in the verse as the lover enjoys himself at the thought of a union with her.

This verse is a fine example of romantic image-making, where the aspiring and the aspired ones are represented by their emotional and physical features. The first line speaks of the aspiring one's sense of pleasure, and the second line configures the aspired one metaphorically as a ripe and juicy fruit ready to be sucked on and consumed. The sheen of her lively skin is represented well by her body being filled, with something like juice, which gives the skin its liveliness. The word—*ab* (now)—marks the end of yearning for the much-desired body of the beloved. Mir recalls this experience in another verse: *paanii bhar bhar aayaa mun.h mei.n dekhe jinho.n ke yaa rab / ve kis mazey ke honge lab-ha-i naa-makiida.*

Ghazal 1723 | Verse 2

180

ملتا رہا کشادہ جبیں خوب و زشت سے
کیا آئنہ کرے ہے بسر یاں حیا کے ساتھ

मिलता रहा कुशादा-जबीं ख़ूब-ओ-ज़िश्त से
क्या आइना करे है बसर याँ हया के साथ

miltaa rahaa kushaada jabii.n KHuub-o zisht se
kyaa aaiina kare hai basar yaa.n hayaa ke saath

(*kushaada-jabiin*—liberal, kind;
KHuub-o zisht—beautiful and ugly, seemly and unseemly;
hayaa—modesty, shyness, decency)

She kept on meeting so kindly
with the seemly and the unseemly;
Praise the mirror's modesty, how
she meets the seemly and the unseemly

Even inanimate objects reflect human qualities. In this verse, the speaker uses the example of a mirror that looks at all kinds of decorated and dreadful faces. The mirror does not negate any face that meets her but only reflects her modesty by looking at every face liberally and sympathetically.

The mirror's image-bearing quality reveals some other meanings too in this verse: (a) the mirror is neutral but kind too, which imparts a symbolic value to it (b) good and bad faces are someone else's creation and not the mirror's (c) both the good and the bad faces coexist, as does the mirror along with them and their reflections (d) the mirror being brittle, breaks too easily as do men with negligence or humiliation (e) faces, mirrors and time are archetypal symbols and they convey their mutuality and kinship to those who could appreciate them.

Considering the diction of this verse, one is struck by the array of suggestive phrases such as *kushaada-jabii.n* (liberal, kind), *KHuub-o zisht* (beautiful and ugly), and *hayaa* (modesty). The first phrase personifies the mirror, standing straight with its head and eyes fixed on its object. The second phrase represents the diverse faces in the sea of humans, and the third phrase describes the essential quality of the mirror's modesty. All these, in the order of their arrangement in the two lines, create the imagistic and thematic structure of the verse. Ghalib signifies this idea in a layered manner: *jalva az ba-ske taqaazaa-i nigah kartaa hai / jauhar-e aaiina bhii chaahe hai mizhgaa.n honaa.*

Ghazal 1736 | Verse 2

181

پتا پتا بوٹا بوٹا حال ہمارا جانے ہے
جانے نہ جانے گل ہی نہ جانے باغ تو سارا جانے ہے

पत्ता पत्ता बूटा बूटा हाल हमारा जाने है
जाने न जाने गुल ही न जाने बाग़ तो सारा जाने है

patta patta buuta buuta haal hamaaraa jaane hai
jaane na jaane gul hii na jaane baaGh to saaraa jaane hai

(*buuta*—flower, sprig, twig)

Each leaf, each twig, knows my state
wherever I go;
Only the blossom knows not,
though the entire garden does know

The songs of pain and pining reveal the singer's state and earn him sympathy. Arguably, the speaker in this verse is no one else but a bulbul who lies languishing in a state of neglect. She complains that the entire garden knows her suffering well, except the blossom it loved and suffered for.

The essential import of this verse is posited in a symbolic framework: (a) the speaker (seemingly a bulbul) has been, stereotypically, at the receiving end of suffering; as it happens in love (b) she has sympathy from every nook and cranny in the garden, but that does not change anything (c) the blossom is either oblivious of the bulbul's suffering caused by his neglect or is simply unkind to the bulbul (d) although the bulbul and the blossom emerge as the two living spirits of the garden, it is a pity that they lie apart and removed from each other (e) the neglect or unawareness of the one closest to us is ironic as much as it is tragic.

Four seminal microcosmic images—*patta* (leaf), *buta* (twig), *gul* (blossom) and *baagh* (garden)—together constitute the macrocosm of this verse. While leaf and twig represent the garden, blossom represents the beloved, and the garden represents the world, which incorporates everything into itself. The more significant meaning of this verse may also be derived if we cared to read these images as constituting the cosmos that human beings inhabit and suffer at the cruel hands of destiny. There is a rich ambiguity in the word *haal* (condition), which refers to both the speaker's present state and his perennial condition. Mir visits this condition with a difference in another verse: *patta patta gulshan kaa to haal hamaaraa jaane hai / aur kahe to jis se ai gul be-bargii izhaar karei.n.*

Ghazal 1740 | Verse 1

182

عالم عالم عشق و جنوں ہے دنیا دنیا تہمت ہے
دریا دریا روتا ہوں میں صحرا صحرا وحشت ہے

आलम आलम इश्क़-ओ-जुनूँ है दुनिया दुनिया तोहमत है
दरिया दरिया रोता हूँ मैं सहरा सहरा वहशत है

'aalam 'aalam 'ish-o junuu.n hai duniyaa duniyaa tohmat hai
dariyaa dariyaa rotaa huu.n mai.n sahraa sahraa vahshat hai

(*junuu.n*—frenzy, passion, insanity;
tohmat—blame, slander, calumny, allegation;
sahraa—wilderness, desert;
vahshat—wildness, dreariness)

All the universe—love and passion,
all the world—a blame
I weep rivers and streams,
all wilderness—the desolation claims

While the universe offers love and passion to men, the world brings them blame and slander. A man, a recipient of both, weeps at the deprivations and failures that come his way and finds the deserts a picture of wilderness. The verse presents both—the convex and concave views—to visualize what man receives as gifts in the form of love and deprivations in the form of suffering.

The rhetorical nature of this verse plays up many a finer point of philosophical depth: (a) the universe representing space, time, matter and energy is the place for higher things like love and passion (b) the world, being a home of specificities is a place to hurl, and bear blames (c) lovers, being destined to suffer in love, shed their tears and live in the rivers of sorrow (d) in the states of their frenzy, they represent the picture of wilderness and suffering (e) the conditions of love on the one hand and deprivation on the other develop a larger picture of life marked by myriad conditions of bliss and suffering.

The verse encompasses four terrestrial zones—*'aalam* (universe), *duniyaa* (world), *dariyaa* (river), and *sahra* (wilds). While the universe is characterized by *'ishq* (love) and *junuun* (passion), the world is characterized by *tohmat* (blame). Man, being a subject of suffering, is subject to *ronaa* (weeping). Thus, he creates a river with his tears and wanders in a state of *vahshat* (wilderness). It is remarkable that while *'ishq* (love) and *junuu.n* (passion) create one force, *tohmat* (blame) and *ronaa* (weeping) and wandering in *sahra* (wildness), make another, opposing one. This uniquely musical verse may be read loudly and with pauses in two clauses in the first line: *'aalam 'aalam 'ish-o junuu.n hai* and *duniyaa duniyaa tohmat hai,* and again with another set of two clauses in the second line as: *dariyaa dariyaa rotaa huu.n mai.n* and *sahraa sahraa vahshat hai.* The musicality of the verse comes from the punctuated movement of the lines and the interposed induction of thoughts. The repetitions of *'aalam 'aalam, duniya duniyaa, dariyaa, dariyaa,* and *sahraa, sahraa* contribute cumulatively to the architectonics of the sound and meaning in this verse. Cumulatively, this condition is epitomized in two verses from two poets of the classical and the modernist temper, respectively. Qayem Chandpuri has this: *vahshat-e dil koii shahro.n mei.n samaa saktii hai / kaash le jaae junuu.n su-e bayabaa.n mujh ko,* but Zeeshan Sahil develops a different perspective: *kisii kii dain hai lekin miri zuruurat hai / junuu.n kamaal nahii.n hai kamaal-e vahshat hai.*

Ghazal 1758 | Verse 2

183

گریزاں ہوں سائے سے خورشید ساں
جہاں جب سے ہے مجھ کو تجرید ہے

गुरेज़ाँ हूँ साए से ख़ुर्शीद-साँ
जहाँ जब से है मुझ को तजरीद है

gurezaa.n huu.n saae se KHurshiid saa.n
jahaa.n jab se hai mujh ko tajriid hai

(*gurezaa.n*—fleeing, fugitive;
KHurshiid—sun;
saa.n—as, like
tajriid—separation, solitude, isolation, celibacy)

I flee from the shadows
like the sun
Ever since the world's birth,
I am—isolation

The world and human beings share a curious relationship with each other. In a highly philosophical moment, the speaker suggests that he has been fleeing from the shadows, just as the sun, the source of light on this earth. He also says that in this process of being on the run, the speaker has been divested of companionship and remained in solitude since the beginning of time.

We can read deeper meanings into the verse: (a) as the moon keeps the earth cool, the sun keeps it warm with its rays and maintains a balance, but both maintain a strange relationship with each other (b) this represents the sun as a quintessential provider of energy (c) the speaker also assumes a similar position of superiority and denies the casting of any shadows arising out of himself like the sun (d) further, he acquires a larger identity for himself by extending the comparison with the sun—always on the run, surviving in a state of separation or isolation, which helps him retain his independence (e) he thus lives in this splendid isolation and values his solitude.

The word *tajriid*, with its multiple meanings of stripping, divesting, separation, solitude and celibacy, adds extra vitality to the verse in terms of its philosophical content. The hidden comparison with the sun lends extraordinary strength to the speaker, who appears to speak from a lofty pedestal of pride. The condition of solitude and stripping is philosophically presented in Mir's major predecessor Vali Mohammad Vali: *husn thaa parada-i tajriid mei.n sab suu.n aazaad / taalib-e 'ishq huaa suurat-e insaan mei.n aa.*

Ghazal 1759 | Verse 3

184

طرح چھریوں کی پلکوں سے ڈالی
نکلی تلوار ابرو کے خم سے

तरह छुरियों की पलकों से डाली
निकली तलवार अबरू के ख़म से

Tar'ha chhuriyo.n kii palko.n se daalii
niklii talvaar abruu ke KHam se

(*tar'ha*—style, manner;
abruu—eyebrows;
KHam—curve)

Knives got their style
from her eyelashes
The curve of her eyebrows showed up
like the sword's flashes

The face of the beloved is a thing of beauty to adore. The speaker praises her in a highly creative manner. He compares her eyelashes with the knife's blade and the curve of her eyebrows with the sword.

This verse of great imaginative novelty celebrates the beauty of the beloved's face with great precision: (a) a knife for eyelashes and a sword for eyebrows are the similes that represent a delicate face that can be lethal (b) knife and sword do not only cut or kill, they are also used to carve and create (c) far from being an exaggeration, this representation categorizes the beloved as a typical female figure in the ghazal tradition (d) on seeing such a face with sharp eyelashes and curved eyebrows, the lover falls for her.

An idea like this could be executed best using figures of speech rather than literal styles. The tone of the verse is straightforward yet effective, plain yet penetrating, for the reader who wonders how inventive and ingenious methods work in poetic representations. Mir executes the image of eyebrows in two of his other verses with remarkable expertise: *dekh ve palkei.n barchhiyaa.n chaliyaa.n / teGh niklii us abruu-e KHam se* and *ab to ham ho chukte hai.n tuk tere abruu KHam hote / kyaa kyaa ranj uThaate the jab jii mei.n taaqat rakhte the.*

DIIVAAN 6

Ghazal 1785 | Verse 2

185

ہو کے بے پردہ ملتفت بھی ہوا
ناکسی سے ہمیں حجاب رہا

हो के बे-पर्दा मुल्तफ़ित भी हुआ
नाकसी से हमें हिजाब रहा

ho ke be-parda multafit bhii huaa
naakasii se hamei.n hijaab rahaa

(*multafit*—being kind, showing attention and respect;
naakasii—disgrace, disrepute, meanness;
hijaab—reservation, concealment, veil)

She showed me her kindness,
appeared without a veil;
But only before disgrace
I put forth a veil

The lover here appreciates that the veiled beloved shows up before him—without a veil—and behaves kindly. This is such a happy turn in his relationship with her that it has given him immense confidence. He is no longer introverted or shy, nor does he care for any disgrace.

We can also infer the following from this verse: (a) appearing without a veil before the lover is the beloved's acknowledgement of her love for her lover (b) this is an act of kindness which contributes towards further bonding between the two (c) it makes the lover bold, and he does not feel shy any longer before anyone, since he has received the love and kindness of one who was seemingly withdrawn from him (d) it's also interesting to note how the lover is imbued with a certain confidence in the aftermath of this gesture from the beloved.

Two words in particular—*be-parda* (without a veil) and *hijab* (veil)—are central to the thematic composition of the verse. Being without a veil and wearing a veil are the two ways of making one's choice, and choosing one or the other defines a person's predilections, which the beloved does here, and the lover enjoys its advantage. Mir's play with a related idea is fascinating: *kaun mil saktaa hai us aubash se / iKhtilaat us se hamei.n ik Dhab se thaa.*

Ghazal 1786 | Verse 2

186

دروازے پر کھڑا ہوں کئی دن سے یار کے
حیرت نے حسن کی مجھے دیوار کر دیا

दरवाज़े पर खड़ा हूँ कई दिन से यार के
हैरत ने हुस्न की मुझे दीवार कर दिया

darvaaze pe khaRaa huu.n kaii din se yaar ke
hairat ne husn kii mujhe diivaar kar diyaa

For many days, I have stood
at the door of my beloved;
Her stunning beauty turned me to a wall
at the door of the beloved

In matters of the heart, fruitless waiting is easier to romanticize than fruitful waiting. In this verse, the lover says that he has been waiting at his beloved's door for several days now, but only fruitlessly. This has rendered him insensate like a wall.

There are more profound suggestions to consider in this verse: (a) the lover is devout and does not really care about the time lost in realizing his dream of seeing the beloved (b) this makes him a seeker, a beggar of a beauteous look but he remains disappointed even after waiting for several days (c) her beauty has overawed him, and he wants to see her once again, but failure to do so has made him into a statue of despair (d) he thus appears as inanimate as a wall, at the threshold of her abode, persistent in his endeavour to catch a glimpse of her.

The verse projects two visible images: the lover in waiting and the beloved's door. It also projects the lover's image as an insensate wall that can only stand still and keep waiting. This aspect of the verse adds exceptional meaning and appeal to it. Here is another strikingly contiguous and unique verse from Mir: *raat majlis mei.n tiri ham bhii khaRe the chupke / jaise diivaar lagaa de koii diivaar ke saath.*

Ghazal 1794 | Verse 4

187

پھیلے شگاف سینے کے اطراف درد سے
کوچہ ہر ایک زخم کا بازار ہو گیا

फैले शिगाफ़ सीने के अतराफ़ दर्द से
कूचा हर एक ज़ख़्म का बाज़ार हो गया

phaile shigaaf siine ke atraaf dard se
kuucha har ek zaKHm kaa baazaar ho gayaa

(*shigaaf*—fissure, slit, crack, incision;
atraaf—all around, sides, limits, extremes)

All around my chest,
fissures became wider;
Each lane of a wound,
a *baazaar*, ever wider

In this verse, the bearer of pain confesses that he has been subjected to pain to such an extent that the fissures in his heart have widened more than ever before into broad lanes. This idea, in turn, is extended when the speaker says that each lane of the wound appears like a market of its own.

We must draw our attention to some other aspects of the speaker's suffering: (a) the chest is the traditional site of pain-bearing and has ever been a kind of playground for wounds to manifest in poetry (b) fissures on the chest or in the heart were too many and much more than the speaker could bear, which made them spread across (c) with the abundance of fissures, it's as if a whole market of wounds comes into being (d) more than lamenting the pain suffered, the lover possibly seeks pride in seeing the wounds on his chest as a spectacle.

The word *atraaf* is used in this verse with the usual meaning of 'sides' and a less popular but loaded meaning of 'extremes', which enriches the verse with a double entendre. It should be interesting to take note of another similar-sounding word *itraaf*, which means viewing or inspecting something pleasant. Depending on how we read the line, the verse would bring two ways of reading to the fore and add rich ambiguity to the verse. Additionally, the verse gains a rare visual quality with the images of *kuucha* and *baazaar* brought together to create an actual marketplace scenario common at the time. Let us look at another verse by Mir for a different perspective on this experience: *hamaarii aaho.n se siine pe ho gayaa baazaar / har ek zaKHm ka kuuchaa jo tang thaa aage.*

Ghazal 1799 | Verse 7

188

موسم آیا تو نخل دار میں میرؔ
سر منصور ہی کا بار آیا

मौसम आया तो नख़्ल-ए दार में 'मीर'
सर-ए मंसूर ही का बार आया

mausam aayaa to naKHl-e daar mei.n Mir
sar-e Mansuur hii kaa baar aayaa

(*naKHl*—tree, plant, sapling, festoon;
daar—gibbet, scaffold, gallows;
baar—burden, load)

When the season arrived,
saplings appeared on the gallows;
It was Mansuur's head
that appeared on the gallows

Reward and punishment mark the turns of human destiny and history. This is best illustrated with reference to the great mystic and scholar extraordinaire Mansur (Abul Mughees al-Hussain bin Mansur al-Hallaj), who chanted *An-al Haq* (I am the truth) and was first hung on an altar, then cut to pieces and burnt, before his ashes were scattered in the air.

Several complex suggestions may be drawn here: (a) truth, when wrongly conceived as false, has ever been sacrificed at the altar of this world (b) Mansur visualized God's effulgence in the phenomenon all over and stressed on *vahdat-ul vujuud* (unity of God), but his call was wasted and he was punished for his allegedly heretical ideas (c) Mansur is an archetypal figure in the chronology of characters whose proclamations of truth were considered heresy (d) figures like him are comparable to saplings that sprout on the altars but are only sacrificial (e) humanity remains a mute witness to unjust punishment and history records it but only in literal terms (f) Mansur knew what lay in store for him, yet he remained steadfast and foresaw that many like him would be sacrificed on the altar across different seasons of history.

Two incredibly ironic words—*mausam* (season) and *naKHl* (sapling)—complement each other to pedestalize Mansur as a champion of appropriate faith rather than as a heretic. The words *daar*, which bears the two meanings of scaffold and home, and *baar*, which implies both a burden and a turn, are also profoundly ironic and enrich the verse with an ambiguous allusion. The element of ironic helplessness and melancholia represented here may be noticed in another verse by Mir: *Mansur kii nazar thii jo daar kii taraf so / phal vo daraKht laayaa aaKHir sar-e buriidan.*

Ghazal 1807 | Verse 2

189

جو قافلے گئے تھے انھوں کی اٹھی بھی گرد
کیا جانیے غبار ہمارا کہاں رہا

जो क़ाफ़िले गए थे उन्हों की उठी भी गर्द
क्या जानिए ग़ुबार हमारा कहाँ रहा

jo qaafile gaye the unho.n kii uThii bhii gard
kyaa jaaniye Ghubaar hamaaraa kahaa.n rahaa

(*Ghubaar*—haze, foulness, affliction)

Only the caravans that passed by
left their dust behind,
But who knows why and where
our own haze hovered behind

Generations follow one another, leaving their marks as they move along the track of life and time. The speaker asserts that the generations gone by have raised their clouds of dust behind them, but he wonders if the haze he or his generation left behind is still traceable anywhere.

A close reading of this verse reveals: (a) each generation lives as a unit in a broader framework of time and space, and it creates an existential paradigm of its own kind (b) every succeeding generation looks back but only to discover the haze left behind by the preceding generation (c) the moving generations are likened to caravans that know no stopping but only faring forward (d) every subsequent generation can only look at the haze of dust which is the ultimate reality of life and time (e) the speaker wonders if the haze raised by his generation is traceable anywhere in the larger framework of time and space (f) there is an impending sense of sorrow as he suffers a sense of loss as his own generation seems to be misplaced in the haze of dust.

The words *gard* (dust) and *Ghubaar* (haze) represent two distinct images that are, in effect, intertwined as the gathered dust turns into haze. This aspect of the verse, created by these two words, imparts a unique layer of meaning as it suggests that even though images remain alive, they become invisible in the haze. The first line makes a logical path for the second one to follow. Another Mir verse echoes this sentiment quite closely: *gaye un qaafilo.n se bhii uThii gard / hamaarii KHaak kyaa jaane kahaa.n hai.*

Ghazal 1820 | Verse 8

190

صاف میداں لامکاں سا ہو تو میرا دل کھلے
تنگ ہوں معمورۂ دنیا کی دیواروں کے بیچ

साफ़ मैदाँ ला-मकाँ सा हो तो मेरा दिल खुले
तंग हूँ मामूरा-ए दुनिया की दीवारों के बीच

(*laamakaa.n*—limitless, expansive;
tang—narrow, confined;
m'amuura—inhabited place)

My heart will open if I have
a boundless space laid out before me;
I am confined within the walls
of the world around I see

Here is an individual who finds his world too limiting. He thus aspires for a limitless space that can afford him the bliss of freedom to realize his creative potential.

The uniquely aspiring individual of this verse unfolds many facets of his personality: (a) arguably, this is the poet himself speaking in the first person who is imaginatively charged and capable of taking massive leaps (b) he eyes the limitless expanse as a condition for his heart to open, both as a person and a poet (c) while considering the world as a limited space enclosed with walls from all sides, he wishes to seek his release from there and realize his vast potential in the worlds beyond this world (d) he also pays the highest compliment to man's immense imaginative prowess that can transcend terrestrial space and reach out to infinity (e) the limitless space is his ultimate space of belonging for exercising his imaginative prowess and configure the world anew.

The design of meaning in this verse is posited in two conflicting expressions—*tang* (narrow) and *lamakaa.n* (limitless). Although they represent physical spaces on the surface, they symbolize imaginative spaces in poetic terms. The rejection of the narrow imaginative space and the choice for the limitless one—a space beyond spaces—further underlines Mir's poetics. Another word—*m'amuura*—also contributes towards enhancing the importance of the verse as it carries two different meanings of an inhabited place and a delightful location. He rejects both as he wishes to create a personal space of imaginative fulfilment like Coleridge's Kubla Khan. Here is Mir again in this reference: *jaan ko qaid-e 'anaasir se nahii.n hai vaarahii / tang aayaa mai.n bahut is chaar diivaarii ke biich.* This is further reminiscent of Ghalib: *be-dar-o diivaar saa ik ghar banaayaa chaahiye / koii hamsaaya na ho aur paasbaa.n koii na ho.*

Ghazal 1855 | Verse 4

191

کیا جنوں ہے تم کو جو تم طالب ویرانہ ہو
جس کو فردوس بریں کہتے ہیں واں آدم کہاں

क्या जुनूँ है तुम को जो तुम तालिब-ए वीराना हो
जिस को फ़िरदौस-ए बरीं कहते हैं वाँ आदम कहाँ

kyaa junuu.n hai tum ko jo tum taalib-e viiraana ho
jis ko firdaus-e barii.n kahte hai.n vaa.n Aadam kahaa.n

(*junuu.n*—frenzy, insanity, fit of passion;
taalib-e viiraana—desirous of desolate space;
firdaus-e barii.n—the superior level of heaven)

What frenzy is this; why do you seek
a desolate space around
That which is called the superior heavens
has no Adam around

Man's quest for the desired object is endless, and this desire also distinguishes him. The seeker in this verse is warned against aspiring for a desolate space like the most supreme heavens. He is warned against his choice, as the heaven he aspires for has no Adam there, which would leave him lonely yet again.

This desire of the speaker brings about philosophical ideas to the fore: (a) man's desire for a space away from human habitat and distinguished by desertion underlines his impatience with the world of hum and buzz that indeed is hollow (b) one who seeks such a forsaken and desolate space must be called a fallacious being in worldly terms (c) Adam, being the archetypal man of all, is no longer in the heavens and has been already driven out of that hallowed space (d) thus he cannot offer any company to his progeny either in the heavens or even upon this earth which implies that any craving for him or this other world is entirely futile (e) in this respect, both the heavens and the earth are deprived of the first man who lived in the heavens and then upon this earth as a consequence of a sin he committed in heaven.

Junuu.n (frenzy) is the verse's central word, distinguishing the seeker's essential features. He is marked not merely by frenzy but also by insanity, which is yet another connotation of the word *junuu.n*. He is being persuaded by a saner voice to abstain from his unwise yearning. Still, he persists with his penchant for seeking a lonely space where he sees the possibility of finding serenity. The penchant for desolate spaces is romantic and wishful but a genuine human urge of the differently inspired. Haider Ali Atish's protagonist echoes Mir's protagonist here: *baguule kii tarah kis kis KHushii se KHaak uRataa huu.n / talaash-e ganj mei.n jo saamne viiraana aataa hai.*

Ghazal 1864 | Verse 4

192

محو صورت نہ آرسی میں رہو
اہل معنی سے ٹک حجاب کرو

महव-ए सूरत न आरसी में रहो
अहल-ए मअ'नी से टुक हिजाब करो

mahv-e suurat na aarsii mei.n raho
ahl-e m'anii se tuk hijab karo

(*mahv*—lost, devoted;
aarsii—mirror;
ahl-e m'anii—embodiments/seekers of meaning)

Fascinated by your face alone,
don't only be stuck in the mirror
Be in the veil before those who hold
meaning beyond the mirror

Self-adoration is blinding, and it prevents one from looking beyond or within. A word of advice is offered here for those who lack this wisdom. It is, therefore, advised not to be self-enamoured but to respect those who see beyond themselves.

The act of seeing and the object seen hold multiple messages in this verse: (a) self-absorbed beings must shake the shackles of the self as the world offers much more meaningful objects to look at and observe (b) looking at one's image in water like Narcissus prevents the seer from looking at the river and realize its potential (c) those who visualize beyond the visible put the pitiably self-obsessed ones to shame (d) it is thus proper that one observes restraint and looks at the enlightened ones in humility as their faces bear more than what appears on their faces rather than look at the mirror that shows only one's own face.

A tone of kind and courteous counselling marks the verse. It contains two pieces of advice in the two lines of the verse. The first line reinforces the second line, and vice versa. Mir finds the beloved's face in the mirror and responds with envy and anger in another verse: *patthar se toRne ke qaabil hai arsii to / per kyaa karei.n ke pyaare mu.nh teraa darmiyaa.n hai.*

Ghazal 1867 | Verse 4

193

آزاد پر شکستہ کو صد رنگ قید ہے
یا رب اسیر ایسا قفس سے رہا نہ ہو

आज़ाद-ए पर-शिकस्ता को सद-रंग क़ैद है
या-रब असीर ऐसा क़फ़स से रिहा न हो

aazaad-e par-shikasta ko sad-rang qaid hai
yaa Rab asiir aisaa qafas se rihaa na ho

(*aazaad-e par-shikasta*—free but with broken wings;
sad-rang—hundred ways/colours;
asiir—captive;
qafas—cage)

A free bird with a broken wing is imprisoned
in a thousand ways in the cage
O God! May not such an enslaved one
be ever set free from the cage

A free bird cannot ever fly if its wings are broken. For such a bird, life is like living in a thousand forms of imprisonments. Therefore, an ironic prayer is that such a bird may never be set free from the cage since it can never fly.

The pathos underlying the verse reflects upon striking existential conditions: (a) both the free and the imprisoned ones live, but their predicaments spell out the marked difference between living and surviving (b) the importance of freedom is realized only in imprisonment since freedom is a bliss and imprisonment a bane (c) even though imprisonment evokes sympathy, it makes the imprisoned ones comprehend the sufferings of deprivation and renders him pitiably helpless (d) at a broader level, all human and non-human lives are lives of imprisonment and freedom separately and together.

The imagistic and ironic quality of the verse draws attention at the very first reading. Irony operates at three levels. First, the phrase—*azaad-e par-shikasta* ([a bird] who is free, but with a broken wing)—characterizes the helpless bird and represents the dichotomy of life caught between paradoxical situations. Second, *sad-rang qaid* (a hundred ways of imprisonment)—portrays the inescapable intensity of punishment. Third, *yaa Rab asiir aisaa qafas se rihaa na ho* (O God! May not such an enslaved one be ever set free from the cage)—highlights an adverse condition for the enslaved one. This irony highlights the existential crisis of life. The one who sympathizes with the bird in the second line appears as the alter ego of the bird itself, which makes the verse all the more ironic. Haider Ali Atish sensitively recreates the ironic predicament of the imprisoned bird with a difference: *sayyad-d gul-azaar dikhaataa hai sair-e baaGh / bulbul qafas mei.n yaad kare aashiyaana kyaa.*

Ghazal 1871 | Verse 7

194

خوش ہیں دیوانگیٔ میرؔ سے سب
کیا جنوں کر گیا شعور سے وہ

ख़ुश हैं दीवानगी-ए 'मीर' से सब
क्या जुनूँ कर गया शुऊ'र से वो

KHush hai.n diivaangii-e Mir se sab
kyaa junuu.n kar gayaa sh'uur se vo

(*diivaangii*—madness, lunacy, insanity;
junuu.n—frenzy, passion;
shu'uur—wisdom, discernment)

All are happy indeed
with Mir's frenzied being;
How well he played his wits
despite his frenzied being

Poets receive praise, but not all of them get it in good measure. However, Mir is praised here for his hypersensitivity, which is likened to a kind of madness. The speaker lavishes praise upon him because he is the one who can play with his insights and sense of discernment, rolling out verses that have never lost their value.

This praise for Mir means so much more: (a) the speaker in this verse may be his ardent admirer over generations, or he may be Mir himself, who praised himself in many other verses as well (b) poets are known to be divinely inspired, and poetry is an expression of divine madness in Platonic terms (c) with their surfeit of intellect and heightened imaginative power, poets turn the ordinary into extraordinary and give a shock of recognition to the reader (d) they are the gods in Coleridgean terms who rule the domains of wit and wisdom as did Mir with his extraordinary faculty (e) they play with wit to create wisdom like Mir to charge their arts and ideas.

The first line of this verse is self-congratulatory, which is justified by the subsequent line. Two words—*junuu.n* (frenzy) and *shu'uur* (wisdom)—contradict each other, but Mir puts them in a delicate embrace to define his poetry. Frenzy, a condition to be wary of, appears to be a prized condition of being for the poet. This is Mir's intriguingly individual way of defining poetry in the broadest sense. Out of several verses where Mir venerates his frenzy, here is one more, for example: *zamii.n se aasmaa.n tak Mir hai shor-e junuu.n meraa / tah-o baalaa kiyaa dono.n mei.n is uudham ne duniyaa ko.*

Ghazal 1873 | Verse 3

195

خواریٔ عشق اپنی عزت ہے
کی ہے ہموار ہم نے ہموارہ

ख़्वारी-ए इश्क़ अपनी इज़्ज़त है
की है हमवार हम ने हमवारा

KHvaarii-i- 'ishq apnii 'izzat hai
kii hai hamvaar hum ne hamvaara

(*KHvarii-i 'ishq*—insult/vileness/meanness in love;
hamvaar—level, smooth, equable, seamless;
hamvaara—always, ever, continuously, seamless)

Insult in love is the cause
of my pride in love;
In ways so plain, I levelled
my ground in love

True lovers are never shy of loving, even if treated with vileness by the beloved. Such a treatment is thus not a disgrace to the lover, as it appears here. This, indeed, is a way of respecting them for loving. With his forbearance or courtesy, this lover has levelled the rough passage of love and made it smooth for himself to fare forward.

The implied meanings could be traced furthermore: (a) travails and punishment in love are no travails or punishments if love is genuine (b) even a blatantly unwelcome attitude in love may be given a positive turn (c) a genuine lover appreciates the goal of love and how it may be earned even from quarters unwelcoming or disapproving (d) the effort to level the rough patches is in itself a positive act of love, worthy of respect.

The most remarkable quality of the verse lies in the play on the word *hamvaar* (level). Coupled with *hamvaar*, the word *hamvaara,* which means doing something continuously, adds immense value to this verse. An opposing view of this, which also highlights the significance of unevenness, can be seen in Dagh Dehlavi: *Thokar bhii raah-e 'ishq mei.n khaanii zuruur hai / chaltaa nahi.n huu.n raah ko hamvaar dekh kar.*

Ghazal 1874 | Verse 1

196

مکتوب دیر پہنچا پر دو طرف سے سادہ
کیا شوخ طبع ہے وہ پرکار سادہ سادہ

मक्तूब देर पहुँचा पर दो तरफ़ से सादा
क्या शोख़-तब्अ है वो पुरकार सादा सादा

maktuub der pahu.nchaa per do taraf se saada
kyaa shoKH tab'a hai vo purkaar saada saada

(*maktuub*—letter;
shoKH-tab'a—of a naughty/sprightly/playful nature;
*pur-kaa*r—skilful, crafty)

Her letter came late, but all blank—
on both sides!
How naughty, crafty, simple
she looks from all sides

Playfulness in love makes the act of loving all the more joyful. In this verse, the beloved plays upon her lover's emotions. She replies late to her lover's letter but without a word on either side of the paper. This does not deter the lover but instead makes him praise her ingenuity.

The lover–beloved relationship unfolds more layers here: (a) the lover waits for a reply, but a blank reply makes two suggestions of either a rejection of the lover's proposal or her inability to reply because of her shyness (b) a blank sheet of paper too is a reply of some curious consent from her side (c) silence or coyness in love is also a way of sweet consent (d) the lover assigns her blank reply to her naughty ways and her skilful and joyous mannerism (e) as the letter is blank and non-committal on both sides, so is the beloved blank and non-committal on both the sides of her eloquence and silence.

The word—*maktuub* (letter)—has a deeper meaning as it refers to a letter and also God's script of the lover's destiny. Applying the second meaning, the verse gains significantly in its implicational meaning because the beloved's blank reply is not from the beloved, but rather it is God's script, which does not favour the lover. Quite close to Mir is Amir Minai in this verse: *misl-e maktuub na kahne mei.n hai kahnaa kyaa kyaa / na miri tarz-e KHamoshii na kisii kaa kahnaa.*

Ghazal 1874 | Verse 2

197

جب میکدے گئے ہیں پابوس ہی کیا ہے
ہے مغبچہ ہمارا گویا کہ پیر زادہ

जब मय-कदे गए हैं पा-बोस ही किया है
है मुग़बचा हमारा गोया कि पीर-ज़ादा

jab mai-kade gae hai.n paa-bos hii kiyaa hai
hai muGh-bacha hamaaraa goyaa ke piirzaada

(*paa-bos*—kissing the feet;
muGh-bacha—young wine server in a tavern;
piirzaada—spiritual master)

I have kissed his feet whenever
I have visited the tavern
My boy bartender alone was
my mystic master in the tavern

The tavern, the visitor, and the bartender make a curious trio, and together, they weave many stories of pleasure and displeasure. In this verse, the tavern visitor respects the boy bartender and metaphorically kisses his feet in appreciation for his care and services. In a sudden leap of thought, he reaches elsewhere and considers his boy bartender a mystic master.

The verse does not tell the tavern's story alone; it tells much more: (a) there is one drinker who drinks the worldly wine from the hands of the bartender in the tavern (b) there is another drinker who drinks the mystical wine from the divine sources as heaven promises the best of wine as it is believed that there is a river of it there, from which the Prophet himself would serve the believers (c) both the wines intoxicate but in two different ways and their intoxication lasts for two different durations (d) the tavern's bartender for this drinker is his mystic master as he possibly sees the image of the divine server of wine in him.

MuGh-bacha is a Persian word and a curious combination of *muGh* and *bacha*, one implying a cup and the other a boy. So, this boy bartender emerges as a curious character and is often referenced in the classical ghazal to illustrate the intricate plots of tavern, wine, drinker and server. Mir has constructed and reconstructed this figure several times with variations. Here is one that reflects on the verse under discussion: *shaaed sharaab KHaane mei.n shab ko rahe the Mir / khele thaa ek muGhbacha mehr-e namaaz se.*

Ghazal 1887 | Verse 5

198

مستی شراب کی ہی سی ہے آمد شباب
ایسا نہ ہو کہ تم کو جوانی نشہ کرے

मस्ती शराब की ही सी है आमद-ए शबाब
ऐसा न हो कि तुम को जवानी नशा करे

mastii sharaab kii hii sii hai aamad-e shabaab
aisaa na ho ke tum ko javaanii nashaa kare

(*shabaab*—youth)

Youth's onset is much like
getting drunk on wine;
Take care, lest your youth
gets drunk on your own youth's wine

Bubbling youth is a charming age to bear witness to. One who embodies this prime of life looks like a person possessed, drunk on the wine of youth. The speaker warns this youth to be careful lest he should get too drunk on his own youth's wine.

This verse has stimulating suggestions to make: (a) youth intoxicates as wine intoxicates both body and senses (b) being drunk on wine is as close as being drunk on one's youth (c) it is better to be drunk on youth than allow the wine to drink on a youth instead and consume him for good (d) a youthful individual may thus overpower his youthfulness than allow his youthfulness to overpower him and subject him to its fire.

Youth, wine and intoxication compose an interactive plot in this verse. The interchangeability of exuberant youth for intoxicating wine adds an extra edge of appeal to this verse. The speaker, who addresses the youthful being, adores him but also warns him to retain his supremacy over intoxication and enjoy the moment's bliss, which the passing of time will snatch away from him. A comparable verse from Mir himself would be proper to quote here to appreciate the central import of the verse: *ab to javaanii kaa nassha hii be-KHud tujh ko rakkhegaa / hosh gayaa phir aavegaa to der talk pachhtaavegaa.*

Ghazal 1903 | Verse 10

199

معقول اگر سمجھتے تو میرؔ بھی نہ کرتے
لڑکوں سے عشق بازی ہنگام کہنہ سالی

माक़ूल अगर समझते तो 'मीर' भी न करते
लड़कों से इश्क़-बाज़ी हंगाम-ए कोहना-साली

m'aquul gar samajhte to Mir bhii na karte
ladko.n se 'ishq-baazii hangaam-e kohna-saalii

(*m'aquul*—proper, right;
ha.ngaam-e kohna-saali—at the season/time of old age)

If Mir thought it were proper,
wouldn't Mir do that too—
Loving the boys in his old age
wouldn't he do that too

Desire and age are no friends, and the desire to make love knows no difference of age, nor gender. A self-reflective person wonders here if he would have loved young boys in the mellow days of his life. He refuses to indulge in such an act not because of any other reason but because of his age, which is not on his side.

As an expression of human desire irrespective of age and gender, this verse goes deeper into the mysteries of sexual indulgence: (a) sexual acts between mature males is one kind of an indulgence but the act between mature males and young boys is of another kind altogether (b) such indulgences do not adhere to social or ethical taboos (c) this kind of love-making substitutes the otherwise more commonly accepted heterosexual relations and makes the speaker take pride in his preference for a same-sex partner (d) sexual preferences and acts are diverse and they have existed in all forms in various social orders across time and space.

Mir has several verses on this subject, and there are indications of this in his autobiographical writing also. The first line of the verse declares nonchalantly that he does not consider it proper to indulge in same-sex love in the declining years of his life, which implies that he would have indulged in it had he been younger. Rather than veiling it for fear of social taboo, his frankness presents him as a stark liberalist concerning the expression of his sexual urges. Hakim Agha Khan 'Aish offers an opposite view, but here again, same-sex love is the point of reference: *taak jhaa. nk aap kii vaisii hii buRhaape mei.n bhii hai / 'Aish buuRhe bhi huve per vo na lapkaa chhuutaa.*

Ghazal 1911 | Verse 1

200

فلک کرنے کے قابل آسماں ہے
کہ یہ پیرانہ سر جاہل جواں ہے

फ़लक करने के क़ाबिल आसमाँ है
कि ये पीराना-सर जाहिल जवाँ है

falak karne ke qaabil aasmaa.n hai
ke ye piiraana-sar jaahil java.n hai

(*falak*—sky, firmament, heaven, celestial sphere;
also canvas, sheet of paper;
piiraana-sar—old head, old age, condition of old age)

The sky is worthy of being one
with the firmament above;
This old head is young still—
the sky one with the firmament above

The sky covers the Earth like an enormous umbrella and is an omnipresent force. However, this umbrella is younger than the bigger firmament that encompasses all. A small fragment of this wider entity, the sky is oblivious to much that the firmament knows. The speaker argues that the sky deserves to become one with the firmament in its own right.

Interrogating the meaning of this verse further, we find: (a) firmament is the vault, and a massive arch of the sky, whereas sky is only a space that can be seen from the earth with its clouds, sun, moon and the stars (b) both have been manifestations of divine creation and deny any human control—but drive human ambition (c) both exist on their own and regulate the life of the earth (d) the sky, however, is only a fragment of the firmament, it looks younger and unlettered—which is also compared with the speaker's seemingly old but *jaahil* head—and deserves to be more than just the immense blue cover of the earth and become one with the firmament.

Two adjectives—*piiraana-sar* (old-head) and *jaahil javaa.n* (oblivious but young)—qualify the sky (and the speaker), but the firmament remains undescribed in the verse. However, it has been implied that it is far greater than the sky in terms of its potential and value. So, being young and oblivious to many realities, the sky needs to grow greater and become one with the firmament. The verse gains in its value with reference to the multiple potentials and multiple meanings of *falak,* comprising God, heaven and firmament on the one hand and a canvas, palm of the hand, and a sheet of paper on the other. Mir underscores the value of *falak* and man as such: *mat sahl hamei.n jaano phirtaa hai falak barso.n / phir KHaak ke parde se insaan nikalte hai.n.* In contrast, he emphasizes the worth of *aasma.n* thus: *aastaa.n kii kisuu ke khaak huaa / aasmaa.n kaa bi kyaa sitaaraa thaa.*

The Transliteration Key pertaining to this book is available on the HarperCollins Publishers India website. Scan this QR code to access the same.

ACKNOWLEDGEMENTS

I gratefully acknowledge and thank the following individuals for their assistance and goodwill in helping me accomplish my Mir project.

Harish Trivedi, Khalid Jawed, Geeta Patel, Mahmood Farooqui, Muneeza Shamsie, and Timsal Masood for their generous endorsements of the book.

Udayan Mitra, Amrita Mukerji and Kartik Chauhan at HarperCollins for configuring the book brilliantly, both editorially and aesthetically, and Devangana Dash for the brilliant cover design befitting Mir's genius.

Abdur Rasheed, Safdar Imam Quadri, Ahmad Mahfooz, and Vipin Garg for numerous consultations during the writing of this book.

Rabee, Munazzah, Yasser, Tabrez, and Maria, who were delighted to watch me in conversation with Mir over the years. Thanks are due to Tabassum, in particular, to whom this book is dedicated.

ABOUT THE AUTHOR

Anisur Rahman is a literary critic, translator, and bilingual poet in English and Urdu. Formerly a Professor of English at Jamia Millia Islamia, a Central University in New Delhi, and a Senior Advisor at Rekhta Foundation, he has worked and published in the areas of comparative literature, translation, postcolonial and Urdu studies. His recent publications include *Earthenware: Sixty Poems* (Rubric Publishing, 2018); *In Translation: Positions and Paradigms* (Orient Blackswan, 2019); *Socioliterary Cultures in South Asia* (Niyogi Books, 2019); *Hazaaron Khwahishein Aisi: The Wonderful World of Urdu Ghazals* (HarperCollins, 2019); *Hazaar Rang Shaairi: The Wonderful World of the Urdu Nazm* (HarperCollins, 2022); and *The Essential Ghalib* (HarperCollins, 2024). Rahman has been a Shastri Fellow at the University of Alberta, Canada (2001–2002) and a Visiting Scholar at Purdue University, USA (2007). He received the Translation Award (2018–19) from the Delhi Urdu Academy. His *Hazaaron Khwahishein Aisi: The Wonderful World of Urdu Ghazals* won the Sahitya Akademi translation prize for 2024.

HarperCollins *Publishers* India

At HarperCollins India, we believe in telling the best stories and finding the widest readership for our books in every format possible. We started publishing in 1992; a great deal has changed since then, but what has remained constant is the passion with which our authors write their books, the love with which readers receive them, and the sheer joy and excitement that we as publishers feel in being a part of the publishing process.

Over the years, we've had the pleasure of publishing some of the finest writing from the subcontinent and around the world, including several award-winning titles and some of the biggest bestsellers in India's publishing history. But nothing has meant more to us than the fact that millions of people have read the books we published, and that somewhere, a book of ours might have made a difference.

As we look to the future, we go back to that one word—a word which has been a driving force for us all these years.

Read.